BREAD

BREAD

the breads of the world and how to bake them at home

CHRISTINE INGRAM and **JENNIE SHAPTER**

HERMES
HOUSE

This edition is published by Hermes House

Hermes House is an imprint of Anness Publishing Ltd
Hermes House, 88–89 Blackfriars Road, London SE1 8HA
tel. 020 7401 2077; fax 020 7633 9499
info@anness.com

A CIP catalogue record for this book is available from the British Library.

PUBLISHER: Joanna Lorenz
EXECUTIVE EDITOR: Linda Fraser
EDITORS: Janet Charatan, Jo Lethaby and Jenni Fleetwood
DESIGNER: Nigel Partridge
PHOTOGRAPHERS: Nicki Dowey (recipes) and Amanda Heywood
HOME ECONOMISTS: Jennie Shapter (recipes) and Jill Jones
EDITORIAL READER: Catherine Sillence
PRODUCTION CONTROLLER: Julie Hadingham

Previously published as T*he World Encyclopedia of Bread and Bread Making*

1 3 5 7 9 10 8 6 4 2

NOTES

For all recipes, quantities are given in both metric and imperial measures
and, where appropriate, measures are also given in standard cups and
spoons. Follow one set, but not a mixture, because they are not
interchangeable.

Standard spoon and cup measures are level.
1 tsp = 5ml, 1 tbsp = 15ml, 1 cup = 250ml/8fl oz

Australian standard tablespoons are 20ml. Australian readers should
use 3 tsp in place of 1 tbsp for measuring small quantities of gelatine,
cornflour, salt, etc.

Medium eggs are used unless otherwise stated.

CONTENTS

INTRODUCTION

There is something undeniably special about bread. The flavor of a good loaf, the texture of the soft crumb contrasting with the crispness of the crust, is almost a sensual experience. Who can walk home with a fresh baguette without slowly, almost absent-mindedly breaking off pieces to eat en route? Or resist the promise of a slice of a soft white farmhouse loaf, spread simply with butter? Most people have their own favorite: ciabatta, rich with olive oil; dark, malty rye; honeyed *challah* or a Middle Eastern bread, freshly baked and redolent of herbs and spices. Whatever the shape or texture, bread has a special place in our affections.

Even today, at the turn of the century, when bread is taken largely for granted, seen as an accompaniment or a "carrier" for other foods, we still have a sense of its supreme significance. In some languages the word "bread" means "food," and in certain of the more rural parts of Spain and Italy, for example, you may find that bread is blessed or kissed before being broken or eaten. There are numerous rituals and traditions attached to bread. Slashing the dough with a cross or making a sign of the cross over the loaf before baking was believed to let the devil out. Cutting the bread at both ends was also recommended to rid the house of the devil. One extraordinary custom was sin-eating, a practice at funerals, where someone

BELOW: Cutting a cross in an unbaked loaf was believed to let the devil out.

ABOVE: Just a few of the many shapes and types of bread.

would eat a loaf of bread and by so doing would take on the sins of the dead person.

The obvious explanation for bread's importance is that until quite recently, it was for many, quite literally the "staff of life"—the single essential food. Today, most people have more varied diets. Potatoes, pasta and rice are all enjoyed in the West and are important staple foods, but in some countries, France and Italy, for example, bread is easily the most popular of the carbohydrates, eaten with every meal and in many cases with every course.

Like wine tasters, true aficionados taste bread *au naturel* in order to savor its unique taste and texture, unadulterated by other flavors. Good as plain bread can be, the best thing about bread is that it goes so well with other foods. Throughout Europe bread is most frequently cut or broken into pieces to be eaten with a meal—to mop up soups and sauces or to eat with hams, pâtés and cheese. Dark rye breads, spread with strongly-flavored cheese or topped with smoked fish, are popular in northern Europe, and in the Middle East breads are split and stuffed with meats and salads—a tradition that has been warmly embraced in the West too. In Britain and the United States, the European custom of serving bread with a

meal, with or instead of potatoes or rice, is catching on, but sandwiches are probably still the favorite way of enjoying bread. Sandwiches have been going strong for a couple of hundred years—invented, it is said, by John Montagu, 4th Earl of Sandwich, so that he could eat a meal without having to leave the gaming table. Although baguettes and bagels are naturally suited for linking bread with meat, the sandwich, clearly an English concept, is unique and continues to be the perfect vehicle for fillings that become more and more adventurous.

BREADS OF TODAY

Figures show that throughout Europe bread consumption declined after World War II. Until then it was the single most important food in the diet, but due to increased prosperity, which meant a wider choice of other foods, and mass production, which led to bread becoming increasingly insipid and tasteless, people moved away from their "daily bread." The situation was more noticeable in some countries than others. In France, Italy and Spain, where people continued to demand the best, bread consumption did not decline so sharply, although even in these countries, the quality did deteriorate for a time. In Britain, however, most bread was notoriously bland—the ubiquitous

BELOW: In northern Europe, dark rye bread is served sliced with colorful, rich-tasting toppings.

white sliced loaf being little more than a convenient shape for the toaster. In supermarkets, certainly, there was a time, not so long ago, when other than the standard pre-wrapped white loaf, the only baked goods on sale were croissants and a selection of fruited teabreads, vaguely labeled as "Continental." Yet within the last ten years, things have improved by leaps and bounds. Perhaps supermarkets, finding that the smell of freshly baking bread enticed shoppers into their stores, installed more in-store bakeries. Or perhaps shoppers who traveled abroad and sampled the breads of other countries created a demand for better breads made with better flours, using more imaginative recipes and untreated with additives.

Nowadays there is a wide variety of breads available both from independent bakeries and large supermarkets. Italian ciabatta and focaccia are now a regular sight, even in the smallest food stores, as are various Spanish, Indian and Middle Eastern breads. There is an increasingly wide variety of German, Danish, Scandinavian and Eastern European breads and, among the French breads, there is now a truly good range. If the supermarket has an in-store bakery, baguettes are likely to be freshly baked, and some are now as good as the real thing. The availability of *pain de campagnes*, *levains* and other rustic breads means that you can choose breads to suit the style of meal you are serving, while sweet breads, such as brioches and croissants from France, *pane al cioccolato* from Italy and numerous offerings from Germany, mean that there is much more to choose from than simply toast at breakfast and rolls with dinner.

Local bakers, although competing with the supermarkets, have paradoxically benefited from the range available at supermarkets. The more breads there are available, the more people feel inclined to try other baked goods. Small bakers who could have easily lost customers to the big stores, have risen to the challenge by producing their own range of country-style and fine breads. Craft bakers are producing traditional breads, at the same

ABOVE: A huge range of traditionally baked French breads are offered for sale at this specialty bakery.

time experimenting with recipes they have devised themselves. Bread making has never been a tradition that stood still. The best craft bakers have ensured that bread making has continued to evolve, resulting in the emergence of all kinds of corn and barley breads, mixed grain loaves and a range of new sourdoughs.

Added to this are the many European-style bakeries. Set up and run by émigrés from all parts of Europe and beyond, these bakeries are the best source of many of the most authentic European breads. In supermarkets you will invariably find ciabatta or focaccia, but for

BELOW: Traditional country-style breads are enjoying a renaissance.

paesano, *pagnotta* or *pane sciocco* you are likely to need an Italian baker, who will be only too happy to provide you with the loaves and tell you all about them while they are being wrapped.

Once you have found a bakery you like, there are no particular tips for buying bread; the baker will be pleased to explain the different styles of loaves and advise on their keeping qualities. Crusty breads, such as baguettes and Italian country loaves are known as "oven bottom" or "oven bottom-baked," which means they have been baked, without pans or containers, on the bottom of the oven or on flat baking sheets or stones. They are evenly crusty, although the type of dough, the humidity during proving, the steam in the oven and the heat itself determines whether the crust is fragile or chewy. Loaves such as the English farmhouse ones, baked in metal pans, characteristically have a golden top, but with thinner crust on the sides. Rolls or breads baked packed up against each other have even softer sides and are described as "batch-baked." Sourdough breads are made without yeast —using a natural leaven instead—and are often labeled as "yeast-free" breads or "naturally leavened." There are many varieties, some made entirely from wheat, some from rye, others from a blend of both of these or other grains. They are normally heavier than an average loaf, with a dense texture and pleasantly tart flavor.

HISTORY

—

Bread seems to be a recurring theme in history. Most people could be forgiven for thinking that history was driven by great scientists and ambitious men. But look closer and you will find that the incentive behind many of our greatest inventions was the availability, production and delivery of food—our "daily bread" in the widest terms. The wheel, the plough and the windmill right through to steam and motorization all plot a course that was concerned specifically with agriculture and producing food. Similarly, the aspirations of any king or queen were intimately connected with the feeding of their people. The poorer and hungrier the pop-ulation, the more insecure was their ruler's position. Give them "bread and circuses!" said Juvenal in the first century A.D., referring to the Roman mob, in a constant state of unrest because of poverty and starvation; and Queen Marie Antoinette famously said "Let them eat cake," on being told that the peasants were rioting because they had no bread. Almost all revolutions came about because of famine, and bread was the single food that might alone have averted some of them.

BELOW: By the first century A.D., bakers in many parts of the world were baking a variety of leavened breads.

THE FIRST BREAD

Archaeology and history show that bread has been eaten since the earliest times. Remains of stone querns indicate that cereal was ground in prehistoric Britain to make a bran-like grain. It is likely that this would have been fashioned into cakes

ABOVE: Distributing bread to the poor in Paris after the famine in 1662.

and cooked over an open fire to make a coarse flat cake. At the same time, in Egypt, where civilization was considerably more advanced, bread was a regular part of daily life, and indeed the Egyptians are credited with being the first people to make bread. Paintings on the walls of tombs depict bread being offered to the gods, and the flat oval-shaped breads look uncannily like *aiysh*, the Egyptian bread still eaten today. Other pictures show round or cone-shaped breads, and it is likely that they were all leavened, since the water from the Nile contains the same strain of yeast that is used in baking today. The Greeks initially made unleavened breads, but during the last millennium B.C. leavens were introduced to raise their breads, and the loaves were baked in bread ovens. Once wheat flour replaced barley meal, the Greeks became very partial to bread, their bakers producing a huge range of different breads made with honey or milk or sprinkled with sesame or poppy seed, according to one account written in the first century A.D.

Elsewhere, the leavening of bread became commonplace, even if at first it might have come about by accident. Natural yeasts exist in the air around us, and a warm paste of flour and water will

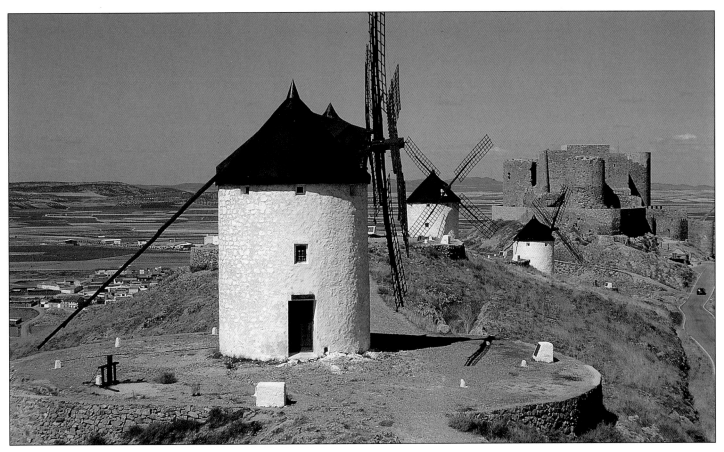

ABOVE: Throughout Europe, windmills were built to make milling easier.

spontaneously start to ferment if left for a couple of hours, so leavened bread is probably almost as ancient as the unleavened cakes baked over hot stones. Sourdoughs made by this natural method became popular in many parts of Europe, and the traditions continue to this day with sourdough ryes from eastern Europe and Germany, wheaten *levains* such as *pain de campagne* and Italian country loaves from southern regions.

In ancient Britain, about the time of the Roman invasion, beer barm—the yeasty froth on fermenting liquor—began to be used as a leaven. Barley was by far the most important crop at that time, and ale was widely brewed. Once the use of natural leavens had become widespread, it would have been but a small step to realize that beer barm, with the same sweet/sour smell, could be used as well.

In Biblical times, leavened bread was common. In the Book of Genesis, Lot, the son of Abraham, welcomes two angels to his house and "baked for them unleavened bread," which suggests that leavened

bread was the more usual food for non-angels. Today, Jews bake unleavened bread—*matzos*—for Passover, in remembrance of the Hebrews' escape from Egypt, and unleavened bread is frequently the bread for ritual or sacred occasions.

Bread also plays a central role in Christianity. Jesus fed the five thousand

BELOW: Originally, bread ovens were made of fireproof stone or bricks.

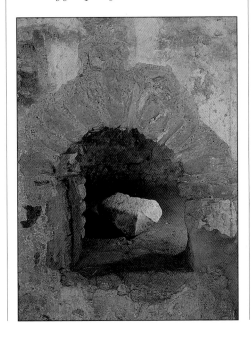

with bread, and at the last supper he broke unleavened bread (it being Passover), giving thanks to the Lord and literally identifying with it, with the words "this is my body," the act of which is recalled in every Christian Mass.

BREAD IN BRITAIN AND EUROPE DURING THE MIDDLE AGES

The Romans brought wheat, oats and rye to Britain along with many of their bread-making techniques. However, while for a time bread making became more sophisticated, it suffered a setback once the Romans left. During the Dark Ages, the growing and harvesting of cereal and then the making and baking of bread would have been a hit-or-miss affair. Families would have gathered cereals from their local fields and threshed the grain either in their own home or by using a quern stone belonging to the village.

By the Middle Ages, however, horses had begun to be used for ploughing and cultivation began to be more organized. The watermill and then the windmill were invented, probably first in England and then elsewhere in Europe. Perhaps this was something of a mixed blessing, for while the mill certainly took the backache out of the task, the lord of the manor retained rights over the mill and would oblige the serfs who worked his land to pay a tithe for the use of the mill. To add insult to injury, the bakehouse, often adjoining the mill, also made a charge to the families who used it, and in a period when cottages were flimsy constructions without ovens or even chimneys, families often had little option but to take their bread to the communal oven.

The loaves themselves were normally huge, weighing more than ten pounds, and would be expected to feed the family for several days. Made of a mixture of grain—wheat, barley, millet and rye—they would have been coarse mealy loaves. If the winters were not too harsh, the summers warm and the rainfall neither too great nor too little, harvests would be good and people could survive on a diet of bread, ale and pottage—a kind of stew made of pulses and meat. However, after a poor harvest, cereal became scarce and people would have to scratch around for almost anything that could be ground to a meal. Acorns and crushed roots were often the stand-bys in times of famine in Europe, while in England the poor would have to resort to horse bread, a type of mealy cake made of ground beans, so-called as it was normally fed to animals.

BELOW: In 15th century France bread was still cooked over an open fire.

ABOVE: This sixteenth century bake-house in Scandinavia was built next door to a public bath—perhaps the oven also warmed the water.

In 1266, laws were introduced in England, known as the Assizes of Bread, which stated that the weight of bread should be fixed to a certain price. For the price of one penny it was set down that three types of bread should be available: white loaves made from bolted (sifted) flour, which were the lightest breads, wheaten loaves made of more coarsely sifted meal and weighing half as much again, and finally the household loaf, the heaviest of all three and made of unrefined meal. The Assize system was deeply unpopular with bakers, but it nevertheless continued for some 450 years, which testifies to the importance the government attached to bread being available and affordable for all the populace.

BRITAIN IN TUDOR TIMES

Bread and stew continued to be the staple foods for most people of England under the Tudors, and while the wealthier people could afford a more varied diet, bread was still the most important food at the table. All large households baked their own bread, and bread also became available at bakeries that sprang up in most towns. These professional bakers would bake some customers' loaves for them, in addition to making and selling their own, although most breads by this time were baked at home, normally over a hearth, since an open oven continued to be a considerable fire risk.

For the poor, most bread was made of a mixture of grains, which would vary depending on the part of the country: rye in Norfolk; barley in northwest England and the lowlands of Scotland, Wales and Cornwall; and oats in the uplands of Wales and the Scottish Highlands. For the poorest, a mixed grain called maslin was often used, while peasant bread made from peas and beans continued to be made during severe hardship.

Although the more affluent people did eat plain brown bread, they also began to acquire a liking for white bread. White bread was considered superior for several reasons: it was more expensive, owing to the time and effort required to sift out the bran, and it implied prestige—some churches used a white bread called Pandemain, by definition more refined, as the sacramental bread. People took this to mean better, and white bread acquired a cachet which has only really been dented in the last 20 years.

Known by various names, this white bread eventually came to be known as manchet. Manchets were made from the finest wheat flour and were relatively small, sometimes not much bigger than a large roll; compared with the large plain breads, they were not considered sufficient for one person at a meal.

Another common practice, dating from the Middle Ages and surviving until the end of the sixteenth century, was the use of trenchers. These were thick slices of bread from large four-day-old whole-wheat loaves, which served as plates for both the less affluent and the wealthy, hard-baked for the purpose and cut into squares or rectangles. The custom was also practiced in France, and trencher breads were made in Corbeil and sold in the markets of Paris. Meat and fish would be placed on top of each slice, the bread soaking up any gravy. Those who were still hungry would then eat their trencher—from where we get the expression "trencherman," someone renowned for the amount he eats. In wealthy families it would have been unseemly to eat the trencher, not to say unnecessary, as there would have been sufficient food offered at table. Instead, the servants would take the pieces of bread and give them to the almshouses.

LATER CENTURIES

Within the British Isles and across Europe, the lot of the peasant farmer contrasted sharply with that of the wealthy. During the eighteenth century, the price of wheat rose sharply. In Britain, the Corn Laws, which were largely responsible for the price increases, were finally repealed in 1846. In France, the State's failure to respond to the crisis resulted in revolution. Around this time, the potato—introduced to Europe at the beginning of the seventeenth century—finally gained acceptance. In France and the south of England, wheat continued to be the favored staple, but potatoes were used increasingly, and by the middle of the nineteenth century, potatoes were as much a staple as bread. For the poor, bread and potatoes together formed the basis of a meager diet. In Ireland, however, potatoes were often the only food, resulting in the catastrophic famine of the 1840s when potato blight struck.

BELOW: Wood-fired ovens in homes were a rarity because of the fire risk.

ABOVE: In Victorian times all large households baked their own bread.

BAKING METHODS

The first means of baking or cooking a bread was simply by placing the dough on a heated stone over the dying embers of a fire. This technique is not dissimilar to that used today by the Australian bushmen when making their damper bread. The first English settlers in Virginia also used the same principle for their maize breads, baking the dough over hot ashes or in hot sand. The advantage is that no hardware or utensils are required; the disadvantage is that the bread, even if leavened, is mainly flat. At some point someone came up with the idea of placing a pot over the bread. The steamy heat caused the bread to rise, and variations on this theme continued for hundreds of years among the poorer people.

At the same time, most villages had a bakehouse, either attached to the mill or owned by the baker. Farmers and larger households often had their own bread ovens, fired with wood and furze (gorse). Although these fuels were cheap to collect, lighting and heating the oven would have been a time-consuming process, and for most households it would be lit only once a week. After the week's bread had been baked, cookies and cakes, which required lower temperatures, would be placed in the cooling oven.

Originally, ovens were heated using wood that was burnt on the oven floor. Once the oven was hot, the embers were removed using a long-handled tool, called a peel. These ancient ovens were built of fire-proof stone, and later replaced by bricks. The stone or bricks would become white hot, and then very gradually the heat would decrease as the bread was baked. Flat breads, such as the Italian *focaccia*, would have been the first breads to go into these immensely hot ovens, where they would be baked quickly. Larger loaves would then be baked, the slowly decreasing heat ensuring that the bread had a good thick crust, which meant that it kept well for the days ahead.

In the United States, Australia, Britain, France and other parts of Europe, enthusiasts have restored these wood-burning ovens and their bread, which is made according to traditional recipes, is quite delicious.

In Ireland, bread was cooked in a type of Dutch oven, which was set in peat with burning embers piled around it. A similar type of oven is still used by the people of Dutch ancestry in South Africa, who make their pot bread by baking it in a cast-iron pot piled high with smoldering embers.

GRAINS AND MILLING

Wheat is by far the most popular cereal for bread making. First grown in Asia Minor, it has been cultivated for some ten thousand years. For most of that time, the sowing and cultivating, threshing and milling were laborious jobs that required toil and effort for both farmer and miller. Today, mechanization makes the task of getting bread to our table far less arduous, and the skills acquired from our ancestors, although refined, are still very much with us today.

Wheat is a member of the grass family, and flour is produced from the grains in the ear. It is a tolerant cereal and grows in a wide range of climates, although it prefers cooler temperatures. There are two basic species of wheat: bread wheat used in baking, and durum used for pasta. Of the bread wheats, the so-called hard ones, which contain a higher proportion of protein, are best for bread flour.

THE WHEAT GRAIN

The wheat grain is one of nature's perfect foods. Crammed with energy and low in fat, it contains fiber, carbohydrates, protein and important vitamins and minerals.

The wheat grain is 1/4-inch long and golden when ripe. The ripeness of wheat is determined by its color; a farmer may also chew a few grains to check that the wheat is dry and crunchy.

WHOLE-WHEAT GRAIN

This is the whole grain from which whole wheat flour is made. Wheat grains are cleaned to remove grit and debris before milling, but nothing else is removed.

BRAN

The bran is the thin, papery skin covering the wheat grain. Some or all of it is removed for whole wheat and white flour respectively. Bran cannot be digested, but it does provide valuable fiber in the diet and can be bought separately for use in bran loaves and for other baking purposes.

WHEAT KERNEL

This is the inner part of the wheat grain, revealed when the bran has been peeled off. It is made up of starch bound together by gluten, the protein needed for bread making to give dough its elasticity. Strong wheats tend to contain a greater proportion of gluten and are therefore the preferred wheats for bread making.

WHEAT GERM

This tiny wheat seed is rich in vitamins B and E, salts, proteins and fatty acids. It is usually present in some degree whole wheat flour. Wheat germ can be bought

BELOW: Nowadays, most of the barley grown in Europe is used for brewing.

ABOVE: The ripeness of wheat grain is determined by its golden color.

separately for adding to loaves or sprinkling over the sides of the baking pans prior to cooking bread. Since its natural oil eventually becomes rancid, wheat germ will keep for only a short period. Store in the refrigerator and check the "use-by" date on the package.

OTHER GRAINS
BARLEY

Barley has been grown across Europe for centuries, and was used for bread making when wheat was expensive and rye was unavailable. Today, the grain is mostly grown for brewing.

BUCKWHEAT

Buckwheat is a member of the same family as rhubarb and sorrel and is therefore not strictly a cereal. It is now mostly grown in northeast Europe.

CORN (MAIZE)

The term "corn" has given rise to considerable confusion. In Britain it was historically used to describe the predominant cereal crop of a region (for instance, wheat in England and oats in Scotland). An English field of corn, therefore, meant a field of wheat, not the tall annual grass with yellow edible grains, which was also known by its sixteenth century Spanish name—maize (*maiz*).

Sailors from Spain and Portugal, who accompanied the early explorers, were

ABOVE:: At Crowdy Mill in North Devon, England, flour is still milled in the traditional way.

responsible for introducing corn into Europe. Until then it was unknown in the Old World, although it was a staple crop in the southern parts of America. It needs higher temperatures and more sunshine than wheat and is therefore grown mainly in the more southern parts of Europe. It is still widely grown in Mexico and in the southern United States.

MILLET

Mostly grown for animal feeds, millet thrives in both tropical and arid countries.

OATS

Oats have been cultivated in northern Europe for centuries, but although among the most nutritious of all cereals, they were mostly grown for animal feed. Thanks, however, to the Scots' love of porridge, this grain continues to be cultivated for human consumption.

RICE

Widely grown in China and other parts of Asia, as well as the United States and parts of Spain and Italy, rice is an important cereal crop. Rice flour is a low-gluten flour, which is used in much the same way as cornstarch.

RYE

Rye prefers colder, dry climates and acid soils and is therefore ideally suited to the cooler parts of Europe, such as Germany, Scandinavia, northern Russia and Poland.

SPELT

This is one of the oldest cultivated species of wheat. It continues to be grown, but only in small areas in Germany and other parts of northern Europe.

MILLING

Flour is milled by passing the grain through a series of grinders. Traditionally, these were huge stones that were placed closer and closer together and turned by water or wind power. Nowadays the stones have been replaced by steel rollers, driven by machine. The ribbed cylinders separate the bran and wheat germ from the white kernel, and the flour is sifted through a series of increasingly fine meshes. The advantage of roller mills, apart from the obvious one of not being dependent upon the weather for power, is that the rollers themselves wear far better than grindstones, which needed replacing regularly. The disadvantages are that the rollers automatically expel the bran and wheat germ and the faster process means that the flour loses some of its flavor and character.

GRIST

The grist is the blend of different wheats a miller selects to make flour. Most flours are made from a mixture of wheats.

WINDMILLS

The stone towers of old windmills are still dotted across Europe. Although they are a reminder of a simpler age, windmills were complex machines that required a great deal of skill. The miller was consequently an important and respected member of the community. Farmers who had spent much of a year growing and harvesting their crop, relied on the miller to turn their efforts into flour so that they could feed their families.

The principle of the windmill is very simple. Huge grindstones, turned by the action of the wind on the sails, slowly milled the grain into flour. The miller's task was to make sure the stones turned at a steady speed: too slowly and the grain would pile up, too quickly and it would overheat and spoil. It was most important to ensure that the hopper remained full of grain, for if there was no grist on the mill, the stones would spark and the whole mill could catch on fire.

Nowadays only a small amount of flour is milled using windmills. Compared with modern methods, the process is very slow. Nevertheless, a few smaller flour producers use windmills for their stoneground flours and thus keep this tradition alive.

BELOW: This seventeenth century windmill is a reminder of a simpler age.

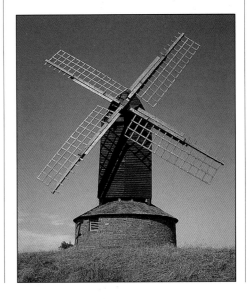

INGREDIENTS FOR BREAD MAKING

WHEAT FLOURS

The simplest breads are a mixture of flour and water and some type of leavening agent. Beyond that narrow definition, however, lies an infinite number of possibilities. The flour is most likely to come from wheat, but may be derived from another type of grain or, even, in the case of buckwheat, from another source entirely. The liquid may be water, but could just as easily be milk, or a mixture. Yeast is the obvious raising agent, but there are other options. Salt is essential, fats are often added, and other ingredients range from sweeteners like sugar or molasses to dried fruit, spices and savory flavorings.

WHITE FLOUR

This flour contains about 75 percent of the wheat grain with most of the bran and the wheat germ extracted. Plain flour is used for pastry, sauces and cookies, while self-rising flour, which contains a raising agent, is used for cakes, scones and other desserts. It can also be used for soda bread. American all-purpose flour is a medium-strength flour, somewhere between the British plain and strong white flour. Soft flour, sometimes known as American cake flour, has been milled very finely for sponge cake and similar baked goods.

UNBLEACHED WHITE FLOUR

Unbleached flour is more creamy in color than other white flours, which have been whitened artificially. Bleaching, which involves treating the flour with chlorine, is becoming increasingly rare and the majority of white flours are unbleached, although check the package to be sure. In Britain, flour producers are required by law to add, or fortify their white flours with certain nutrients such as vitamin B1, nictinic acid, iron and calcium. These are often added in the form of white soy flour, which has a natural bleaching effect.

RIGHT: Organic flours are being used increasingly for bread making.

STRONG WHITE/WHITE BREAD FLOUR

For almost all bread making, the best type of flour to use is one that is largely derived from wheat that is high in protein. This type of flour is described as "strong" and is often labeled "bread flour," which underlines its suitability for the task. It is the proteins that combine to form gluten when mixed with water, and it is this that gives dough its elasticity when kneaded, and allows it to trap the bubbles of carbon dioxide given off by the yeast. A soft flour produces flat loaves that stale quickly; conversely, if the flour is too hard, the bread will have a coarse texture. A balance is required and most millers blend hard and soft wheats to make a flour that produces a well-flavored loaf with good volume. Most strong white flours have a lower protein content than their whole-wheat equivalent and a baker would probably use a flour with a protein level of 12 percent. The protein value of a flour can be found listed on the side of the package under "Nutritional Value."

FINE FRENCH PLAIN FLOUR

French bakers use a mixture of white bread flour and all-purpose flour to make baguettes and other specialties. French all-purpose flour is called *farine fluide* in its country of origin because it is so light and free-flowing. Such is the popularity of French-style baked goods that this type of flour is now available in European supermarkets.

WHOLE-WHEAT FLOUR

This flour is made using the whole of the wheat grain and is sometimes called 100 percent extraction flour: nothing is added and nothing is taken away. The bran and wheat germ, which are automatically separated from the white inner portion if milled between rollers, are returned to the white flour at the end of the process. *Atta* is a fine whole-wheat flour used for Indian breads (see Other Flours).

STONEGROUND WHOLE-WHEAT FLOUR

This whole-wheat flour has been ground in the traditional way between two stones. The bran and wheat germ are milled with the rest of the wheat grain, so there is no separation of the flour at any stage. Stoneground flour is also considered to have a better flavor, owing to the slow grinding of the stones. However, because the oily wheat germ is squashed into the flour, rather than churned in later, stoneground flour has a higher fat content and may become rancid if stored for too long.

ORGANIC WHOLE-WHEAT FLOUR

This flour has been milled from organic wheat, which is wheat produced without the use of artificial fertilizers or pesticides. There are organic versions of all varieties of whole-wheat and white flours available at most large supermarkets and health-food stores.

STRONG WHOLE-WHEAT/ WHOLE-WHEAT BREAD FLOUR

A higher proportion of high gluten wheat is necessary in whole-wheat flours to counteract the heaviness of the bran. If the flour is not strong enough, the dough may rise unevenly and is likely to collapse in the oven. The miller selects his grist (the blend) of hard and soft wheat grains, according to the type of flour required. Bakers would probably look for a protein content of about 13.5 percent; the strong flours available in supermarkets are normally between 11.5 and 13 percent.

ABOVE: A selection of different wheat flours and grains. Clockwise from top right: strong white flour, stoneground whole-wheat, whole-wheat, wheat germ, organic whole-wheat, plain flour, organic plain flour, semolina, organic stoneground whole-wheat and Granary flour. The three flours in the center are (clockwise from top) brown, spelt and self-rising flour.

GRANARY FLOUR
Granary is the proprietary name of a blend of brown and rye flours and malted wheat grain. The malted grain gives this bread its characteristic sweet and slightly sticky flavor and texture. It is available at health-food stores and supermarkets.

MALTHOUSE FLOUR
A specialty flour available at some large supermarkets and healthfood stores, this is a combination of stoneground brown flour, rye flour and malted wheat flour with malted wheat flakes. It resembles Granary flour.

GRAHAM FLOUR
This popular American flour is slightly coarser than ordinary whole-wheat. It is named after a 19th-century Massachusetts cleric, Reverend Sylvestor Graham, who developed the flour and advocated using the whole grain for bread making because of the beneficial effects of the bran.

BROWN FLOUR
This flour contains about 85 percent of the original grain, with some of the bran and wheat germ extracted. It produces a lighter loaf than 100 percent whole-wheat flour, while still retaining a high percentage of wheat germ, which gives bread so much of its flavor.

WHEAT GERM FLOUR
A wheat germ flour can be brown or white but must contain at least 10 percent added wheat germ. Wheat germ is highly nutritious and this bread is considered particularly healthy. Wheat germ bread has a pleasant nutty flavor.

SEMOLINA
This is the wheat kernel or endosperm, once the bran and wheat germ have been removed from the grain by milling, but before it is fully milled into flour. Semolina can be ground either coarsely or finely and is used for certain Indian breads, including *bhatura*.

SPELT
Although spelt, a variety of wheat, is no longer widely grown, some flour mills still produce a spelt flour, which is available at healthfood stores.

OTHER FLOURS

Alternative grains, such as barley, corn-meal and oatmeal, are full of flavor but contain little or no gluten. Breads made solely from them would rise poorly and would be extremely dense. The milled grains are therefore often mixed with strong wheat flour. Rye is rich in gluten, but pure rye doughs are difficult to handle; once again the addition of strong wheat flour can provide a solution.

BARLEY MEAL

Barley is low in gluten and is seldom used for bread making in Britain and western Europe. In Russia and Eastern European countries, however, barley loaves continue to be produced, the flour mostly blended with some proportion of wheat or rye flour to give the loaf volume. These loaves are definitely on the robust side. They tend to be rather gray and flat and have an earthy, rather mealy flavor. Similar loaves must have been baked in parts of the British Isles in the past, when times were hard or the wheat harvest had failed. There are several old Welsh recipes for barley bread, which was rolled out flat before being baked on a baking stone. Finnish barley bread is made in much the same way.

Barley meal is the ground whole grain of the barley, while barley flour is ground pearl barley, with the outer skin removed. Either can be added in small quantities to

BELOW: Finnish barley bread

whole-wheat or to white flour to produce a bread with a slightly rustic flavor.

BUCKWHEAT FLOUR

This grain is blackish in color, hence its French name, *blé noir*. It is not strictly a cereal but is the fruit of a plant belonging to the sorrel family. The three-cornered grains are milled to a flour and used for pancakes, blinis and, in France, for crêpes or galettes. It can also be added to wheat flour and is popular mixed with other grains in multigrained loaves. It has a distinctive, earthy flavor and is best used in small quantities.

CORNMEAL (MAIZEMEAL)

This meal is ground from white or yellow corn and is normally available in coarse, medium or fine grinds. Coarse-ground cornmeal is used for the Italian dish of polenta; for bread making, choose one of the finer grinds, available at most healthfood stores. There are numerous cornbreads from the southern United States, including cornbread made with fresh corn kernels. Corn was brought back to Europe by the Spanish and Portuguese and corn breads are still popular in these countries today, particularly in Portugal. Corn contains no gluten so will not make a loaf unless it is blended with wheat flour, in which case the corn adds a pleasant flavor and color.

MILLET FLOUR

Although high in protein, millet flour is low in gluten and is not commonly used by itself in bread making. It is pale yellow in color, with a gritty texture. The addition of wheat flour produces an interesting, slightly nutty flavor.

OATMEAL

Oatmeal does not contain gluten and is only very rarely used by itself for bread making. The exception is in Scotland where flat yeast-leavened oatmeal biscuits have been popular for centuries. These are baked on a griddle and served with butter or marmalade. Oatmeal can also be used in wheat or multigrain loaves. Choose finely ground oatmeal for making oatcakes or for using in loaves. Rolled oats are not a flour but are the steamed and flattened whole oats. They look good sprinkled on the crust of loaves and rolls, and add a pleasant flavor.

RICE FLOUR

Polished rice, if ground very finely, becomes rice flour. It can be used as a thickening agent and is useful for people with wheat allergies. It is also occasionally used for some Indian breads.

STORAGE

Although most flours keep well, they do not last indefinitely, and it is important to pay attention to the "use-by" date on the package. Old flour will begin to taste stale and will make a disappointing loaf. Always store flour on a cool dry shelf. Ideally, the flour should be kept in its bag and placed in a tin or storage jar with a tight-fitting lid. Wash and dry the jar thoroughly whenever replacing with new flour and avoid adding new flour to old. Whole-wheat flour, because it contains the oils in wheatgerm, keeps less well than white flours. Consequently, do not buy large quantities at a time and keep it in a very cool place or in the salad drawer of the refrigerator.

ABOVE: A selection of non-wheat grains and specialty flours. Clockwise from top center: rye flour, buckwheat flour, cornmeal, bajra flour, organic rye flour, millet grain, jowar flour, gram flour and atta or chapati flour. In the center are (clockwise from top) barley meal, fine oatmeal and rice flour.

RYE FLOUR

Rye is the only other cereal, apart from wheat, that is widely used to make bread. It has a good gluten content, although the gluten in rye is different from wheat gluten, and rye doughs are notoriously sticky and difficult to handle. For this reason, rye meal is often blended with other flours to create a dough that is more manageable. There are as many different rye meals as there are wheat flours, ranging in color and in type of grind. Pumpernickel and other dense and steamed box-shaped rye breads use a coarsely ground whole-wheat rye, while finer flour, which contains neither the bran nor the germ, is used for the popular crusty black breads.

INDIAN FLOURS
ATTA/CHAPATI FLOUR

This is a very fine whole-wheat flour, which is normally found only in Indian grocers where it is sometimes labeled *ata*. As well as being used to make chapatis, it is also the type of flour used for making rotis and other Indian flat breads.

BAJRA FLOUR

This plant grows along the west coast of India. The grains are a mixture of yellow and gray but when ground, the flour is a more uniform gray. It has a strong nutty aroma and a distinct flavor. *Bajra* bread or *rotla* is cooked, like all unleavened breads, on a griddle.

JOWAR FLOUR

Jowar grows over most of central and southern India. The flour, ground from the pretty pale yellow grains, is a creamy-white color. The flat breads usually made from this flour, called *bhakris*, are roasted on a griddle and are traditionally served with a rich-flavored, spicy, coconut, garlic and red chili chutney.

GRAM FLOUR

This is a flour made from ground chickpeas. It is also known as *besan*. The Indian *missi rotis*—spicy, unleavened breads from northern India—are made using gram flour or a mixture of whole-wheat and gram flours.

YEAST AND OTHER LEAVENS

Almost all breads today are leavened in one way or another, which means that a substance has been added to the dough to initiate fermentation and make the dough rise.

Without yeast or another leavening agent, the mixture of flour and water, once cooked, would be merely a flat, unappetizing cake. At some point in our history, our ancestors discovered how dough, if left to ferment in warm air, produced a lighter and airier bread when cooked.

The transformation of dough into bread is caused by yeast or another leavening ingredient producing carbon dioxide. The carbon dioxide expands, the dough stretches and tiny pockets of air are introduced into the dough. When the bread is cooked the process is set and the air becomes locked in.

LEAVENING AGENTS

The most popular and most widely known leavening ingredient in bread making is

BELOW: Clockwise from top left: fresh yeast, dried yeast, fast-action dried yeast and easy-blend dried yeast.

yeast. However, raising agents such as baking soda and baking powder are also used for making certain breads.

YEAST

Yeast is the most popular leavening agent for bread making. It is simple to use, more reliable than a natural leaven and considerably quicker to activate. Conventional dried yeast, easy-blend and fast-action yeast are all types of dried yeast, produced for the convenience of those making bread at home. Almost all bakers prefer fresh yeast, since it is considered to have a superior flavor and to be more manageable and reliable. However, when fresh yeast is not available or convenient, dried yeast is a handy substitute.

There are several ways of adding yeast to flour. Fresh yeast is usually blended with lukewarm water before being mixed into the flour; conventional dried yeast is first reconstituted in warm water and then left until frothy; easy-blend and fast-action dried yeasts are added directly to the flour.

THE SPONGE METHOD

Some yeasted breads are made by the sponge method, whereby the yeast is dissolved in more water than usual, and then mixed with some of the

flour to make a batter. This can be done in a bowl, or the batter can be made in a well in the center of the flour, with only some surrounding flour included at the start, as in the recipe for Split Pan Loaf. The batter is left for at least 20 minutes—often much longer—until bubbles appear on the surface, a process known as sponging. It is then mixed with the remaining flour, and any other ingredients are added. The advantage of this method is that it enables the yeast to start working without being inhibited by ingredients like eggs, fat and sugar, which slow down its action.

Many French breads are also sponged. A slightly different technique is used and the batter is left to ferment for a lot longer —for 2–12 hours. The slow fermentation creates what is described as a *poolish* sponge, and makes for a wonderfully flavored bread, with very little acidity, yet with a fragile and crunchy crust. *Pain polka* is made by this method, as are the best baguettes. Two factors affect the rise: the temperature of the room and the wetness of the mixture. A wet sponge will rise more quickly than a firmer one. Italian bakers employ a similar process called a *biga*. This uses less liquid, and the sponge takes about 12–15 hours to mature. For an example of the use of a *biga* starter, see the recipe for ciabatta.

BAKING POWDER

This is made up of a mixture of acid and alkaline chemicals. When these come into contact with moisture, as in a dough or a batter, the reaction of the chemicals produces tiny bubbles of air so the dough rises and becomes spongy, just as it does with yeast. Unlike when making yeast-leavened breads, however, it is important to work fast as the carbon dioxide will quickly escape and the loaf will collapse.

BAKING SODA

Baking soda, sometimes just called soda, is the leavening ingredient in Irish soda bread. It is an alkaline chemical which, when mixed with an acid in a moisture-rich environment, reacts to produce carbon dioxide. Cream of tartar, an acid that is made from fermented grapes, is commonly used in conjunction with baking soda for soda breads, or else the soda is combined with sour milk, which is naturally acidic. Buttermilk may also be used.

BREWER'S YEAST

Old cook books sometimes call for brewer's yeast or ale or beer barm. Until the last century, this was the only leavening ingredient. Since then, brewer's yeast has acquired something of a cult status, and during the 1950s in the United States and Britain it was considered a wonder food owing to its nutritional value. It is not however, suitable for bread making, being too bitter, and should only be used for making beer.

NATURAL LEAVENS

Natural leavens, made using a medium of flour, or grown from potatoes, yogurt, molasses or buttermilk were once very popular and are enjoying a renaissance.

SOURDOUGHS

Sourdoughs are breads based on a natural leaven. An authentic sourdough relies entirely on the wild yeasts that exist in the air. Given the right conditions, any dough of flour and water or batter of vegetable origin will start to ferment spontaneously and will continue to do so if starch or sugar is added to feed it. Recipes for some of the traditional American and German breads use a variety of rather surprising starters for their sourdoughs, from potatoes to molasses. With the renewed interest in rustic breads, there are all sorts of sourdough breads in supermarkets and specialty bakeries, and numerous books explaining how to make them at home. There are many, many types of sourdough. In France the sourdough method is known as the *chef* or *levain*, and is used

LEFT: Pain de campagne is one of the many French sourdough breads.

for *pain de campagne* as well as for sourdough baguettes.

Despite their many variations, sourdoughs do have some elements in common. Each begins with a "starter," which can take anything up to a week to ferment and become established. This "starter" or leaven is used, daily by bakers or less frequently by home bread makers, for the day's bread. A small amount of the dough is then kept back and used for the next batch of bread. Alternatively, a slightly more liquid starter can be made and kept in the refrigerator until it is ready for use. Each time part of the starter is used, the remaining starter is refreshed with equal amounts of flour and water. Replenished in this way, starters have been known to survive for many years.

Starters for sourdoughs, as well as the breads themselves, vary widely—not only from country to country but from village to village. Many recipes, and indeed many bakers, recommend using a little yeast to get started, as a true starter is likely to be rather a hit-or-miss affair. Wild yeasts may be all around us, but for some reason they seem to vanish as soon as you decide to make a sourdough. Starters also improve with age, so do not be discouraged if your first sourdoughs are rather bland. After a few attempts, you should find your breads developing their own tangy personality.

YEAST KNOW-HOW

◆ Yeast needs warmth to activate it, but must not be subjected to too hot a temperature or it will die. Whether dissolving yeast in water or adding liquid to the yeast and flour, make sure the liquid is not too warm. The optimum heat is 100°F. If you do not have a thermometer, experts recommend mixing 1¼ cups boiling water with 2½ cups cold water, and measuring the required water from the mixture.

◆ If you are using easy-blend or fast-action dried yeast you can afford to have the water slightly hotter, since the yeast is mixed with the flour, and the heat of the water will rapidly dissipate.

◆ Check "use-by" dates on dried and fast-action yeasts. If a product is past its "use-by" date, replace it. If it is marginal and you cannot immediately replace it, take a measuring cup and pour in ½ cup warm water (110–115°F). Add 1 teaspoon sugar, stir to dissolve and then sprinkle over 2 teaspoons dried yeast. Stir and leave for 10 minutes. The yeast should begin to rise to the surface after the first 5 minutes, and by 10 minutes there should have developed a rounded crown of foam that reaches to the 1 cup level of the measuring cup. If this happens the yeast is active, if not, the yeast has lost its potency and should be discarded.

◆ The amount of yeast you require should not increase proportionally as the amount of flour increases, so take care if you decide to double the quantities in a recipe. You will not need to double the amount of yeast. Similarly, if you halve a recipe, you are likely to need proportionally more yeast or be prepared to wait longer for the bread to rise.

ADDITIONAL INGREDIENTS

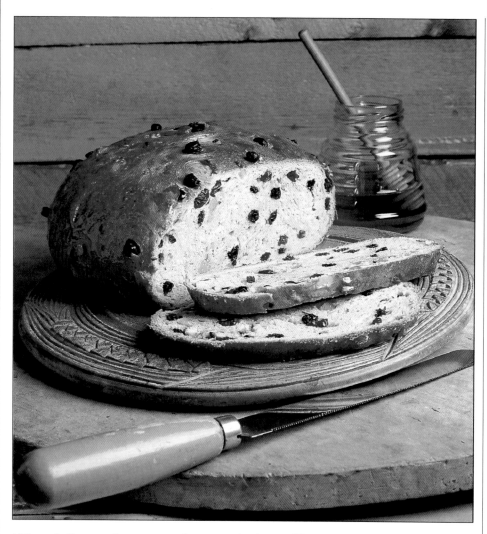

Although flour and yeast are the most obvious ingredients used in bread making, there are a number of other ingredients that are just as important.

WATER OR MILK

As a general rule, savory loaves are made using water; teabreads and sweeter breads use milk. Whatever the liquid, it is always heated slightly. Breads made with milk are softer both in the crumb and the crust than those using water.

ABOVE: Welsh bara brith is packed with dried fruits.

SALT

Almost all bread recipes add salt at the beginning, stirring or sifting it into right the flour.

Salt is one of the few essential ingredients in bread making. It is important for both flavor and the effect it has on the yeast and dough. Essentially, it slows down the yeast's action—which is why it should not be added directly to the yeast. This means that the dough rises in a controlled and even way, giving a well-risen even loaf. Too little salt means the loaf will stale more quickly; too much and the crust will harden, so do take care when measuring salt.

LEFT: The French petit pains au lait, made with milk rather than water, have a lovely soft crumb and crust.

SUGAR

Sugar, once invariably added to all breads (usually with the yeast), is now no longer necessary for savory breads since modern yeasts can be activated without it. However, some bakers still prefer to add a little sugar, even when making savory baked goods, contending that results with sugar are better than when it is omitted.

White and brown sugar, honey, molasses and golden syrup can be used to sweeten teabreads and fruit breads. Sugars are normally added with the flour, while liquids, such as molasses and honey, are more often stirred into the lukewarm liquid so that they are gently warmed as well.

BUTTER AND EGGS

Enriched breads are made with the addition of both butter and eggs and normally use milk rather than water. These breads, such as Sally Lunn, barm brack and many of the festive European breads, have a delicious cake-like texture and soft crust. The butter is either melted or diced and the eggs beaten before being worked into other ingredients to make a fairly sticky batter. This is then beaten by hand or in an electric mixer. In some instances, the butter is kneaded into the dough after the initial rising, since large quantities of butter can inhibit the action of the yeast.

BELOW: Sally Lunn, one of the richest breads of all, is served in Britain sandwiched with clotted cream.

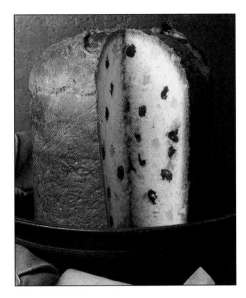

ABOVE: Pannetone is enriched with eggs and egg yolks.

BELOW: Red lentil dosas are spiced with turmeric and black pepper.

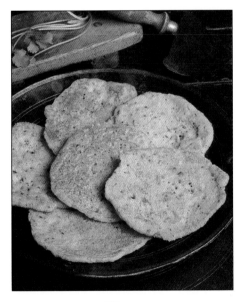

FRUIT

Almost any dried fruit can be added to bread. Raisins, currants and mixed peel have always been popular for fruit loaves. Chopped dates, apricots and prunes can all be kneaded in, as can more exotic fruits, such as dried mango or papaya. Fruit can be added to a dough during mixing or left until the second kneading. If adding at the second kneading, warm the fruit first, so that it does not inhibit the action of the yeast. If you are using an electric mixer or food processor for kneading, note that the blades, particularly on the food processor, will chop the fruit. This spoils both the appearance and the flavor of the loaf, so only knead by machine to begin with, then knead the fruit in by hand after the initial rising.

FATS

Fats, in the form of butter, oil, lard or vegetable shortening, are sometimes added to savory loaves. They add flavor and help preserve the freshness of the loaf. The Italians particularly love adding olive oil to their breads, which they do in generous quantities. Although oils and melted butter can be poured into the flour with the yeast and liquid, solid butter or fats are normally kneaded into the flour before the liquid is added.

NUTS, HERBS AND OTHER SAVORY INGREDIENTS

Some of our favorite breads today are flavored with herbs, nuts and other

BELOW: Ciabatta, like many Italian breads, is made with olive oil.

such savory ingredients. *Manoucher*, "Mediterranean nights" bread, is a rainbow of colors. Based on the Italian *focaccia*, it contains rosemary, red, green and yellow bell peppers along with goat cheese. The Italians add olives or sun-dried tomatoes to their ciabatta, while walnut bread (*pain aux noix* in France, *pane con noci* in Italy) is one of the best-known and best-loved savory loaves.

Nuts, herbs, pitted olives and sun-dried tomatoes should be roughly chopped before being kneaded into the dough after the first rising.

SPICES

The sweet spices are cinnamon, nutmeg, cloves and ginger, and for savory breads cumin, fennel, caraway and anise impart a delicious flavor. Mace, pepper and coriander seeds can be used for both sweet and savory breads. Spices can be added with the flour or kneaded in with fruit or nuts, or other ingredients.

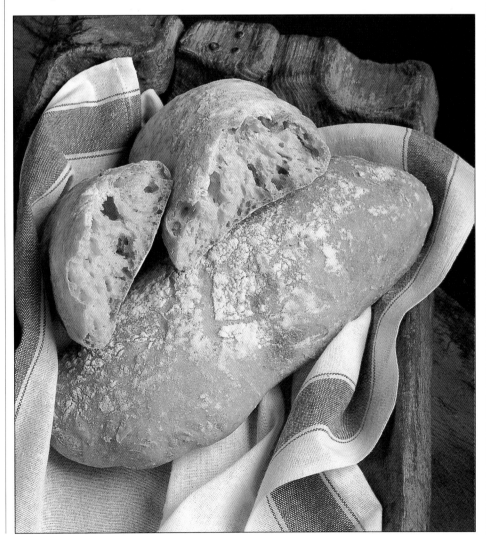

TECHNIQUES

—

USING YEAST

There are several different forms of yeast, some easier to use than others, but none of them particularly tricky if you follow a few simple rules. Whichever yeast you use, it must be in good condition—neither old nor stale—and must not be subjected to too much heat.

USING COMPRESSED CAKE YEAST

Compressed cake yeast is occasionally available at baker's stores, healthfood stores and gourmet supermarkets with in-store bakeries. It is pale beige in color, has a sweet, fruity smell and should crumble easily. It can be stored in the refrigerator, wrapped in plastic wrap for up to 2 weeks or frozen for up to 3 months. A quantity of ½ ounce should be sufficient for 6–8 cups flour, although this will depend on the recipe.

1 Put the yeast in a small bowl. Using a spoon, mash or "cream" it with a little of the measured water until smooth.

2 Pour in the remaining measured liquid, which may be water, milk or a mixture of the two. Mix well. Use as directed in the recipe.

USING ACTIVE DRIED YEAST

Active dried yeast is simply the dehydrated equivalent of fresh yeast, but it needs to be blended with lukewarm liquid before use. Store dried yeast in a cool dry place and check the "use-by" date on the package. You will need about ½ ounce (1½ teaspoons) active dried yeast for 6 cups flour. Some bakers add sugar or honey to the liquid to which the yeast is added, but this is not necessary, as the granules contain enough nourishment to enable the yeast to work.

1 Pour the measured lukewarm liquid into a small bowl and sprinkle the dried yeast evenly over the surface.

2 Cover with plastic wrap and let sit in a warm room for 10–15 minutes until frothy. Stir well and use as directed.

WATER TEMPERATURE

For fresh and regular dried yeast, use lukewarm water; for easy-blend and fast-action yeast the water can be a little hotter, as the yeast is mixed with flour before the liquid is added.

USING QUICK-RISE DRIED YEAST

This is the most convenient of the dried yeasts as it can be stirred directly into the flour. This yeast contains a bread improver, which eliminates the need for two kneadings and risings—check the instructions on the package to make sure. Most of these yeasts come in ¼-ounce envelopes, which are sufficient for 6 cups flour. Do not store opened envelopes as the yeast will deteriorate quickly.

Sift together the flour and salt into a medium bowl and rub in the fat, if using. Stir in the easy-blend or fast-action dried yeast, then add warm water or milk, plus any other ingredients, as directed in the recipe.

BELOW: Small, shaped rolls are very quick to make using easy-blend yeast.

MAKING A YEAST DOUGH BY THE SPONGE METHOD

This method produces bread with an excellent flavor and soft texture. The quantities listed are merely an example and can be increased proportionately. See individual recipes.

1 Mix ¼-ounce fresh yeast with 1 cup lukewarm water in a large bowl. Stir in 1 cup unbleached plain flour, using a wooden spoon, then use your fingers to draw the mixture together until you have a smooth liquid with the consistency of a thick batter. (Do not add salt to the sponge, as this would inhibit the yeast.)

2 Cover with a damp dish towel and leave in a warm place. The sponge will double or triple in bulk and then fall back, which indicates it is ready to use (after about 5–6 hours).

3 The sponge starter is now ready to be mixed into a dough with the remaining flour and any other ingredients, such as butter, as directed in the recipe.

MAKING AN ITALIAN STARTER (*BIGA*)

If you wish to make an Italian *biga* for Pugliese or a similar Italian country bread, use 1½ cups unbleached plain flour. Cream the yeast with 6 tablespoons lukewarm water, then pour it into a well in the center of the flour. Gradually mix in the surrounding flour to form a firm dough. The dough should be kneaded for a few minutes and then left, covered with lightly oiled plastic wrap for 12–15 hours.

MAKING A FRENCH SOURDOUGH STARTER (*CHEF*)

It is not difficult to make a sourdough starter. The starter can be kept in the refrigerator for up to 10 days, but for longer than that it should be frozen. Bring the starter to room temperature before adding to the next batch of bread.

1 Place 1 cup flour in a large bowl and add 5 tablespoons water. Combine, then knead for 3–4 minutes to form a dough. Cover the bowl with plastic wrap and set aside at room temperature for 2–3 days. The flour that you choose will depend on the bread you wish to make; it can be whole-wheat, white or rye, or a combination of two or three.

2 After 2–3 days, the mixture will rise and aerate slightly and turn a grayish color. A soft crust may form on top the starter and it should develop a slightly sweet-sour smell.

3 Remove any crust that has formed on top of the starter and discard. Stir in ½ cup lukewarm water to make a paste and then add 1½ cups flour. The flour can be whole-wheat or a mixture of whole-wheat and white. Combine to make a dough, then transfer to a work surface and knead lightly until firm.

SOURDOUGH

The actual word "sourdough" is thought to have come from America as this style of bread was commonly made by pioneers and the word was sometimes used to describe old "Forty-Niners". However bread made by the sourdough method dates back long before the 19th century. Many traditional European rye breads are based on this method, particularly in Germany and Scandinavia where the sour flavor of the leaven complements the flavor of the rye. In Britain sourdoughs are sometimes called acids or acid breads, the precise name depending on the part of the country. Some restaurants and home bread makers have their own favorite acid breads, but generally there is not much of a tradition of sourdoughs in the British Isles.

Except in Ireland, where soda bread was popular, ale barm (the fermentation liquor from beer) was the most commonly used leaven for bread making until it was replaced by baker's yeast around the middle of the last century.

4 Place the ball of dough in a bowl, cover again with plastic wrap and let sit for 1–2 days at room temperature.

5 Remove and discard any crust that forms. What remains—the *chef*—can now be used to make a sourdough bread, such as *pain de campagne rustique*. To keep the *chef* going, save about 8 ounces of the dough each time.

6 Place the dough starter in a crock or bowl, cover and keep in the fridge for up to 10 days or freeze.

MIXING, KNEADING AND RISING

The sequence and method of adding ingredients to make your dough is surprisingly important. For some breads, fresh or dried yeast is dissolved in lukewarm water and then stirred into the flour; if quick-rise dried yeast or fast-action dried yeast is used, this is added directly to the flour with warm water or milk added afterward. Read your recipe carefully before starting and warm your bowls if they are in the least bit chilly, so that the yeast gets off to a good start.

MIXING

The easiest way to mix the dough is with your hand but, if you prefer, start mixing with a spoon until the mixture is too stiff to stir, then mix by hand.

1 If using fresh or regular dried yeast, mix it with lukewarm water or milk as described in the recipe. Sift the flour, salt and any other dry ingredients (including easy-blend or fast-action dried yeast, if using) into a large, warm mixing bowl.

2 If using butter or lard, rub it in. Make a well in the center of the flour mixture and pour in the yeast mixture with the remaining lukewarm water. If oil is being used, add it now.

3 Mix the liquid into the flour using your hand, stirring in a smooth, wide motion so that all the dry ingredients are evenly incorporated and the mixture forms a dough. Knead lightly in the bowl.

KNEADING

Kneading is something you just cannot skip in bread making. If you do not have strong wrists, or simply do not enjoy it, you will have to resort to using the food processor, which takes all the effort—and much of the time—out of kneading. Better still though, learn to love it.

Kneading dough, whether by hand or machine, is the only way of warming and stretching the gluten in the flour. As the strands of gluten warm and become more elastic, so the dough becomes more springy. It is the elasticity of the dough, combined with the action of the yeast, that gives bread its light, springy texture. Insufficient kneading means that the dough cannot hold the little pockets of air, and the bread will collapse in the oven, leaving a heavy and dense loaf.

HOW TO KNEAD BY HAND

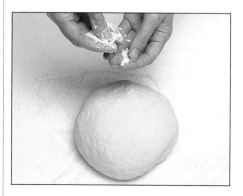

1 Place the mixed dough on a floured surface and flour your hands generously.

2 Press the heel of your hand firmly into the center of the dough, then curl your fingers around the edge of the dough.

3 Pull and stretch the dough toward you and press down again, giving the dough a quarter turn as you do so.

4 Continue pressing and stretching the dough, making quarter turns so that it is evenly kneaded. After about 10 minutes the dough should be supple and elastic; however, some breads need more kneading, so do check the recipe.

ADDING EXTRA INGREDIENTS

Ingredients, such as olives, can be added after kneading or they can be kneaded in after the first rising.

KNEADING IN A FOOD PROCESSOR

Unless you have an industrial-size machine, it is likely that your food processor will only be able to knead moderate amounts of dough. Don't attempt to knead more dough than recommended by the manufacturer, as it may damage the motor. If necessary, knead in small batches and then knead the dough balls together by hand afterward.

Fit the dough blade into the processor and then blend together all the dry ingredients. Add the yeast mixture, and extra lukewarm liquid and butter or oil, if required; process until the mixture comes together. Knead for 60 seconds or according to the manufacturer's instructions, then knead by hand on a floured board for 1–2 minutes.

KNEADING IN A FOOD MIXER

Check the manufacturer's instructions to make sure bread dough can be kneaded in your machine.

Combine the dry ingredients. Add the yeast, liquid and oil or butter, if using, and mix slowly, using the dough hook. The dough will tumble and fall to begin with, and then it will slowly come together. Continue kneading the dough for 3–4 minutes or according to the manufacturer's instructions.

RISING

This is the easy part of bread making—all you need now is to give the dough the right conditions, and nature and chemistry will do the rest. While kneading works and conditions the gluten in the flour, during rising (proving) the yeast does the work. The fermentation process creates carbon dioxide, which is trapped in the dough by the elastic gluten. This process also has the effect of conditioning the flour, improving the flavor and texture of the eventual loaf.

The number of times you let your bread rise will depend on the yeast you are using and the recipe. A quick-rise yeast needs no first rising, but dough using fresh yeast and other dried yeasts normally requires two risings, with some recipes calling for even more.

TEMPERATURE AND TIME

For most recipes, dough is left to rise at a temperature of about 75°–80°F, the equivalent of an airing cupboard or near a warm oven. At a cooler temperature the bread rises more slowly and some of the best-flavored breads, including baguettes, use a slower rising, giving the enzymes and starches in the flour more time to mature. The quantity of yeast used will also determine the time required for rising. More yeast means quicker rising.

1 Place the kneaded dough in a bowl that has been lightly greased. This will prevent the dough from sticking. Cover the bowl with a damp dish towel or a piece of oiled plastic wrap to prevent a skin from forming on top.

2 Let rise until the dough has doubled in bulk. At room temperature, this should take 1½–2 hours—less if the temperature is warmer; more if the room is cool. It can even be left to rise in the refrigerator for about 8 hours.

A FEW SIMPLE RULES

◆ Warm bowls and other equipment.

◆ Use the correct amount of yeast: too much will speed up the rising process but will spoil the flavor and will mean the loaf stales more quickly.

◆ If you have a thermometer, check the temperature of the lukewarm liquid, at least until you can gauge it accurately yourself. It should be between 98°–108°F. Mixing two parts cold water with one part boiling water gives you water at roughly the right temperature.

◆ The amount of liquid required for a dough depends on several factors—type of flour, other ingredients, even the room temperature. Recipes therefore often give approximate quantities of liquid. You will soon learn to judge the ideal consistency of a dough.

◆ Do not skimp on kneading. Kneading is essential for stretching the gluten to give a well-risen, light-textured loaf.

◆ Avoid leaving dough to rise in a draught and make sure the ambient temperature is not too high, or the dough will begin to cook.

◆ Always cover the bowl during rising as a crust will form on top of the dough if the air gets to it. Plastic wrap can be pressed on to the dough itself or can be stretched over the bowl. Either way, oil the plastic wrap first or the dough will stick to it as it rises.

◆ Remember: the slower the rising, the better the taste of the bread.

PUNCHING DOWN, SHAPING AND FINAL RISING

After all the effort by the yeast to create a risen dough, it seems a shame to punch down. However, this is important, as you need to redistribute the gases in the dough that were created by fermentation. Punching down also reinvigorates the yeast, making sure that it is evenly distributed, and ensures that the bread has an even texture. It should take only a few minutes and the bread is then ready for shaping. The dough is fully risen when it has doubled in bulk. If you are not sure that it is ready, test by gently inserting a finger into the center of the dough. The dough should not immediately spring back. If it does, let sit for a little longer.

1 Punch down the risen dough using your knuckles. The British call this "knocking back the dough," which is an accurate description of the process. Having punched down the dough, place it on a floured work surface and knead lightly for 1–2 minutes.

SHAPING

There are several ways of shaping the dough to fit in a loaf pan.

1 The easiest way is to shape the dough roughly into an oval and place it in the pan, with the smooth side on top.

2 Alternatively, roll out the dough into a rectangle, a little longer than the pan. Roll it up like a Swiss roll, tuck in the ends and place the roll in the pan, with the seam-side down.

3 Another method for shaping the dough is to roll it out into a rectangle and fold it in half lengthwise, pinching the edges together on the sides and flattening the dough out slightly with the heel of your hand. Fold the dough over once more to make a double thickness and pinch the edges together again. Now gently roll the dough backward and forward until it has a well-rounded shape.

4 Fold in the two short ends and place the dough in the prepared pan with the seam along the bottom.

1 Shape the dough into a round and then press along the center with your hand. Turn the dough over, so that the smooth side is on top.

2 Shape the dough into a round or oval and place it on a baking sheet.

TIPS

◆ Always punch down the dough after the first rising and knead lightly to redistribute the yeast and the gases formed by fermentation, otherwise you may end up with large holes in the loaf or the crust may lift up and become detached from the crumb.

◆ Rising the dough in a warm place is not always necessary—it is simply a method of speeding up the process. Dough will rise (albeit very slowly) even in the refrigerator. However, wherever you decide to rise your dough the temperature must be constant. Avoid drafts or hot spots, as both will spoil the bread and may cause it to bake unevenly.

◆ Some breads may need slashing either before final rising or during this period (see next section).

SHAPING A BAGUETTE

1 Divide the dough into equal pieces. Shape each piece into a ball and then into a rectangle measuring 6 × 3 inches. Fold the bottom third up and the top third down lengthwise. Press the edges together to seal them. Repeat twice, then stretch each piece to a 13–14-inch loaf.

2 Place within the folds of a pleated, floured dish towel or in *bannetons*.

SHAPING A BRAID

1 Divide the dough into three equal pieces. Roll each piece into a 10-inch "sausage" about 1½ inches thick.

2 Place the three "sausages" on a greased baking sheet. Either start the braid in the center, braiding each end in turn, or pinch the pieces firmly together at one end, then braid.

3 When you have finished, pinch the ends together, and turn them under.

FINAL RISING

After shaping the dough and placing it on the baking sheet or in the pan, there is usually a final rising before baking. Depending on the warmth of the room, this can take ¾–1½ hours, although in a very cool room it may take up to 4 hours. Cover the dough so that the surface does not crust over. Oiled plastic wrap placed over the pan or directly on the bread is the best method. The timing is important as over-rising means the loaf may collapse in the oven, while too little proving will mean the loaf will be heavy and flat.

BELOW: A loaf ready for the final rising.

BELOW: After rising the dough should be doubled in size—no more.

PROVING BASKETS

Professional bakers use proving baskets called *bannetons* for baguettes, and circular *couronnes* for round loaves. Some are lined with linen. Proving baskets are available at good kitchenware shops but, depending on the shape you require, you can improvise with baskets and/or earthenware dishes. Simply dust a linen dish towel liberally with flour and use to line the container.

BELOW: A proving basket will give your loaves a professional finish.

CHOOSING PANS

Choosing the right size loaf pan can be a tricky business. If it is too small, the dough will spill over the top. If it is too large, the final loaf will be badly shaped and uneven. As a general rule the pan should be about twice the size of the dough. Professional bakers use black pans, which are considered to be better than shiny metal ones, as they absorb the heat better, giving a crisper crust. Always warm a pan before using and then grease it with melted lard, vegetable oil or unsalted butter. Experiment to see what you find most successful. Baking sheets should also be greased or buttered to prevent sticking.

TOPPING AND BAKING

The actual baking is perhaps the simplest part of the bread-making process, yet even here the yeast still has a part to play and it is important that you play your part too, by making sure conditions are as ideal as possible. When the loaf goes into the oven the heat kills the yeast, but for the first few minutes, there is a final burst of life and the bread will rise even further before the entire process is set and the air is finally locked in.

PREPARING TO BAKE

While the shaped dough is having its final rise, you will need to preheat the oven to the required temperature. It is important that the oven is at the right temperature when the bread goes in – almost always a hot oven, between 220–230°C/425–450°F/ Gas 7–8, although check the recipe since sweet loaves or those containing a lot of butter cook at a lower temperature. Many recipes suggest that the oven temperature is reduced either immediately after putting the bread in the oven or some time during cooking. This means the bread gets a good blast of heat to start with, and then cooks more gradually. This mimics the original bread ovens, which would have cooled down slowly once the embers had been removed.

SLASHING

Once the loaf is ready for baking, all that is needed is to slash and glaze the loaf. This is done not only for appearance, but also to improve the baking of the loaf. When the loaf goes into the oven, the yeast will continue to produce carbon dioxide for a short time and the loaf will rise. This is called the "spring". Slashing provides escape routes for the gas and gives direction to the spring, so that the loaf will open out around the slashes and retain an even shape. Loaves that have not been allowed enough time to rise will tend to have more spring, and it is therefore important to slash these fairly deeply. If you think your loaf may have over-risen, only slash it gently.

You will also find that some recipes suggest slashing either before the final rising

or some time during it. This will depend on how much you want your loaf to "open up". The earlier it is slashed the more the split will develop. However, unless the recipe specifies otherwise, the general rule is to slash the loaf just before you put it in the oven.

ABOVE: *Cob or coburg – just before baking, slash a deep cross across the top of the loaf.*

ABOVE: *Baguette – slash four or five times on the diagonal just before the baking process.*

ABOVE: *Porcupine – slashing not only looks attractive, but gives a wonderful crunchy crust to this bread. Make five or six cuts across the bread in one direction, then cut again at right angles, chequerboard fashion.*

ABOVE: *Tin loaf – part-way through rising, make one deep slash along the length of the loaf.*

GLAZING

Glazing has two important functions. It gives an attractive finish to the loaf and it introduces moisture during cooking. This moisture produces steam which also helps to expand the gases in the loaf and ensures it cooks through completely. Glazes also change the consistency and taste of the crust. Bread can be glazed before, during or just after baking: sometimes recipes will suggest all three. If you glaze before and during baking, take care not to brush sticky glazes up to the sides of a tin or let the glaze drip on to the baking sheet, thereby gluing the bread to its container. This will cause the loaf to crack and rise unevenly.

All sorts of glazes can be used – egg yolk, egg white, milk, butter, sugar solutions, salt solutions and olive oil are regularly used. They also help the toppings to stick to the surface of the loaf.

ABOVE: *Brushing a plait with beaten egg yolk and milk before baking gives it a golden glaze and a professional-looking finish.*

TOPPINGS

There are as many toppings as there are glazes, if not more, all of which add to the appearance, taste and texture of your finished bread. The dough can be rolled in a topping before the second rising, or it can be glazed and sprinkled with the topping just before baking. Try poppy seeds, grated cheese, caraway seeds, oats, cracked wheat, sea salt, sunflower seeds, sesame seeds, herbs, cornmeal or wheat flakes as alternative toppings.

For basic breads and rolls, toppings are simply a matter of preference – for dinner parties it's always nice to offer people a selection of white and wholemeal rolls, each sprinkled with a different topping. Some breads classically have their own particular topping. *Challah*, for instance, is traditionally sprinkled with poppy seeds, pretzels are covered with sea salt or caraway seeds, while the long thin grissini can either be rolled in sesame or poppy seeds. Rolled oats add a soft texture to loaves, and many traditional British and American loaves, such as

ABOVE: Roll the dough for a Granary loaf in sunflower seeds.

ABOVE: A split tin loaf can be dusted with flour before baking.

ABOVE: Grated cheese

ABOVE: Cornmeal

ABOVE: Cracked wheat

ABOVE: Chopped fresh herbs

ABOVE: Rolled oats

ABOVE: Chopped black olives

ABOVE: Poppy seeds

ABOVE: Sea salt

ABOVE: Sesame seeds

ABOVE: Wheat germ

ABOVE: Sunflower seeds

ABOVE: Caraway seeds

loaf and San Francisco sourdough bread have no toppings as such, but a dusting of flour gives an attractive matte sheen to the finished loaf.

Grated cheese and sautéed onions also make more substantial as well as tasty and attractive toppings and many Italian breads demonstrate a rich variety of toppings—whole green or black olives, chunks of sun-dried tomatoes and roasted bell peppers are frequently added to ciabattas and focaccias. As with glazes, toppings can also be added during and sometimes after cooking. Small breads, such as Vienna rolls, are baked until just golden, brushed with milk or cream and then sprinkled with sea salt, cumin or caraway seeds. They are then returned to the oven for a few more moments until cooked.

BELOW: For a dinner party or a buffet, bake a batch of rolls with assorted toppings.

BAKING TIMES

This will depend on the recipe, the size of the loaf and the heat of the oven. As a general rule, rolls take about 20 minutes, round country breads 40–50 minutes and pan loaves a little longer, 45–60 minutes. To check if bread is ready, remove it from the oven and tap firmly on the base of the loaf with your knuckles. It should have a hollow sound. If it seems soft or does not sound hollow, bake for a little longer.

ABOVE: Check that rolls are ready by gently turning one over in a clean dish towel. The underside should be firm and golden, with no trace of moisture.

ABOVE: To check that a loaf is cooked, tap the base with your knuckles. It should be firm and sound hollow.

ADDING MOISTURE TO THE OVEN

A baker's oven is completely sealed and therefore produces the necessary steam for an evenly risen loaf. At home, glazing helps to produce steam, as does a pan of boiling water placed in the bottom of the oven, or you can spray water into the oven two or three times during cooking.

WHAT WENT WRONG

DOUGH WON'T RISE

You may have forgotten the yeast or the yeast may be past its "use-by" date and is dead. To save the dough, make up another batch, making certain the yeast is active. This dough can then be kneaded into the original dough. Alternatively, dissolve the new yeast in warm water and work it into the dough. Another time, always check that yeast is active before adding to flour.

SIDES AND BOTTOM OF BREAD ARE TOO PALE

The oven temperature was too low, or the pan did not allow heat to penetrate the crust. To remedy this, turn the loaf out of its pan and return it to the oven, placing it upside-down on a shelf, for 5–10 minutes.

CRUST TOO SOFT

There was insufficient steam in the oven. You could glaze the crusts before baking next time and spray the inside of the oven with water. Alternatively, place a little hot water in an ovenproof dish in the bottom of the oven during baking. This problem particularly besets French breads and other crusty loaves, which require a certain amount of steam in the oven.

CRUST TOO HARD

Using too much glaze or having too much steam in the oven can harden the crust, so use less glaze next time. To soften a crusty loaf, leave it overnight in a plastic bag.

CRUST SEPARATES FROM THE BREAD

This is caused either by the dough drying out during rising, or by the oven temperature being too low and the dough expanding unevenly. Next time, cover the dough with plastic wrap or waxed paper to prevent any moisture loss while rising, and ensure that the oven is preheated to the correct temperature, so that heat penetrates uniformly throughout the loaf.

SOFT PALE CRUST

This could be because the bread was not baked for long enough or perhaps the oven temperature was too low. When you think bread is ready, tap it firmly underneath; it should sound hollow. If it does not, return the bread to the oven, only this time placing it directly on the oven shelf.

LOAF IS CRUMBLY AND DRY

Either the bread was baked for too long or you used too much flour. Next time check the quantities in the recipe. It is also possible that the oven was too hot. Next time reduce the temperature and check the loaf when the crust looks golden brown.

LARGE HOLES IN LOAF

Either the dough was not punched down properly before shaping or it was not kneaded enough originally.

BREAD HAS A YEASTY FLAVOR

Too much yeast was used. If doubling recipe quantities, do not double the amount of yeast but use one and a half times the amount. In addition, do not overcompensate for a cool room by adding extra yeast unless you don't mind a yeasty flavor. Wait a little longer instead—the bread will rise in the end.

LOAF COLLAPSES IN THE OVEN

Either the wrong flour was used for a particular recipe or the dough was left too long for the second rising and has over-risen. As a rule, the dough should only double in bulk.

LOAF IS DENSE AND FLAT

Too much liquid was used and the dough has become too soft, or was not kneaded enough. Check the recipe for quantities of liquid needed until you are confident about judging the consistency of the dough. The dough should be kneaded firmly for at least 10 minutes.

BREAD-MAKING MACHINES

Bread machines may take the fun out of bread making, but if you enjoy home-made bread on a daily basis, they make it an incredibly easy process. All you need to do is add the correct ingredients, press the right buttons and—presto—a few hours later, you have a freshly cooked loaf of bread!

Many bread makers have a timer switch, so that you can program your bread to be ready when you get up in the morning. Almost all bread machines will make a variety of different types and sizes of loaves, and many have a feature where the bread machine does the kneading and rising, leaving the baking up to you—useful for French loaves, pizzas or any other breads that are not a standard loaf shape.

THINGS TO LOOK OUT FOR WHEN BUYING A BREAD-MAKING MACHINE

◆ Unless you are likely to need only one small loaf a day, choose a machine with the option of making small, medium and large loaves.
◆ "Rapid-bake": this cuts down on resting time, and by recommending extra yeast, also cuts down on rising. You will get a loaf in under 2 hours.
◆ Dough (or manual) cycle: allows you to remove the dough prior to shaping when making loaves that are not the standard "loaf" shape.
◆ Crust color: some bread makers have the option of a dark, medium or pale crust.
◆ Sweet bread cycle: breads that are high in sugar or fat need to bake at slightly lower temperatures, otherwise these ingredients tend to burn. A sweet bread cycle means that the bread-making machine will automatically adjust the heat to allow for this, if programmed to do so first.
◆ Timer feature: this useful feature allows you to set the bread maker so that the bread is ready for when you get up in the morning or when the children come home from school.

USING A BREAD MACHINE

1 Add the easy-blend or fast-action yeast to the bread pan. If you are making a quick or rapid-bake loaf, you may need to add up to one-and-a-half times the usual quantity of yeast, but check the manufacturer's instructions.

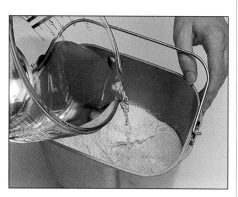

2 Add the remaining ingredients to the bread pan and place in the machine. Select the type of loaf you wish to bake, the size and color of the crust.

3 Dried fruit, olives or other ingredients used to flavor breads are added after the initial kneading. This is to ensure that they are not broken up too much. Depending on the type of loaf you chose to make, your bread will be ready to eat in 2–5 hours.

TIPS FOR CONVERTING RECIPES

Once you're familiar with your bread machine and confident using suggested recipes, you will probably want to adapt some of your own favorite recipes. A loaf baked in a bread-making machine will, of course, always be "loaf-shaped," but since most bread makers have a dough cycle (where the dough is kneaded but not baked), it is possible to prepare rolls, ciabatta and baguettes—indeed most breads featured in this book. It is important that you reduce the recipe according to the maximum capacity of your machine (and even more if you wish to make a small loaf).

Make sure that the proportions of all the essential ingredients for the recipe are approximately as follows:

FOR A 1 POUND LOAF
Flour: 2–2¾ cups
Liquid (water or milk): ¾–1 cup
Salt: ¼–1 teaspoon
Fat: 2 teaspoons–3 tablespoons
Salt: 2 teaspoons–3 tablespoons
Dried yeast: 1½ teaspoons–
1 tablespoon

FOR A 1½ POUND LOAF
Flour: 3–4 cups
Liquid (water or milk): 1–1¼ cups
Salt: ½–1½ teaspoons
Fat: 1–4 tablespoons
Dried yeast: 1½ teaspoons–
1 tablespoon

◆ If adding fruit or other ingredients, reduce the quantities proportionately.
◆ Always use a fast-action yeast.
◆ If adding eggs, remember that one large egg is roughly equal to 4 tablespoons liquid, so reduce the liquid accordingly.
◆ When adapting a recipe, monitor the machine carefully and make a note of any adjustments you may need to make. For instance, pay attention to whether the mixture is too moist or whether the machine struggles to knead the dough. If the loaf is too tall, this may be because you've added too much liquid, yeast or sugar, or added insufficient salt.

BREAD-MAKING EQUIPMENT

Bread making is not an exact science, and you do not need a fully equipped kitchen with state-of-the-art utensils if you decide to try it. In the long run, though, you may decide that some things are essential and others could be useful.

SCALES/WEIGHTS
A scale with weights is more accurate but a spring scale is easier to use and more convenient (especially if you have a tendency to lose the weights). Bear in mind, if buying a scale for bread making, you will probably be using large quantities of flours and will therefore need a large-size scale with a deep basin.

MEASURING CUPS
Heatproof glass cups are most convenient, as liquids can safely be heated in them in

BELOW: Be sure to get a scale with a large measuring bowl.

LEFT: Sieves for flour or spices

the microwave and they are dishwasher safe. Measurements should be clearly marked on the outside; be sure to buy cups with the measurements recorded clearly on the outside so that you can follow any recipe with ease.

MEASURING SPOONS
These are useful in the kitchen for adding small quantities of spices. A set of spoons measures from ¼ teaspoon to 1 tablespoon.

FOOD PROCESSOR
Most food processors can mix and knead dough extremely efficiently and in

a fraction of the time it would take by hand. Always check the instruction book about bread making since only the larger machines can handle large amounts of dough, and you may find that it is necessary to knead the dough in batches.

ELECTRIC MIXER
An electric mixer fitted with a dough hook will knead dough in a time similar to that taken to knead by hand but with much less effort. Small machines can cope with only small amounts of dough, and if you are considering buying a machine for bread-making purposes, make sure that the equipment is suitable for the quantities of bread you are likely to want to make.

SIEVES
Some finer breads may require the flour to be sifted, so it is worth having at least one large sieve for flours and a smaller sieve should you wish to add ground spices or dust the loaves with flour or confectioners' sugar after baking them.

ABOVE: A selection of glass bowls

BOWLS

If you do not have a selection already, it is worth buying some now as it is not possible to make bread (at least in the kitchen) without at least two good-sized bowls. Choose a bowl with a wide mouth, which is still deep enough to contain the batter or dough. A smaller china or glass bowl is also useful (although you can use the measuring cup) for making up dried yeast.

ROLLING PIN

Some doughs need to be rolled out and you will need a large rolling pin for this job. A wooden rolling pin that is long and smooth and has no separate handles is ideal for bread making.

DOUGH KNIFE OR SCRAPER

This is extremely handy when kneading dough by hand. The rectangular piece of steel on a wooden handle is particularly useful in the early part of kneading, for lifting and working sticky or difficult doughs. The blades normally measure about 4 × 5 inches and should ideally be slightly flexible rather than rigid.

COOK'S KNIFE

You will need a sharp knife for slashing the dough—either during rising or just before baking. Some recipe books suggest using a razor for this job but the blade does need to be very sharp indeed. Since a good cook's knife can be kept in razor-sharp condition, this is the preferable option and adds a professional touch to your loaves.

ABOVE: Bread knife and cook's knife

LEFT: Dough knife/scraper

ABOVE: Rolling pin

ABOVE: Pastry brushes

BREAD KNIFE

A dull knife can wreak havoc on a fresh loaf of bread, so make sure you use a good bread knife. Bread should be cut in a sawing motion, which is why bread knives have long serrated blades. A plain cook's knife, although it will cut through the bread, will spoil the texture of the crumb.

PASTRY BRUSH

This is essential for glazing loaves and rolls. Choose a good, wide brush. It is worth spending extra for a brush that will not lose its bristles. Use a brush made from natural fibers; nylon will melt if used for brushing hot loaves during cooking.

BREAD PANS

Bread pans come in all sizes, and it is worth having a selection. Include a 1-pound and preferably two 2¼-pound pans so that you can make loaves in a variety of shapes and sizes. If the pans are labeled with their dimensions, rather than

BELOW: Shallow loaf and cake pans

their capacity, look for 7 × 3-inch (equivalent to 1 pound) and 9 × 5-inch (equivalent to 2¼-pound). Other useful sizes are 12 × 4-inch and 10 × 4-inch. Professional bakers prefer matte black pans, which absorb the heat better than the shiny ones and therefore make the crust crisper. The wider shallow pans are

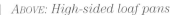

ABOVE: High-sided loaf pans

mostly used for fruit breads. Pan loaves are baked in plain, high-sided pans; farmhouse loaves are slightly shallower and pans may be stamped with the word "Farmhouse." Cake pans are sometimes used for bread making. Monkey bread, for instance, is baked in a 9-inch springform ring cake pan, while buchty—breakfast rolls that are batch-baked—require a square, loose-bottomed cake pan with straight sides that will support the rolls as they rise.

Several speciality breads are baked in a deep 6-inch cake pan. These breads include *panettone* and Sally Lunn.

If you are fond of baking focaccia, you will find a 10-inch pizza pan or shallow round cake pan invaluable.

MOLDS

There are various sizes of brioche molds for the traditional, fluted brioche, including individual bun size. A *kugelhopf* mold is a fluted ring mold essential for making the Alsace or German *kugelhopf* or the Viennese *gugelhupf*. A savarin mold is a straight-sided ring mold for savarins and other ring-shaped breads. If you don't have the correct mold, it is sometimes possible to improvise. Boston brown bread, for instance, can be baked in a special mold, but the heatproof glass jar from a cafetière coffee maker can be used instead, or even two 1-pound coffee cans, without the lids, work perfectly well once they have been washed and dried.

BELOW: Baking sheets and patty tins

BAKING SHEETS

When buying baking sheets, look for ones that are either completely flat, or have a lip only on one long edge. This makes it easier to slide bread or rolls on to a wire rack. Strong, heavy baking sheets distribute the heat evenly.

MUFFIN PANS

Muffin pans with 3-inch cups are very useful for making elaborately shaped rolls like the aptly named New England Fantans, while larger popover pans come into their own for specialties like Georgian Khachapuri. The pans support the dough while it is filled with cheese and then tied into a topknot.

FLOWER POTS

Earthenware flower pots can also be used for baking. These need to be tempered before being used for bread. Brush the new, perfectly clean pots liberally inside and out with oil and place in a hot oven (about 400°F) for about 30 minutes. (This can conveniently be done while you are cooking something else.) Do this several times until the pots are impregnated with oil. They can then be used for baking bread and will need very little greasing.

BELOW: Earthenware flower pots make unusual molds for loaves.

LEFT: A French fluted brioche mold and a savarin or ring mold

LONGUETS

Longuets are molded pieces of steel, like corrugated iron, used for baking baguettes. They are designed with the professional baker in mind but will probably fit in an average size oven.

BAKING STONE

Baking stones are now widely available, sold principally for pizzas but also useful for making thick crusted loaves. They are the nearest thing to replicating an authentic brick-floored oven. The stones are heated in the oven and then the bread is placed on top.

BANNETONS AND COURONNES

These are the canvas-lined proving baskets used by French bakers for their bread: *bannetons* are used for baguettes, *couronnes* for round loaves. In Germany, sourdough bread is sometimes proved in a floured basket, which has the effect of creating a crust that looks like wicker.

GRIDDLE

This is a heavy cast-iron pan used on top of the stove for griddle cakes, soda farls, bannocks and even Indian breads like missi rotis and chapatis. Weight is the important feature with griddles, so that heat can be evenly dispersed.

Griddles can have handles or have the more old-fashioned design of a hooped handle over the entire pan, often with a small hoop in the center which would have been used to hang the griddle over a peat fire. In Scotland, where they are still widely used, griddles are also known as girdles.

Square-shaped griddles that come with metal hoops for English muffins and crumpets are also available at good kitchen supply stores. The hoops have a diameter of about 4 inches and are about 1-inch-deep.

BELOW: This short, deep banneton is ideal for shorter French loaves.

ABOVE: Very long bannetons are designed for supporting baguettes during the final rising.

BELOW: A griddle for pikelets and other free form breads, such as griddle-baked soda bread and oatcakes.

BREADS OF THE WORLD

Bread is a particularly fundamental aspect of a country's cuisine—it reflects the climate and geography, as well as the customs, culture and religious beliefs of the people. This comprehensive guide includes the world's best-loved breads and many less well-known loaves, too. It will help you recognize the different breads that are sold in supermarkets and bakeries, act as a guide if you are traveling abroad, and encourage you to sample local breads, whether you've traveled halfway across the world, or simply moved to a new area.

BRITISH BREADS

British bread is now considered as good as any bread in Europe, something that could not have been said 20, or even 10 years ago. In the 1970s and 80s British vacationers discovered the delights of French baguettes, Italian ciabatta and all the other wonderful breads of Europe, and began asking why their own bread was so uninteresting. Many small bakers, of course, had been producing excellent bread for years, a delight for their customers but unknown to all those who shopped mostly in supermarkets. Things changed when supermarkets introduced their own in-store bakeries. Suddenly fresh bread was readily available. The equation was simple. Fresh bread tasted great; people started eating more of it, and thus more bread, and in greater diversity, was made and sold. It's an equation where everyone wins. Bread is relatively cheap; it's an excellent food; it can be eaten with almost any meal and there is now a huge choice for the consumer. Small bakers have risen to the challenge of the supermarkets by producing their own specialty breads. All sorts of sourdoughs, ryes and corn breads are now available, along with a vast range of the more traditional British breads. The following breads are among the better known shapes, and are the breads you are likely to find at almost any

RIGHT: A bloomer can be distinguished by the diagonal slashes across the top.

good bakery and at most supermarkets, too. White breads are defined by their shape rather than the dough, and the majority of loaves are made using the same dough. However, once you start tasting and comparing breads, you will discover that the shape, the method of cooking and even the amount of slashing on the loaf will alter the flavor.

BATCHED BREAD

These loaves are baked together without pans so that there are no crusts along the sides, the individual loaves being broken apart when baked. The top crust is normally soft. Brick or sister brick loaves are two loaves baked together in large square or rectangular pans and then broken apart to give a half-batched effect.

BLOOMER

This is a popular oven bottom-baked loaf, i.e. one that is baked without a pan, either on a tray or on the bottom of the oven. It has a plump, oval shape and is distinguished by five or six diagonal slashes across the upper crust. A bloomer from a good baker's has a soft crumb and a fragile but crisp crust. However, store-bought bloomers that have been pre-wrapped in plastic often have a disappointingly soft crust. Bloomers can be made using brown, whole-wheat flour, rye

ABOVE: Batched loaves are not necessarily uniform in shape, but always have soft sides. White and brown loaves can be made.

ABOVE: Cornmeal loaf (top) and brown and white cobs. The even texture of the crumb on the cob loaves means that they make excellent toast.

or multigrain flour; however, the most popular type is white.

COB

The cob is perhaps the oldest and most basic of British loaves. The loaf is round and completely plain without slashes or decoration, and is oven-baked and crusty. The word "cob" is an old English word for a head, and plain round loaves made with coarse, brown meal would have been the basic loaf for many families for genera-tions. Cobs today can be white, but are usually brown, whole-wheat or Granary.

COBURG

This white, round, oven bottom-baked loaf has a cross slash on the upper crust, distinguishing it from the cob. Some bakers slash the loaf before the final ris-ing to produce a wide-spread loaf with four clover-leaf corners. Others slash more conservatively for a loaf that retains its basic round shape.

PAN COBURG

This loaf is baked in a shallow round pan, the diagonally slashed crust rising up and over the sides of the pan to look a bit like a cauliflower, a name by which it is also known. Bakeries sometimes make this loaf, either on order or because they have an appreciative clientele, but it is also a popular bread to make at home.

CHECKERBOARD

Also known as a porcupine or rumpy loaf, this bread is cross-hatched to make a "checkerboard" crust. The loaf is usually floured before being cut, and the deeper the cuts, the more the crust will spread.

CORNMEAL

This is not a traditional British loaf, but is becoming increasingly popular, especially among some of the small bakeries who have developed their own recipes, blending cornmeal with a strong white or whole-wheat flour. Sometimes whole corn kernels are also added to give a delicious loaf with good texture.

DANISH

A traditional—or proper—Danish loaf is a round loaf with one central lengthwise cut. Originally oven bottom-baked to give a good crust, it was always made using white flour—unlike the cobs and coburgs that

RIGHT: A good Danish loaf should have a soft floury crust and a fairly dense crumb.

BELOW: Hovis loaves come in various sizes but all have the familiar pan shape with "Hovis" on the sides.

would have used the cheaper and more widely available brown flour. Danish loaves today, however, are as likely to be more oval in shape. A good Danish bread from a bakery still has the firm crust and is cut with frequent and deep diagonal slashes on the top. A common supermarket version of a Danish bread is a pre-wrapped, cylindrical sliced loaf that is distinguished mainly by the lightness of the crumb. Although this is advertised as virtue, there is very little that can be said in its favor, since it is bland to the extent of being quite tasteless. So, whenever possible, buy from your local bakery instead.

FARMHOUSE LOAF

Farmhouse pans are shallow and somewhat squat,

RIGHT: Braids can be elaborate. Most are enriched with eggs and butter.

producing the characteristic plump pan loaves. At one time special bread pans were used, which had the word "Farmhouse" impressed along the side of the loaf. This was introduced toward the end of the last century when there was a move away from the "whiter-than-white" breads that had become immensely popular, to a more healthy bread. The original farmhouse loaves were made using brown flour to satisfy the instincts of the more health conscious, although ironically today most farmhouse loaves are white. Today some artisan bakers make their own special farmhouse breads using a dough that has been fermented for longer than usual, but the majority of farmhouse loaves are made using exactly the same dough as other white breads. The difference, as is often the case, is in the shape.

HOVIS

No sooner had the poor in Britain been converted to the values and merits of white bread, than a movement began to persuade people that breads containing wheat germ, the bits discarded by the roller mills, were highly valuable nutritionally. A flour was developed that put the wheat germ back into the flour, after first stabilizing it to prevent rancidity. The flour was called Hovis (from the Latin *hominis vis*, meaning "the life of man") and one of the most enduring proprietary breads was born. All Hovis loaves, whether baked at home or bought from a bakery, are made using Hovis flour, although there are a variety of different mixes, some containing

more of the whole-wheat along with other grains. Hovis loaves have their name impressed along the side and some are quite delicious. Pre-packed and sliced loaves have less character.

INNES

Innes Original is one of the few sourdough loaves widely available in Britain today, although individual bakers may well make their own favorite sourdough.

BRAID

Specialty bakers often produce their own braided loaves, which can be made from anything between three and eight strands of dough. They

mimic the popular European and Jewish breads but are no less British for all that, having been made by artisan bakers for generations. They are normally white and can be crusty, made using plain dough, or they can be enriched with butter, eggs and milk and are therefore soft.

SPIRAL

Several of the European breads are shaped by rolling the dough into a sausage shape and then twisting it around to make a spiral or snail shape. Specialty bakers may produce their own particular favorite, which may be white and crusty or enriched and sprinkled with poppy seeds or glazed with egg.

ABOVE: A spiral loaf

RIGHT: Ground nuts give this walnut bread a slightly beige color.

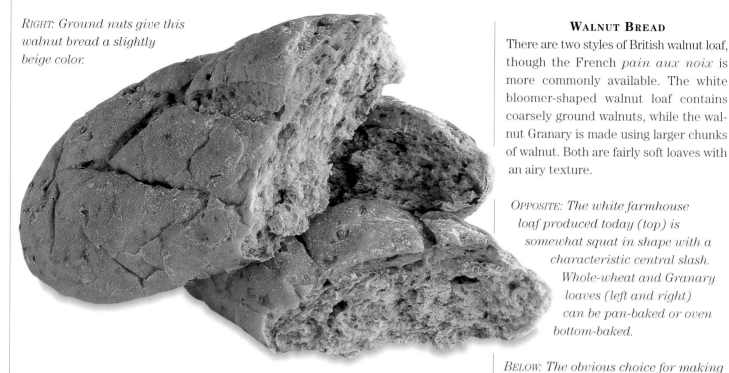

WALNUT BREAD

There are two styles of British walnut loaf, though the French *pain aux noix* is more commonly available. The white bloomer-shaped walnut loaf contains coarsely ground walnuts, while the walnut Granary is made using larger chunks of walnut. Both are fairly soft loaves with an airy texture.

OPPOSITE: The white farmhouse loaf produced today (top) is somewhat squat in shape with a characteristic central slash. Whole-wheat and Granary loaves (left and right) can be pan-baked or oven bottom-baked.

BELOW: The obvious choice for making sandwiches is the eponymous sandwich loaf, but any pan or split pan loaf works well, despite the more irregular shape.

PAN/SPLIT PAN LOAVES

These loaves are baked in pans, the crust either forming a domed shape (pan), or being slashed along the center before baking (split pan), so that there is a larger crust area. The crust is normally fairly soft, particularly on loaves that have been pre-packed. A sandwich loaf, which is baked in a completely enclosed pan, is—as the name suggests—popular for making sandwiches, since all the slices are conveniently square.

VIENNA BATONS

A Vienna baton is a slashed long loaf which was, until very recently, the British approximation of the French baguette. The crumb is light and airy, the crust crisp and flaky.

The French baguette was developed partly from a process that originated in Vienna where steam was injected into the oven. Known as the "Vienna" technique, the process was adopted by British bakers in the forlorn hope of reproducing the increasingly popular baguette. The experiment wasn't entirely successful. Vienna batons resemble baguettes only in shape. Their light airy crumb and crisp flaky crust nevertheless has a character of its own and they are surprisingly good sliced, topped with grated cheese, then toasted and added to French onion soup.

VITBE

Like Hovis, this is another loaf made from a proprietary brand of flour, which also returns the stabilized wheat germ to the white flour. There are two kinds of VitBe loaves: the original wheat germ bread and a Hi-Bran loaf.

ENGLISH BREADS

ENGLISH OATMEAL BREAD

Oats have always been an important crop in England and other parts of the British Isles, although mainly for animal feed. Oatmeal contains no gluten, so breads made entirely using oats were inevitably flat, baked on stones or on a griddle. Many parts of England, as well as Wales and Scotland, have their own traditional oatmeal cakes, but the meal can be used for baking loaves if it is mixed with wheat flour.

CORNISH SAFFRON CAKE

This Cornish sweet bread is yeast-leavened, enriched with fruit and spiced with nutmeg, cinnamon and saffron. Saffron was an important crop in England in the sixteenth century and although it gradually declined, it continued to survive in the West Country, where numerous traditional breads and cakes include tiny strands of saffron, adding a delicate flavor and pretty coloring.

RIGHT: Cornish saffron cake is one of the best known of the English currant breads.

LEFT: The cottage loaf—an English favorite

COTTAGE LOAF

The cottage loaf must be among the oldest shapes of English breads. The distinctive arrangement of a smallish round loaf baked on top of a larger round loaf seems to be a peculiarity to England, and Elizabeth David in her *English Bread and Yeast Cookery* suggests that it might have originated as an improvised way of economizing on baking space in a small oven. The two loaves are wedded together by pushing a wooden spoon handle or fingers down the center of the two rounds and sometimes the sides are snipped to give an extra crusty finish. Traditionally, cottage loaves would have been baked on the bottom of the oven, and the best cottage loaves today have a thick, dark bottom crust. Sadly, few bakers have the time or oven space for these celebrated loaves and they are not widely available. For special occasions or on request, some of the smaller specialty bakers will bake a cottage loaf and, no doubt, take great pleasure in doing so.

GUERNSEY GÂCHE

From this small British island off the coast of Normandy come two breads that are both known as "gâche." The French, brioche-style gâche is highly spiced with cloves and made in proper Normandy style with apples. The British version is heavier, enriched with candied peel and golden raisins, and made with eggs and rich Guernsey butter and milk.

HARVEST LOAF

Harvest loaves are not really intended for eating but are made by bakers in the autumn to coincide with harvest festivals in churches and schools. It is a tradition that has happily endured in many of the smaller villages of England, and bakers clearly enjoy the opportunity to demonstrate their skill and expertise.

HOT CROSS BUNS

Small yeasted buns have been popular in England since medieval times. Small breads, enriched with eggs, currants and raisins and spiced with nutmeg and cinnamon, were served to accompany wine at the end of a feast. They became a particular Lent favorite among the Elizabethans, who enjoyed displaying their wealth and sophistication by using

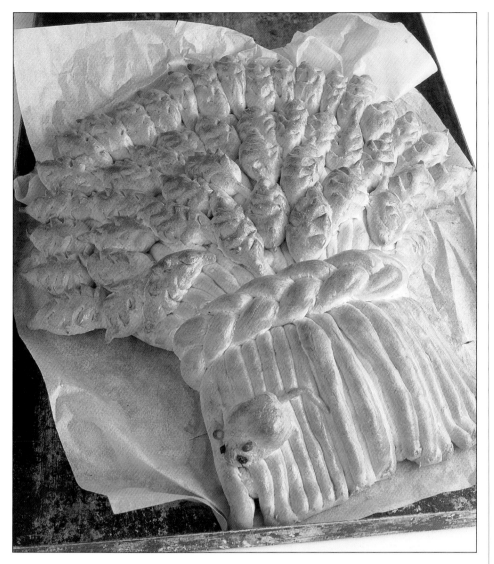

ABOVE: A harvest loaf gives bakers an opportunity to practice their skill and can be quite spectacular.

CRUMPETS

Crumpets are another traditional bread, and are similar to pikelets and muffins. Recipes for crumpets date from the eighteenth century and then, just as now, they were always toasted and eaten with butter. Today, crumpets are made using yeast and baking powder (or baking soda and cream of tartar), which accounts for their characteristic holey surface. Crumpets are available pre-packaged at supermarkets but the superior crumpets from specialty bakers are harder to find and it might be simpler in the long run to make your own.

LEFT: Crumpets are traditionally served warm with butter.

the expensive and much sought-after spices from the Far East. During the Middle Ages it was common practice to mark loaves with a deep cross before baking to ward off evil spirits and, although the custom was abandoned after the Reformation, the buns made for Good Friday continued the custom for this most significant of religious days. Hot cross buns are now available almost all year round. They normally make an appearance shortly after Christmas. Some bakers, however, continue to bake their own hot cross buns only during Lent and most have the attraction of not being over-spiced.

LEFT: Hot cross buns are the traditional Easter treat.

LARDY CAKE

There are many different versions of this unequivocally English bread, but all go by the same name and all are very rich. Originally, lardy cakes were made for celebrations, notably harvest festivals, but as sugar and fruit became more affordable they became popular all year round. Various English counties lay claim to lardy cake. You can certainly eat delicious lardy cake in Lancashire and Yorkshire, and Northumberland, too, has its own speciality. The Midlands and Derbyshire are partial to a very sweet variety, while further south, in Surrey and Hampshire, there are versions of fruitless lardy cakes. The round, flattish breads are made using a basic white dough, which is layered with fat, sugar and fruit. Lardy cake, almost by definition, is very caloric (so be warned) and it contains pork lard and is therefore a prohibited food for vegetarians. The cake is still often sold by weight or by the piece.

ABOVE: A sticky, rich and tasty lardy cake

RIGHT: Lincolnshire plum bread makes a pleasant snack, spread with butter or damson jelly.

LINCOLNSHIRE PLUM BREAD

Just as with plum pudding or plum cake, plum means dried fruit in this context, namely currants, raisins and golden raisins. There are several of these plum breads—fruited breads—sold at supermarkets, distributed by a variety of producers. However, the Lincolnshire plum bread seems to be the best known. This, too, is widely available, but visitors to Lincolnshire should try if possible to sample the non-commercial version, as baked by smaller specialty bakers.

MUFFINS

English muffins—to give them their correct name and to differentiate them from regular muffins, which resemble cupcakes—belong to the same tradition as crumpets, although there are several differences, as enthusiasts would be only too ready to point out. Like crumpets, they are a part of an English folk memory that includes the muffin man, winter afternoons in front of the fire, toasting forks and tea time. Although muffins and crumpets are made from the same, or similar, basic recipes, muffins use a stiffer mixture and are consequently thicker with a thin skin or crust on each side and without the characteristic holes of crumpets. Like crumpets, muffins are delicious toasted, either split and then toasted or toasted and then split (it makes a difference!) and served with butter. Pre-packaged English muffins are available at any supermarket. Bakers also occasionally make their own. (Look for those made by small artisanal bakeries, which are likely to have a better flavor and a crisper crust.)

BELOW: Once mostly white, brown muffins are now almost as popular.

LEFT: Pikelets are a specialty of northern England.

to the townspeople. The story goes that Sally Lunn, a Huguenot, brought her recipe from France and adapted it to the English oven. Alternatively, although less romantically, the word is thought to be a corruption of the French *soleil lune* or "sun and moon" cake. Either way, Sally Lunn is a distinctive-looking bread with tall sides and a billowing top like the *kugelhopf* of Alsace. Although there is no one authorized version, Sally Lunn is always made using white flour and yeast, enriched with butter and cream. It can be lightly spiced and slightly citrusy, but should not be over-flavored. In England, it is often sold at pastry shops, split and spread with butter or clotted cream.

SOURDOUGH

There is no tradition of making sourdoughs in England but many of the more adventurous bakers are now producing loaves using a sourdough leaven. There are all sorts of breads using various blends of wheat and rye flours, some using a potato starter. Most loaves of this type are, however, flattish and fairly dense with a definite sour/acid flavor.

PIKELETS

Some people say pikelet is just another name for crumpet, and in some parts of England the words are synonymous. However, while both pikelets and crumpets have the distinctive holey tops, pikelets are not cooked in rings but are free form in shape, being cooked straight on the griddle like Scotch pancakes or the Welsh crumpets *bara pyglyd* (pronounced piglet, and from which pikelets may well get their name). The mixture for pikelets is very much the same as crumpets, but perhaps a bit thinner for pikelets. Bakers in the counties of Leicestershire, Derbyshire, Yorkshire and Lancashire may produce them on a regular basis, and they are sometimes available at larger supermarkets. Otherwise you will need to find a baker who specializes in regional breads and cakes.

SALLY LUNN

This brioche-style cake is a speciality of the West Country or, more particularly, Bath, where supposedly a lass called Sally Lunn once sold her cakes

ABOVE: Sally Lunn, with its delicate citrus flavor, is often sliced into three layers and filled with clotted cream.

BELOW: Sourdough bread

STOTTIE

This flattish bread is native to the north-east of England, where it is widely available, although almost unheard of anywhere else. Almost always white, it is flat with a soft, floury crust, often (but not always) scored with a single slash or cross. Local bakers explain that stotties were traditionally the last things to be baked in the oven at the end of the day, the name itself coming from the local word "stott," meaning to throw to the ground. The bread apparently was ready for eating if it rebounded from the floor! Stottie bread (perhaps as a result of such bad treatment) is rather dry with an open crumb and fairly chewy texture. It is, however, delicious with another regional dish, ham and pease pudding (based on split peas).

STAFFORDSHIRE OATCAKES

Unlike the small, crumbly Scottish oatcake, Staffordshire oatcakes are soft and floppy and are the size of small pancakes. They are known locally as "turnstall tortillas" and they are indeed similar to a tortilla, although unlike the Mexican bread, these are eaten in true English fashion with eggs and bacon for breakfast or butter and honey for tea.

The oatcakes are made from a mixture of oatmeal and flour, yeast and milk or water. It is likely that they have been made in Staffordshire for centuries, as all sorts of oatcakes and griddle cakes were common in the north of England from Tudor times. With the Industrial Revolution, though, they became associated with the Staffordshire potteries, and while available at many supermarkets, the best are those that are baked on the premises of local bakers in places such as Stoke-on-Trent.

YORKSHIRE FARL

This is a round soda bread, similar to the Irish soda breads, that is cross-slashed into quarters (farls) before being baked.

BELOW: Stotties are a favorite in the north of England.

WELSH BREADS

BARA BRITH

Bara brith is one of the best-known fruit breads of the British Isles. "Bara" is the Welsh word for bread, while "brith," meaning spotted, describes the currants that are an essential ingredient. Although there are brown or whole-wheat versions, bara brith is normally made using white flour. A good bara brith is yeast-leavened, lightly spiced and fairly dense in texture. Today, raisins and mixed citrus peel are often added, but currants are the essential ingredient, and bakers in Wales will commonly plump these first in cold tea, perhaps to emulate the juicy blackcurrants thought to have been the original fruit in bara brith. The bread is sold at most large supermarkets and some delicatessens, but for a really traditional bara brith you may need to travel to Wales, where there are many different versions from which you can choose your own particular favorite.

RIGHT: Bara brith was considered a luxury loaf when dried fruit was expensive. It is still one of the most delicious teabreads.

WELSH COB

Unlike the round English cob, a Welsh cob is something like a cross between an English farmhouse and a stottie. It is baked oven crusty and is normally made from white flour. Usually dusted with flour before baking, these loaves may also have a cut along the center.

ABOVE: Welsh cob

WELSH COTTAGE

The Welsh cottage loaf, like its English equivalent, is not often made by bakers, as it is time-consuming and takes up a lot of oven space. However specialty bakers and some restaurants may produce these loaves for their customers. The bottom half of the loaf is sometimes slashed vertically before the final rising.

WELSH POT BREAD

In the days before families had ovens for baking, people improvised in the most ingenious ways. Dough, which would normally have been fairly coarse and brown, would be molded in an iron pot and then turned upside-down onto a flat stone lying over a wood-burning fire. Alternatively, the dough was baked in a three-legged pot, which also would be placed over an open fire, and smoldering peat would then have been piled on top. Pot breads like these are not made these days, but occasionally some restaurants will make their own version, using earthenware pots to create interesting and crusty loaves.

LEFT: Welsh cottage

WELSH PANS

Welsh pans have a crusty appearance with a pleasant soft crumb. The white loaves are sometimes cross-hatched but are often, like the whole-wheat and Granary versions, left plain. Like most pan loaves, this bread makes great toast and is often served buttered with the delicious, slightly salty Welsh butter.

LEFT: Swansea loaf, now made only rarely, was a popular bread in the eighteenth century.

BELOW: Left to right: white, whole-wheat and Granary Welsh pan loaves

SWANSEA LOAF

Although nowadays fairly rare, this was once the basic loaf for all who lived in Swansea and its environs. It was normally a batch-baked bread, made with a white wheat flour, and would have been sold in the markets. Some local restaurants that specialize in Welsh food may bake this bread for guests, or there are museums around Swansea that give regular exhibitions of bread making: the bread is made and baked as you watch, so you have the opportunity of tasting it as it once really was—made by traditional methods, baked in old-fashioned ovens and served still warm.

SCOTTISH BREADS

ABERDEEN BUTTERY ROWIES

Scottish bakers, especially when explaining their wares to the uninitiated, may well describe these delicious little rolls as Scottish croissants. There are certainly similarities. Although the shape differs, rowies being round or oval, they are both made in a similar way: layered with butter so they have a delicious texture that resembles pastry. Rowies, however, are lighter and more savory than croissants, using less butter but more salt. They are widely available in Scotland, less so as you move further south.

LEFT: Despite the name, soft rolls are slightly crusty.

SELKIRK BANNOCK

This fruited loaf is popular throughout Britain and is available at most large supermarkets, although there was once a time when these breads were only made in the town of Selkirk. It is a round loaf (normally white) and, unlike barm brack and bara brith to which it is often compared, should be completely unspiced. It, too, contains fruit, some versions using only golden raisins, others containing currants and candied peel as well. Traditionally it would have been made with lard, making it similar to lardy cake, but most store-bought versions today use butter or vegetable fat instead, although some older recipes may still suggest a mixture of butter and lard.

BARLEY BANNOCK

"Bannock" is an Old English word of Celtic origin and was probably the first word used to describe bread, as long ago as the fifth century A.D. The word still has a rather antiquated ring to it. It generally describes a type of flat, scone-like bread, and in Scotland the two words "bannock" and "scone" are used interchangeably. Bannocks were originally unleavened breads, made with barley or oatmeal and cooked on a griddle. Such flat, dense breads are unheard of these days. Most of today's bannocks are made using baking powder or baking soda as a raising agent, which gives them a light, airy texture. Some bakeries produce bannocks using a natural leaven. The sour flavor is something of an acquired taste, especially when coupled with that of the barley. The breads are still cooked on a griddle and have the characteristic earthy flavor of barley.

MELROSE LOAF

This is Scotland's best-known soda bread. It is a proprietary bread, made by a bakery in the south of Scotland. It is a whole-wheat, malted loaf with a dense texture and is a popular bread for breakfast, often being spread with butter and marmalade.

LEFT: Aberdeen buttery rowies

SCOTCH BREAD

Scottish bakers are renowned for their bread, and these fine loaves are the most popular bread in Scotland, used for sandwiches and toast. Often simply called a "plain" loaf, the bread has the characteristic soft sides of a batch-baked loaf and the top is baked to a dark brown. It has a particularly good flavor, thanks to the longer than usual fermentation period.

MORNING ROLLS

These soft and flattish, floury rolls are to be found at every bakery and supermarket in Scotland. They are called "baps" in some parts of Scotland; in other parts such a word is completely unheard of and the rolls are called "morning rolls" or just "rolls." The product, however, is clearly the same: made with plain, rather than strong flour, the rolls can be whole-wheat or brown, but are more commonly white. They are made with lard, which is rubbed into the flour. This is mixed to a dough with milk and water and, of course, yeast, creating the characteristic soft texture. The rolls are normally batched together on large baking sheets and are pulled apart after cooking so, like batched bread, they have little or no side crust and are often almost square in shape. A little dimple in the center of the roll, pressed into the dough just before baking to stop the tops from blistering, is a sign of a true traditional

ABOVE: Scotch bread is mostly used for sandwiches.

morning roll, but these marks frequently disappear in the oven and their absence should not deter you from buying the rolls if they look and smell fresh. They are best eaten very fresh, and are noticeably salty, like most Scottish bread. They are popular almost any time of the day, but are a favorite at breakfast, for bacon "butties" and with various fillings. A variation of Scottish "baps" or morning rolls is soft rolls. Confusingly, these rolls are often not as soft as morning rolls. They have a golden glaze, which is produced by brushing the rolls with cream both before and after they are baked.

RIGHT: Morning rolls may be known by different names in Scotland but are all similar, being white, flattish and soft.

IRISH BREADS

WHITE SODA BREAD

Soda bread is the traditional bread of Ireland, which has quite different bread-baking traditions from mainland Britain. The old Irish hearth had no built-in oven, and bread was cooked either on a griddle set over the fire, or in a *bastable*, a type of Dutch oven or oven-pot that would have been set in the smoldering peat. These methods continued to be popular even when iron stores were introduced to Ireland, and even today specialty Irish bakers will make their traditional breads in cast-iron casseroles with the lid on. Another significant difference in bread making in Ireland was the popularity of baking soda, as opposed to yeast, as a raising agent. Buttermilk provides the necessary acid to the alkaline baking soda, and the best soda breads are made using this, although cream of tartar is often used as an alternative to the buttermilk.

There is a vast range of different soda breads, and almost every bakery in Ireland, as well as almost every restaurant, has its own favorite recipe. Outside Ireland there is still a reasonable selection of white, brown and whole-wheat soda breads available at most supermarkets. Better still are those breads made on the premises by artisanal bakers. If the baker is Irish, so much the better.

Irish round soda bread is normally

RIGHT: Soda bread can be baked whole and then broken into farls.

marked with a cross. Cut the bread into quarters before cooking, and you have soda farls. These are either baked in the oven or cooked on a covered griddle and have a pale, crusty, floury appearance.

RIGHT: Barm brack is one of Ireland's most delicious teabreads. Toast and eat with butter or just cut into chunks and serve with jam.

OATMEAL SODA BREAD

In a country with a history of more than its fair share of poverty, almost any edible material that could be ground into a meal would have been used for making bread. Oatmeal is high in protein and would have made a nourishing if flattish bread.

BARM BRACK

This is the Irish version of the Welsh bara brith, the words also translating as "speckled bread." It is linked with several Irish festivals, notably St Brighid's Day—February 1 and the first day of spring—and the festival of Luanasa, which celebrated the start of harvest on August 1. Barm brack is associated with Halloween and there is also a tradition of baking a wedding ring into the bread, the finder being thus assured of becoming engaged before the year is out. The traditional barm brack, normally made with white flour, is one of the few yeasted Irish breads. Made with sugar, raisins, mixed citrus peel and currants, it is enriched with butter and eggs. Barm brack is quite delicious by itself, spread with jam or toasted and buttered. It is widely available in Britain and is well worth looking for.

POTATO BREAD

Potatoes, since their introduction in the seventeenth century, have been an essential food in Ireland. At various times, up to and including the early parts of the twentieth century, wheat was scarce and expensive. Potatoes were regularly used to help "stretch" the flour, producing a nourishing and (if lard was available) a well-flavored griddle bread. Today, potato breads made by blending mashed potatoes with some proportion of white flour are baked by Irish bakers and some restaurants. The dough is then normally marked or cut into farls and either cooked on a griddle or baked in the oven.

RIGHT: This potato bread was formed into a star shape before being baked.

RIGHT: Soda farls are wedges of soda bread, either cut from a loaf before baking or after.

SODA FARLS

As already mentioned in the entry on white soda bread, the term "farl" describes a wedge-shaped soda bread (usually a quarter of a loaf). The word derives from "fardel," which meant "fourth part," and in Ireland, soda bread is often marked into quarters, or "farls," before baking, as indeed is the Yorkshire farl. In addition, some are actually cut into farls (either into quarters or thirds) before baking, to make a thick wedge-shaped bread with a good crust. Most of these soda farls are made using a white flour, although some are whole-wheat breads, made with Irish-milled flour and creamy buttermilk. Properly made, soda farls, like soda bread, are delicious. Their main problem is that they go stale quickly, so if possible consume on the day of purchase.

WHEATEN LOAF

This wheaten loaf is a soda bread that is baked in a pan, so that it is "loaf" shaped, rather than the usual rough round. In Ireland, round soda breads are often called "cakes" or "cakes of bread"; whereas a pan-baked soda bread is called a loaf. Wheaten loaves are normally made with soft Irish whole-wheat flour.

BELOW: An Irish wheaten loaf, which is a type of soda bread.

FRENCH BREADS

The French are passionate about their bread. A baguette is one of France's most potent symbols and, whether carried in a basket, strapped to a bicycle or simply tucked under a schoolboy's arm on the way to school, it is as much a sign that you are in France as are the streets of Paris or the vineyards of Provence.

Bread is eaten with every meal and with every course apart from sweet desserts. Although, as in most countries, pre-packaged bread is available, the French seem to attach much importance to their bread, and consequently most families eat fresh bread bought daily—if not at their local *boulangerie*, then at least from the fresh bread counter at the supermarket.

By far the majority of loaves consumed in France are baguettes, but there are nevertheless many other types of French bread. The *pain de campagne* and the *levains* are popular throughout the country but there are also countless regional breads of all shapes and sizes. Homemade bread is relatively unusual in France, which surely must be because excellent fresh bread is so easily and readily available. Every village has at least one *boulangerie* where bread is made three or four times a day. French people shop daily—sometimes twice daily—for their bread. Baguettes have to be eaten as fresh as possible, and walking or cycling to the bakery is a small price to pay for the treat.

BAGUETTE

The baguette was developed in Paris in the 1930s and came about due to a combination of factors. White bread was becoming increasingly popular, being synonymous, so it was believed at the time, with quality and excellence. The new baker's yeasts that had been developed meant bakers could experiment with other ways of adding yeast to flour, and mechanized kneading and steam ovens led to substantial improvements in techniques and baking. There are many explanations today for why the best baguettes (and they are not all excellent, even in France) are such a delight, yet so difficult to recreate. The soft French flours certainly play a significant part, producing a soft, light crumb with a wonderful wheaty flavor. The small amounts of yeast used, together with a long kneading and rising period and finally, but not least, the skill of the baker, all contribute to the flavor and texture of a baguette, with its crisp, thin crust and delicious, soft crumb.

The baguette was first known as *pain de fantaisie* ("fancy bread"), but the word baguette, meaning "stick," was soon adopted, being obviously the more descriptive nomenclature. *Flutes*, *bâtards*, *ficelles*, *pains* and *petits pains* all belong to the same family and are, made using the same dough and method. *Pain* is a rounder French bread, normally found only in rural areas. The *bâtard* ("bastard") is a cross between the baguette and the *pain*. It is shorter and slightly fatter than a baguette but weighs about the same. The *flute* is a slim 7-ounce baguette, while the little *ficelle* ("string") is slimmer still, weighing half as much as a baguette. The baguette itself measures some 27 inches in length and weighs 9 ounces. *Petits pains* are individual sized breads and are often eaten for breakfast.

The baguette has been available outside France for some 20 years and thankfully continues to get better and better.

ABOVE: There are many different varieties of French baguettes, but they should all have a crisp crust and a soft crumb.

Other baguette-style breads are *baguette à l'ancienne* or *baguette de tradition*, *baguette rustique* and *baguette campagne*, often dark, slightly floury and with small paper labels. These breads are an effort by some traditional bakers to recreate the original baguette, as opposed to the modern version, which has, particularly since the 1970s, been subject to ever-faster production methods. These "traditional" baguettes may be made by a sourdough method, can contain rye or other grains or may be a whole-wheat or bran version. You will need to ask to find out.

Although breads sold in the United States as French bread are sometimes worth avoiding, more and more baguettes, sold either by French-style bakeries or discerning supermarkets, can be very good. They are likely to contain the essential soft wheat and may have been imported from France partially-baked.

VIENNA ROLLS

These little milk breads and their cousins, *petits pains au lait*, are enriched with milk and egg and are normally served for breakfast. Do not confuse French Vienna rolls with British rolls of the same name, which are a crusty torpedo-shape and made with a plain dough. French Vienna rolls are similar to bridge rolls and are fairly small and soft. They may be slashed three or four times across the top, while *petits pains au lait* are rounded, often with a cross cut on top, or long and tapered at either end. They sometimes have a sprinkling of sugar on top.

BRIOCHE

Brioche is one of France's favorite breakfast breads, made with white flour and yeast, enriched with butter, milk and eggs and sweetened with just a little sugar. It is similar to many of the British enriched breads, such as Sally Lunn, although generally richer, using a half to three-quarters butter to flour ratio, which is as rich or richer than most pastries. Although not as popular as croissants outside France, brioche makes a perfect bread for breakfast, with its soft texture and rich flavor. It tastes wonderful served with marmalade or fruit preserves.

Brioche is made in a variety of shapes and sizes. The most

ABOVE: A loaf-shaped brioche and small individual brioche buns.

RIGHT: The unmistakable crescent-shaped croissant is popular at breakfast almost everywhere.

famous is undoubtedly the *brioche à tête*, with its fluted sides and little brioche cap perched on top, and which in turn comes in various sizes—from individual buns to large loaves. The *brioche Nanterre* is made by arranging six or eight balls of brioche dough in a zigzag pattern along the bottom of a loaf pan, while the *brioche Parisienne* is made in a similar way, but with nine or ten balls of dough placed in a circle. Both rise to fill out the pan but the divisions still exist so that small chunks can be broken off.

Savory brioche, made using cheese in place of some of the butter, is becoming more widely available outside France. This is likely to be loaf-shaped, rather than the traditional round, and can be used for savory dishes (as indeed can the sweeter versions). One of the most delicious ways of using savory brioche is to hollow out the center and stuff with wild mushrooms or grilled bell peppers.

CROISSANTS

Another essentially French creation, these popular pastries are available almost everywhere, served not only for breakfast but stuffed with savory fillings and sold wherever there is a demand for food that can be eaten on the run. In France, a distinction is drawn between the *croissant au beurre*, which is small and straight and is made using butter, and the *croissant ordinaire*, which is the more familiar crescent shape made with vegetable fat. The distinction is by no means clear cut, however, as some producers who use only butter in their croissants favor the crescent shape. If the croissants are pre-packaged, you can check the package; otherwise you will need to ask your baker. Ideally, buy croissants fresh in the morning from a local baker, when they will be soft inside, with a flaky crust.

ÉPI

This translates as "wheat ear" and is the traditional bread at harvest festivals, the French equivalent of a harvest loaf. The little ears of bread are made separately and fashioned into sticks or into a large round called a *couronne* ("crown"). The breads can then be broken off, piece by piece, for eating. *Épis* are normally made using a baguette-style dough and are light and crusty.

FOUGASSE

These large, flat breads are quite unmistakable with their deep cuts representing branches of a tree, cogwheels or even the grate of a fire. They are a specialty of Languedoc and Provence, although they originally came from Italy and are closely akin to the Italian focaccia. Sometimes known as *fouacés*, or "hearth bread," they were traditionally baked on the bottom of the oven after the embers had been

ABOVE: Épi is an unusual bread.

scraped out, but while it was still too hot to bake a normal loaf. There are several varieties of *fougasse*—most use a sourdough-style leaven and all are flat, deeply cut and baked in a very hot oven.

PAIN DE CAMPAGNE

Next to baguettes, this is the best-known of French breads. In spite of its name, the loaf was the invention of a Parisian baker and is as much enjoyed in towns and cities as it is in the country. Made using a *chef* starter, it has a thick, slightly gray and floury crust and a discernibly sour smell and taste. No rules exist for its shape, although, like almost all French bread, it is baked on the bottom of the oven (i.e. without using pans) and is therefore a convenient round (or a rather misshapen) baton. Outside France and in French cities, the breads are normally of manageable size, weighing about 1 pound, but visit a rural *boulangerie* in France and you will find huge cartwheel-size breads or sturdy, long loaves, which will keep a large family going for several days. These are sometimes called *pain ménage* ("household bread") and may be sold by weight.

LEFT: Fougasse is the equivalent of Italy's focaccia but has characteristic slashes.

Since it is very much a local product, you will find the bread changes from region to region, even from village to village. Although most use white wheat flour, rye meal and whole-wheat grain are occasionally added, especially for *pain de campagne rustique*, and the flavor and shape will vary enormously. Being a sourdough bread, it keeps well for 4–5 days and indeed is better the day after baking—quite the opposite of the refined baguette.

Pain de campagne is widely available at supermarkets. Shop around for the variety you prefer.

RIGHT: Pain de Campagne comes in many shapes and sizes.

Pain aux Noix

This favorite French bread, although it translates as "nut bread," is understood to be walnut bread. The walnuts give it a teabread feel, but it is very much a savory bread, best served with soft cheese, such as Brie or Camembert or, if you prefer, strong-flavored Cheddar or Stilton. It is made using a whole-wheat bread flour, which contrasts with and complements the nutty and savory walnuts.

Pain de Mie

This is the French version of a British sandwich loaf. It is cooked in a pan with a slide-on lid, so that it has square sides and a soft crust, making it the ideal shape for sandwiches. Unlike the British loaf, however, it is normally enriched with milk and butter so that, in flavor, it is more like brioche than a plain white loaf.

Pain de Seigle/Pain au Seigle

Pain de seigle is French rye and the choice bread for eating with oysters. Regulations insist that it must contain at least two-thirds rye, the remaining proportion made up with wheat flour, which gives it a lighter flavor and color than German and Scandinavian rye breads. *Pain au seigle* ("bread with rye") needs to contain only 10 percent rye and is a lighter bread.

Pain Poilâne

This proprietary loaf is produced and distributed by the famous Poilâne bakers in Paris, not just throughout France, but all

ABOVE: Pain au seigle (left) contains a small amount of rye and has a mild flavor. A brown pain de mie (center) stands alongside pain aux noix (right), a savory walnut loaf that is excellent with a strong cheese.

over the world. Based on the traditional and long-forgotten country loaves of France's past, the bakery prides itself on the methods used for making and baking the bread—a natural sourdough leaven is kneaded briefly but long fermented, then hand-molded and finally baked in wood-fired ovens. Because the sourdough method, by definition, produces a different loaf each time, breads in stores can vary to a surprising degree, some being wonderful, others disappointing.

PAIN POLKA

A specialty bread of the Loire region, this is an oval or round loaf, somewhat flat and criss-crossed with deep slashes. It is baked using the *levain* method of reserving part of the previous day's dough and using this as the starter for the bread.

PAIN BATTU AU FROMAGE

This is a cheese batter bread, which uses Parmesan cheese, a fact that suggests that the bread originally came from Italy or the Alpes-Maritimes region of France. The cheese is stirred into the batter and also sprinkled on top before baking, to give a golden crust. The bread can be loaf-shaped or baked in brioche-style individual pans.

PAIN ALLEMAND AUX FRUITS

This translates as German fruit bread, but is nevertheless a French bread from Strasbourg, a city on the border of Germany. Strasbourg is in the heart of Alsace, a region famous for its rich breads, notably *kugelhopf*. *Pain Allemand* is a rich fruit bread

ABOVE: Pain polka can be plain or may contain chopped olives.

LEFT: Pain Poilâne is easily recognized by the four slashes making a rough square on its top.

ABOVE: There are many variations on pain au levain (back) but all will be made using the sourdough method. The boule de meule is a very substantial loaf best eaten with hearty soups and stews.

that is spiced with cinnamon, cloves and anise seed and rich with raisins, prunes, apricots and figs. It is, needless to say, a festive bread.

PAIN AU LEVAIN

A white or sometimes whole-wheat bread that has become almost as popular in the United Kingdom as it is in France. A *levain* is a bread made by the natural sour-dough method, *levain* being the French term for a sourdough. The breads come in a variety of shapes, often resembling a rather short and flat baguette, or can be molded into rough squares. *Pain rustique* is made using the same sourdough method, but using a proportion of whole-wheat flour or a blend of grains.

BOULE DE MEULE

The word *boulangerie* comes from the French word for a round of dough, *une boule*, which also accounts for the name of this bread. *Boule de meule* translates literally as a round of stoneground dough, which pretty well sums up this bread, except that it is baked, ideally on the bottom of the oven, until it is crusty. *Boules de meule* are normally quite large, with an excellent flavor.

GÂTEAU DE GANNAT

This rich festive bread is popular in the Gannatois region of France. Its principal distinguishing feature is the fromage blanc that is stirred into the batter-like dough with eggs and butter to make a soft crumbly loaf with a sweet/sour flavor. This taste is particularly noticeable if brandy has been added.

PAIN DE PROVENCE

Provence is so rich in all sorts of wonder-ful foods that it would be nonsense to

RIGHT: Cereale is normally a torpedo-shaped loaf.

ascribe a single bread to this region. If you visit Provence you are likely to find a range of pains de Provence, either fashioned roughly into small loaves or made into slender baguettes. Along with the herbs of Provence—savory, thyme and basil—the dough is made with lavender flowers and fennel. It has a heady flavor and is superb served with cheese or to accompany a soup.

CEREALE

This is a well-flavored light brown loaf with a good crust and a tender crumb. It is made from eight cereals and seeds and typically includes wheat, corn, rye, millet, malted wheat and oats, with sunflower and sesame seeds. The shape is quite distinctive. *Cereale* is usually formed into a broad torpedo shape and is lightly dusted with flour.

BELGIAN BREADS

PISTOLET

Pistolets are the Belgian equivalent to the croissants of France. They are small, butter-enriched round rolls, easily distinguished by their central indentation, which is made using a stick dipped in oil before baking. They have a soft texture under a thin, glossy crust and can be found in many parts of northern France, too, where they are just as popular as they are in their native Belgium. *Pistolets* are normally enjoyed for breakfast or for tea, split and spread with preserve or, alternatively, are broken into chunks and eaten French-style dipped in café au lait.

CRAMIQUE

A popular Belgian teabread, this is stuffed with raisins and enriched with butter and milk. It is rather squat in shape and can be made using a whole-wheat or a white flour, or a blend of the two. Whiter versions have a soft crumb with the texture and flavor of brioche, while the whole-wheat *cramique* has a more malted flavor. Bought fresh, *cramique* is wonderful simply buttered or spread with a preserve. Breads that are two or three days old taste good toasted, buttered and spread with jam, or served with a soft cheese, such as brie or camembert.

ABOVE: Fruity cramique

ITALIAN BREADS

Italian bread has had something of a renaissance in the past few years and rightly so. Italian breads are a delight, delicious served with pasta, fish, meats and poultry, as well as cheese. Any Italian baker will tell you that there are thousands of different Italian breads. This could actually be true if anyone ever tried to count! Italy was once made up of a number of independent states, and each developed its own favorite cuisine, including, of course, breads. Geography and climate played a part, as did prosperity. Some of the best-known loaves, such as ciabatta and *pagnotta* are "national" breads, available everywhere. Other breads—the more peasant-style loaves—from rural areas would have been coarse, mealy loaves, made with whatever grain could be gathered together. Olive oil was frequently added, not only for flavor, but to add extra nourishment and to help the keeping qualities of the loaf. Nowadays these rustic loaves are still made using olive oil. They are normally white, although whole-wheat and mixed grain loaves are not unheard of. They can be yeast-leavened but originally would have been made using a natural leaven. Small bakeries, especially those in the south of Italy, a region only mildly influenced by tourism and fashion, still produce these loaves for their loyal customers, made in the traditional way from time-honored recipes. If you visit these parts, be sure to buy and sample some of these regional breads; you will not fail to be delighted. Outside Italy, various country-style breads, such as *pagnotta* and *pugliese*, are available from Italian-style bakers, although these loaves are likely to be standardized. Nevertheless, many first-generation Italian bakers in Britain and North America, who learned their baking skills from their parents and grandparents, bake their own favorite regional bread and these are likely to be as good and authentic as the breads of their homeland.

The distinguishing feature of most Italian breads, especially those bought from an Italian-style baker, is the shape rather than the dough. By and large, bakers do not make up different doughs for different breads—they would not have the time, the space or the labor. The difference lies in the shaping, the slashing and the baking—a small distinction you may think, but wait until you try the bread and you will be surprised.

BIOVA

This regional bread comes from the north of Italy, around Piedmont. It is cylindrical in shape with little pointed horns. Made with lard, it has a thick crust and soft crumb and has an excellent flavor.

CARTA DA MUSICA

This extraordinary harvest sheaf bread from Sardinia, also sometimes called *carasaù* is made with paper thin leaves of dough, piled up to make a tower that looks like a stack of uneven shaped pancakes. The leaves of bread are brittle but can be eaten as a snack with an aperitif or with salads. Alternatively, the leaves of bread can be softened in a light dressing or even just water and olive oil, then wrapped around a filling.

CIABATTA

This ubiquitous loaf has surprisingly not suffered even though it is produced on a massive scale so as to be available at almost every supermarket in the country.

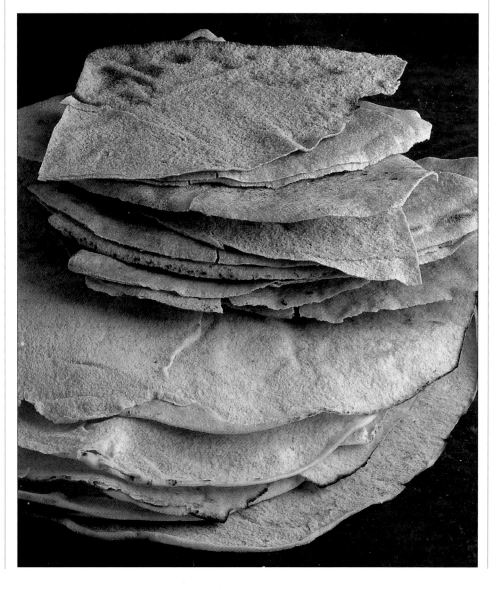

LEFT: Carta da musica means "sheets of music" and does look not unlike sheets of parchment piled on top of each other.

LEFT: Plain ciabatta served with olive and sun-dried tomato versions.

It is an oval, slightly flattish loaf, and looks like a squashed slipper, which is what the word, rather unromantically, means. It is made with generous quantities of olive oil and has a thin, fragile crust. The crumb is light, holey and slightly chewy. Ciabatta is delicious served as an accompaniment to soups or tomato salads, as it will mop up the juices beautifully.

Like the French baguette, ciabatta is a relatively new shape of bread. It is normally a white loaf, made using a sponge dough method—flour, yeast and water are fermented for up to 24 hours before being incorporated into the rest of the dough. Another particular feature of ciabatta, making it a tricky bread to bake at home, is the soft consistency of the dough. It has a minimum of 75 percent water and oil and is thus quite unlike any other kind of bread. A long kneading process also contributes to ciabatta's unique flavor, which should be sweet/sour, as well as its texture: a crisp crust and an open crumb. Numerous flavorings can be added to ciabatta—from olives and sun-dried tomatoes to cheese and walnuts. Many supermarket loaves are sold partially-baked and should be finished in a hot oven before being served. The final baking enhances both the flavor and texture of what is undeniably one of the world's favorite breads.

FOCACCIA AND FOCACCETTE

Focaccia is another Italian bread that has captured the imagination of the rest of the world. Known variously as "Italian country flat bread," *pizza rustica* or *pizza genovese,* it is a large, flat bread, slightly puffy when fresh and dimpled all over the surface with little indentations. It can be round, square or a rather misshapen rectangle; shape is not particularly important. This is the original Italian hearth bread, made from surplus pieces of dough and baked at very high heat before the oven cooled slightly for the massive family loaves. It is easy to imagine the children waiting impatiently for their share of the warm bread as it came out of the oven. Today, most store-bought focaccia, particularly those from supermarkets, are round and can be rather bland in flavor. However, Italian bakers who know and love this bread will produce far more tasty loaves, baking them in a very hot oven so that, like pizzas, they are floury and flecked with black.

Focaccia is a wonderfully versatile bread. Apart from the olive oil that is kneaded into the basic dough, the flattish bread can be sprinkled with sea salt, herbs,

BELOW: Focaccia is often sprinkled with crushed rosemary.

onions, prosciutto or cheese. Smaller versions of focaccia, *focaccette,* are small rolls sprinkled with salt and onions.

GRISSINI

These long, thin breadsticks, mainly popular as a snack with drinks, are made from wheat flour and have been cooked until completely dry, so that they are basically all crust and no crumb. The better grissini are made using olive oil; best of all are those that are handmade by bakers, having considerably more character than the bland, smooth breadsticks available at most supermarkets.

Grissini come from the northwest of Italy, around Turin and Piedmont. Here they also make a more substantial type of breadstick, called *francescine*. These are thicker breadsticks with a softer center, and they not only have a better flavor, but have a decidedly good crunch, too. Grissini are mostly made using white flour, although whole-wheat ones are sometimes available, especially if made on the

BELOW: Paesana

ABOVE: The best grissini are bought at Italian bakeries or delicatessens.

premises by smaller bakers. Grissini are commonly rolled in poppy seeds or sesame seeds or coarsely ground sea salt before baking to add extra flavor.

MICHETTA

This is a round white roll with a well-flavored crust, which is called *rosetta* in Rome.

MEZZA LUNA

This simple crusty loaf is shaped like a half moon. It is made with the standard white dough used for *pagnotta* and other country breads.

PAESANA

This round, simple white loaf that is cross-cut to divide into farls, tastes like focaccia or ciabatta. *Paesana* is generally less rich in olive oil and, without the addition of herbs, sun-dried tomatoes or olives, tends to be a far plainer loaf than its cousins. It is nevertheless very good with soups and stews.

PAGNOTTA

This large, round farmhouse loaf is probably the most common and popular bread in Italy, sold all over the country. Loaves can be small and round, but in Italy some may be huge, cut in portions, each still big enough to feed a large family. The bread is traditionally made using the sourdough method. Outside the country, some Italian delicatessens sell this bread, either imported from Italy or made to an original recipe. Italian-style bakers, however, do not always use the classic but lengthy process for their breads. They argue that for most, *pagnotta* means a standard wheat loaf, so they use the same dough as for other Italian breads. In Italy *pagnotta* can be white, whole-wheat or a mixture, depending on the region, and all types are available outside Italy, with white being the most common.

PANE ALLA CIOCCOLATA

A yeasted bread made with olive oil and studded with dark chocolate, which is kneaded into the dough, it can be whole-wheat, but is more commonly colored a rich brown with cocoa powder. In Italy, chocolate bread is served with mascarpone or Gorgonzola cheese as a snack.

PANE CON NOCI

There are several Italian breads that go under

ABOVE: Pagnotta is Italian country bread; loaves can be huge.

LEFT: Pane al cioccolato, made as rolls.

RIGHT: Pane con noci is a savory nut bread.

the heading "bread with nuts." The oval-shaped bread is similar to the British and French walnut breads, while a slim, flat loaf with golden raisins and walnuts is a sweet version of ciabatta.

PANETTONE

Panettone is a Milanese specialty, sold around Christmas as a traditional festive cake. In Italy and in delicatessens outside the country, it is sold wrapped in cellophane and tied with colored ribbons. For all its richness—made with liberal amounts of butter, eggs and milk, together with golden raisins, candied citrus peel and sometimes chocolate—*panettone* is surprisingly light in texture. This may have something to do with the traditional *panettone* shape, which is like a squat cylinder or dome, slightly wider at the top where the bread has billowed out into a deep golden crust.

PANE DI MAIS

Made using polenta, a coarse ground cornmeal, *pane di*

RIGHT: Panetonne is the classic Christmas bread.

RIGHT: Pugliese is one of the best-known and beloved Italian breads.

mais is one of the few Italian corn breads. It normally also contains some olive oil. It is flatter than most Italian breads, owing to the high proportion of corn, but pieces are perfect for mopping up sauces and salad dressings.

PANE TOSCANO

Alternatively called *pane sciocco* or *pane sciapo Toscano*, this salt-less bread is a favorite among Tuscans, who love it for the flavor of the wheat, which is more pronounced in the absence of salt. The bread was made at a time when salt was heavily taxed. Unlike many Italian breads, *pane sciocco* does not contain olive oil either. If you try it by itself, a common reaction is "something's wrong," or "something's missing from this bread." However, eaten with goat cheese, anchovies, olives or salami, the bread comes into its own.

PUGLIESE

This much-loved Italian bread was once the regional bread from Puglia, in the southern region of Apulia. Perhaps it is the extra-virgin olive oil from this region or the excellence of the wheat, but *pugliese* is considered to be among the

RIGHT: Sfilatino are like small baguettes.

jewels of Italian breads, popular all over the country and beyond as well. The bread is normally white, with a pale, floury crust and a soft crumb, quite dense by Italian standards, compared with the holey ciabatta and the open-textured *pagnotta*.

SFILATINO

Looking something like a French baguette that has perhaps been crossed with a baby ciabatta, these little Italian breads are a wonderful addition to the bread counter at the supermarket and are excellent served with an Italian meal. Although similar in shape to the baguette, any comparison ends there. *Sfilatino* loaves are noticeably smaller than the baguette, without the slashes on top and with a darker, more floury crust. Made using lots of virgin olive oil,

the crust is crisper and less flaky than the baguette, while the crumb is softer.

ITALIAN OLIVE BREAD

Olives are grown throughout Italy, and it's not surprising to find all sorts of olive bread. The more commercially produced loaves are enriched with eggs and butter and normally contain pitted green olives and sometimes whole olives stuffed, Spanish-style,

with red pimiento. Smaller bakers often also produce their own olive breads. These are plainer doughs, which usually contain black olives, sometimes pitted, but sometimes not—so take care when biting into a slice.

TORTINO

Tortino is similar to an olive bread, but is much larger and more rustic with a dense crumb. It can be stuffed with olives, spinach or tomatoes or a mixture of all three.

SICILIAN SCROLL

Sicily has a strong tradition of bread making. Over the centuries, monks and nuns of the island's many monasteries perfected their baking skills as a sign of devotion to God. Sicilian scroll is unusual in that it contains a high proportion of semolina. Shaped into a broad "S," it has a soft, pale yellow crumb and a crisp crust that is traditionally topped with sesame seeds.

ABOVE: Pane Toscano goes by several names, including sciocco and "Tuscan salt-less bread." It has a dense crumb, which to palates unused to its salt-free nature is very bland. However, it has its devotees and is good with cheese.

SPANISH BREADS

Bread is the symbol of all food in Spain. In villages, where bread is still often made at home, the housewife will kiss and make the sign of the cross over the loaf before baking, and children are taught never to snatch bread as this is seen as a sign of disrespect, not only to their parents but also to God.

If you visit Spain, you are likely to find that the first breads of the day are the morning rolls, such as *bollo* or *chica* (meaning "little girl"). Later in the morning, the *panadería* (bakery) will start producing larger breads. These are of almost every conceivable shape and size, but will mostly be yeast-fermented, white, wheat breads. Spain is famous for its simple white breads, with their smooth crust and soft white crumb. Bread is eaten with every meal and with every course. except for sweet desserts. More simple still, and a tradition much loved by the Spanish, is the custom of pouring virgin olive oil over fresh bread to eat as a snack at any time of the day.

While wheat is the principal crop, oats, barley and other cereals are sometimes blended with wheat flour for more rustic loaves. In the northwest corner of the country, in Santiago and La Coruña, whole-wheat and rye breads can be found. Here, near the north of Portugal, cornmeal is blended with wheat flour to make rich yellow loaves. Corn was brought back to Spain from the New World by sailors returning home, but is not as popular today in Spain as it is in Portugal.

PAN CATETO

This is the traditional Spanish country bread, made from a starter called the *levadura de masa*.

BELOW: The pan gallego often looks like a squashy cottage loaf with a top knot.

HORNAZO

This is a Castilian flat bread customarily made at Easter. The dough is filled with chunks of *chorizo* (spicy sausage), cheese and hard-boiled eggs so that when it is baked and cut, everybody receives a different piece of bread. *Horno* is the Spanish word for an oven, from which the bread probably gets its name. At one time in Spain, people would take loaves of bread, as well as large roasts, turkeys or even whole lambs, to the local baker for cooking in the stone *horno*.

PAN GALLEGO

This country-style bread is made using olive oil and has a pleasant, unassuming flavor. It can be a rather misshapen round, and a whole loaf can be huge. Much of the *pan gallego* sold outside Spain are quarters of a large loaf. The crust is soft and floury, the crumb light with an open texture. Seed *gallego* is a similar loaf but is studded with pumpkin and sesame seeds, which give it a delicious flavor and texture.

BELOW: Pan aceite

PAN QUEMADO

This is one of the best-known Spanish sweet breads. It has a rather squashed, sunken look, a bit like an enlarged English lardy cake with its glossy brown top, but in spite of appearances, this is a delicious sweet loaf, a little like a French brioche in texture, although it is made with olive oil rather than butter.

GOFIO

This unusual bread is classified as Spanish, coming as it does from the Canary Islands, but has a fascinating and ancient history that suggests it might more rightly belong with the Arabian or Moroccan breads. Although the Canaries have belonged to Spain for hundreds of years, they were once the home of a group of Berbers called the Guanches. Now extinct, little knowledge of these original people remains other than a few artifacts. *Gofio*, however, is thought to have originated with these North African people. The bread is the shape of a large ball and is made from a variety of flours—wheat, barley, corn and gram (dried chickpeas), which are sometimes blended and always toasted before milling. The dough is mixed with water or milk and, although yeast is used today, originally the dough would have been fermented using a natural leaven. Once risen, the bread is baked, either conventionally in an oven or, even today in some parts of the Canaries, in a Dutch oven, a pot-like construction where the embers of the fire are piled around the outside of the pot.

The result is a crusty round loaf with a fairly dense crumb, quite unlike the light and airy Spanish breads and indeed unlike most traditional Moroccan breads as well, which are mostly flat and baked very quickly in unusually hot ovens. Perhaps the scarcity of wheat meant these ancient people needed to be more inventive, or perhaps their settled life on the islands, as opposed to the nomadic life of the Berbers, meant they had more time for the task of baking.

ENSAIMADAS

A specialty of Majorca (Mallorca), these small yeasted pastry buns are the Spanish answer to the croissant, except that instead of being crescent-shaped they look more like little Moorish turbans. Normally a little sweeter than croissants, they have the same soft texture and are served at breakfast with jam or honey in the island's many hotels. Consignments of these little rolls are regularly sent to Barcelona, where they are much appreciated by both tourists and local city dwellers.

A much larger version of the *ensaimada* can also be found in Majorca. This is often topped with cream or a sweet custard-like topping made with pumpkin pulp, sugar, lemon juice and spices. This dessert is particularly popular at fiestas, when the *ensaimada* is decorated with small pieces of squash and thin slices of *sobrasada*, a type of Majorcan sausage.

MAJORCAN POTATO BUNS

Although a relatively small group of islands, the Balearic Islands have a surprisingly rich and varied cuisine. Along with their own local fish and meat dishes, they have a variety of delicious breads, including these Majorcan potato buns. These small buns are made using either sweet or ordinary potatoes. They have a very sweet taste and are normally eaten at breakfast, during mid-morning or for tea, and are usually served with jam or honey.

PAN ACEITE (OLIVE OIL BREAD)

This is similar to the French *fougasse* and the Italian *focaccia* breads. *Pan Aceite* is commonly a rather misshapen-looking bread. It is baked on the side of the oven, after being brushed liberally with olive oil (hence the name olive oil bread).

TWELFTH NIGHT BREAD

In Spain and Portugal children receive their presents not on Christmas Day but on Twelfth Night (January 6). Appropriately for the Epiphany, the gifts are delivered by a figure representing the Magi, the three wise men who made their journey from the East to bring gifts to the infant Jesus. It is customary for a special bread called *roscon de reyes* in Spain and *bolo-rei* in Portugal to be baked for this day. The rich teabread is stuffed with fruits and candied peel and traditionally contains a coin or figurine, bringing luck to the person who is given the piece of bread in which it is discovered.

PORTUGUESE BREADS

Portuguese bakers, like their counterparts in other countries, frequently use the same basic dough for making loaves and rolls. It is the shape and manner of baking that gives each bread its own idiosyncratic flavor and texture. Many Portuguese breads are made using a yeasted white flour dough.

ALENTEJANO

This is a white bread with a fairly thick crust and a well-flavored crumb, which has a distinctive, salty/sour flavor. Like almost all Portuguese and Spanish breads, the bread is baked on the bottom of the oven and has an even, golden crust.

BROA DE MILO

This simple loaf from Minho in northern Portugal, the name of which translates as "corn bread," is normally referred to simply as *broa* and is eaten by everyone. Corn is a popular grain for making bread in Portugal and Spain. The conquistadors and sailors brought home not only potatoes, tomatoes and bell peppers, but corn

RIGHT: Alentejano has a good flavor.

BELOW: Papo secos are soft yet crusty.

ABOVE: Rosquilha is an attractive round bread.

as well, together with the skills needed to grind it into meal. Corn proved to be a successful crop in the north of Portugal where wheat does not flourish, and it would have been quickly selected as the preferred crop. It is likely that even from the beginning, bakers would have blended cornmeal with wheat in order to provide some gluten, but when this was scarce barley and alfalfa flour were used and, even today, loaves are made from a mixed grain. *Broa de milo* is a robust, well-flavored loaf, which goes well with Portuguese soups and *cozidos*—stewed meat, vegetables and pulses.

ROSQUILHA

This is a ring-shaped white bread with a pleasant crust and a slightly chewy texture and salty flavor. It is usually be made using the same dough as *alentejano* but the shape means *rosquilha* is crustier, although it does not stay fresh as long. *Rosquilha* can be bought and eaten at any time of day but is very popular for breakfast or during mid-morning, and is served with coffee.

CANTELO

This wedding bread is a traditional bread from the northern region of Portugal. The loaf is baked in a ring, and custom dictates that the bride and groom break the bread into pieces to give to their wedding guests with a glass of wine.

PAPO SECOS

These small white rolls are a popular breakfast bread all over Portugal. They have a soft white crumb and a delicious crust that is crisp without being hard. Like

ABOVE: If you live near a Portuguese bakery, try caracas as an alternative to regular hamburger buns.

RIGHT: Bolo do caco is a hearth bread like focaccia and fougasse.

many breads from Portugal, they are baked with lots of steam, which accounts for their good crust yet ensures that the crumb is light and airy.

CARACAS

Caracas are similar in size and shape to *papo secos* but are more like an English or Scottish bap, batch-baked and cooked with less steam so they are softer and less crusty.

BOLO DO CACO

This flattish loaf is similar to the Spanish olive oil bread. It is another type of hearth bread, cooked on the bottom of a very hot oven. It is best eaten very fresh with dressed salads or with other foods that have plenty of liquids that need mopping up.

MAIA BREAD

This is a long white loaf, normally made using a plain white dough. It is popular all over Portugal and is one of the better-known everyday breads, eaten with fish soups and salads, and Portuguese cheese.

BELOW: Maia bread is almost always a white loaf and has a good, slightly chewy crust.

GERMAN BREADS

There is an enormous range of German breads. Outside Germany—in Britain, for example—you could be forgiven for thinking that all German breads come in neat packages wrapped in cellophane. These are in fact the *kastenbrots* (box breads) and include the well-known pumpernickel. In Germany, however, and increasingly available throughout Europe and North America, there are also the German *krustenbrots* (crusty breads). These are the freshly baked breads, bought from a bakery or from the fresh bread counters at supermarkets, and they are as varied and delicious as the loaves to be found in the rest of continental Europe. The German word *brot* means either wheat or rye bread, with other breads named for the type of grain used in their making: oats, corn or barley.

KASTENBROTS

In the customary way that German words very often describe exactly what they mean, *kastenbrots* translates as "box bread." The bread is steam-baked for some 20 hours in apan with a lid, which

BELOW: Pumpernickel is the best-known of the German kastenbrots.

results in a dense and heavy loaf which is both moist and crumbly with a chewy texture. It has a sour flavor but with a certain sweet, malty overtone and, unlike most breads, has a distinctive but not unpleasant aftertaste. *Kastenbrots* are not breads to be eaten with wine, but are best enjoyed with a glass of cool German beer.

These breads almost invariably use rye flour (normally a whole-wheat grain that can be coarsely or more finely ground according to the type of bread). The dough uses a natural, sourdough leaven, which adds to the sour taste of the bread and complements the flavor of the rye, with its own earthy taste. The darkest *kastenbrots* contain only rye but wheat flour is added in varying proportions to give a loaf that is lighter in appearance, texture and flavor. Other grains, such as oats or barley, as well as sunflower and sesame seeds, are added to certain loaves, and there are therefore numerous variations on the basic theme. The bread always comes thinly sliced, wrapped in cellophane and clearly labeled. While moist in texture, the bread, with its sweet/sour yet dry flavor tastes best buttered or spread with a soft cheese. Savory foods, such as smoked salmon, marinated herring or German sausage, are most commonly served with the darker breads, but the lighter breads are excellent with marmalade or other strongly flavored preserves.

PUMPERNICKEL

The best known of all the *kastenbrots*, pumpernickel is also the darkest of these breads. It is usually made with 100 percent coarsely ground rye grain, and has an unmistakable sour, earthy flavor, but

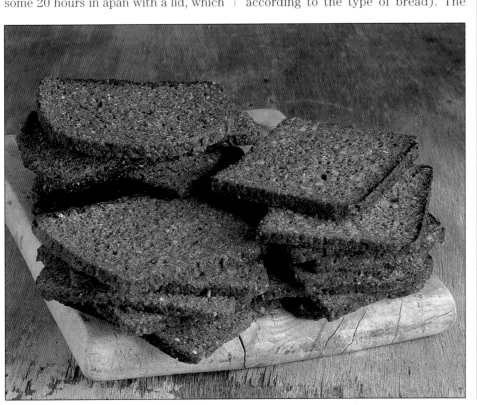

LEFT: Vollkornbrot (left) is a 100 percent rye bread, while roggenbrot (back) is slightly lighter, containing some wheat flour. Sonnenblumenbrot (right) is made with sunflower seeds, which give it a lighter flavor and a good texture.

some are made with slightly less rye flour and a small amount of wheat flour. Like many German breads, pumpernickel is sometimes flavored with caraway seeds.

VOLLKORNBROT OR SCHWARZBROT

This is another strongly flavored bread, the names of which translate as "whole corn" or "black" bread. The whole "corn" in this instance is rye, which again is coarsely ground. The bread also contains molasses, adding to the dark color and the malty flavor of the bread—which is probably for devotees only.

ROGGENBROT

Roggen is German for rye, but, in fact, this bread often contains a small proportion of wheat flour, too. *Roggenbrot* is a dark oblong pan loaf with a hard crust that is sometimes encrusted with whole grains. In spite of the added wheat flour, this is still an intensely flavored bread, best eaten with strong-tasting foods.

SONNENBLUMENBROT

Sunflower seeds give this bread a pleasant crunchy texture. *Sonnenblumenbrut* is made mainly using rye flour, but a small proportion of wheat flour together with the sunflower seeds makes this a more palatable loaf for those sampling *kastenbrot* for the first time.

WEISENKEIMBROT

This means "wheat germ bread" and it is made using the wheat germ, along with rye grain and flour.

Grahamsbrot uses a higher proportion of whole-wheat flour, specifically the American-style graham flour.

ABOVE: Three krustenbrots: Black Forest (left), Bavarian rye (right) and roggenbrot.

MUESLIBROT

This is a multigrain *kastenbrot*, made using a muesli-style mix of cereals, chopped nuts and whole grains. It is a popular choice in Germany for those who want a healthy teabread that has plenty of texture and is not overly sweet.

KRUSTENBROTS

These crusty breads are the day-to-day breads of Germany, and are also popular in parts of Canada and in the American states around the Great Lakes, where German emigrés settled in the 1840s. In other European countries, German-style bakers import the flours from Germany or bake them using locally bought flours and meals, but sometimes import the sourdough culture from their native home. Many, although not all, German breads contain rye flour.

LEFT: Weisenkeimbrot (back) is made with both rye and wheat flours, while mueslibrot contains a mixture of cereals, nuts and whole grains.

ABOVE: Landbrot

BELOW: German square rye

Rye was once the main cereal in northern Europe. It tolerates the cooler dryer climate, and for centuries, while the more affluent enjoyed white bread made with imported wheat, the poor continued to eat bread made with the grain that was cheap and readily available. When wheat became relatively inexpensive in Germany, white wheat flour was used by all but the very poorest, either by itself or with rye flour. There is consequently a great variety of German breads. Some are baked in pans, but the majority are baked on the bottom of the oven and are evenly crusty.

RIGHT: German rye

GERMAN SQUARE RYE

This is an easily recognized bread: it is a large square loaf that is cross-hatched on top. It is often just known as German rye, but unlike other ryes of that name it has a pleasant, gentle flavor, due partly to the blend of rye and wheat flours, and also partly

to the long fermentation process. Like most German ryes, it too uses the sourdough principle and consequently has a noticeable yet mild, sour flavor. It is good with German meats and sausages or with creamy cheeses.

LANDBROT

This is a traditional country bread, made using a large proportion of wheat flour but with enough rye to give a pale, beige-colored crumb. It has an excellent sweet/sour flavor, partly from the rye and partly from the buttermilk, which is used instead of milk or water. It comes in all sorts of shapes and sizes, sometimes with a floury crust and sometimes without. Inside, the bread is always open-textured and slightly chewy, and is good with soups and stews.

ROGGENBROT

Unlike the *kastenbrot* of the same name, this *krustenbrot* contains only rye grain and rye flour. It is a robust, sourdough loaf with a thick, chewy crust.

GERMAN RYE BREAD

There are many varieties of this sturdy loaf, including the well-known Bavarian rye. Rye breads come in various shapes and sizes, but are most often pan or bloomer-shaped. The loaf typically has more rye than usual, but wheat flour is there too, for a lighter texture. Like many

German breads, it is made by the sourdough method. The culture is made by mixing rye flour with water to produce just the right balance of acids to work the dough. Although these cultures can last for many years if fed and reinvigorated correctly, most bakers will start a new culture every week, mainly so that they—and you—know what you are getting.

A 100 percent rye bread contains, as you might expect, only rye flour, and is therefore suitable for anyone with an allergy to wheat. This, too, uses the sourdough method and has a dense texture and strong, sour flavor.

GEBILDBROT (PICTURE BREAD)

Now something of a rarity, these breads can still be found in villages on festive occasions. The bread is molded into complex shapes and patterns, usually with symbolic meanings. Loaves may be embossed with horses, deer, serpents, flowers and sheaves of wheat or fashioned into shapes of men and women. The origin of this custom most likely dates from pagan times when bread would have been offered to appease the gods. Christianity also used breads in many rituals and many of the *gebildbrote* bear Christian symbols, such as crucifixes, loaves and fishes.

PRETZELS

Although extremely popular as snacks in America, pretzels are nevertheless German in origin. Like *gebildbrote*, pretzels have a symbolic meaning, which may have its origins in pagan times. The distinctive knot shape is believed by some to have been a symbol for the solar cycle; others believe the crossed arms symbolize the cross and that pretzels were originally made as a Lenten bread. Whatever the explanation, pretzels clearly have important significance in Germany and beyond—the same symbol of interlocking rings is the sign of a bakery throughout northern Europe.

Pretzels are almost always made using white flour and, according to a decree of 1256 in Landshut, it was a punishable offense for a baker to bake pretzels from anything but the finest white flour. Unlike other salted breads or crackers, German

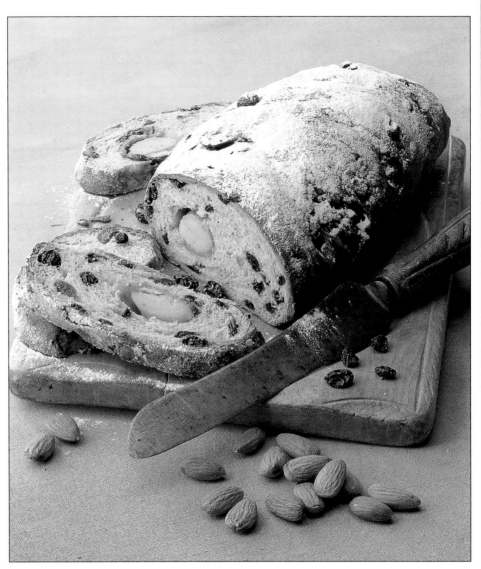

ABOVE: Stollen is a popular Christmas treat in many European countries. It is rich with fruit and often has a sweet marzipan center.

pretzels in many ways resemble a bagel. Along with the white flour, they contain yeast and milk and are poached, sprinkled liberally with sea salt and then baked until the crust is hard and golden. This salty, crunchy crust contrasts with the soft crumb.

ROLLS

There is an enormous variety of German-style rolls. Most are made from white flour and may be sprinkled with caraway or poppy seeds. *Semmel,* with their star-shaped design on top, and *Eiweckerl,* are mainly served at breakfast.

STOLLEN

There are many German sweet breads but perhaps the best-known and most-loved is stollen, sold almost everywhere as a treat at Christmastime. It is an oval-shaped loaf, which tapers at each end. The shape is said to represent the infant Jesus wrapped in swaddling clothes. The bread is packed with golden raisins, currants and mixed citrus peel and is usually spiced and enriched with eggs, butter and milk. Almonds may be finely chopped and added to the dough with the fruit, or they may be ground and made into a paste that is then rolled into the bread, giving it a sweet, moist center. Stollen is unfailingly delicious, although it is predictably high in calories.

FOUR CEREAL BREAD

This dark, solid loaf is made using a blend of cereals but always includes both rye and wheat.

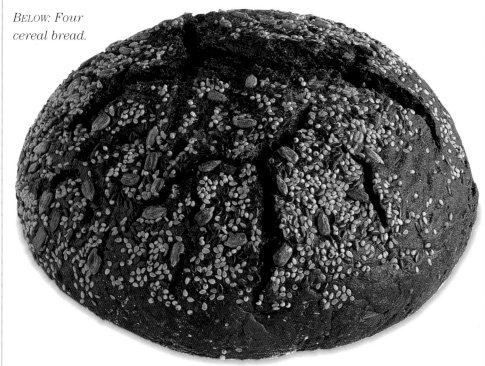

BELOW: Four cereal bread.

GOLDGRAIN

Sometimes called a multi-grain loaf, this baguette-shaped loaf is made using wheat, rye, barley, oats, soy flour, linseed, sunflower seeds, wheat bran, semolina and millet. For all this vast array of ingredients it is not unduly heavy and it has a texture not dissimilar to a Granary bread, with a wholesome, nutty flavor. Goldgrain sometimes is made with the addition of chopped walnuts. Both varieties are popular in health-conscious Germany and are becoming more easily available elsewhere. They are distributed by several producers.

BELOW: Mehrkorn is a comparatively light-textured krustenbrot *made from a mixture of different grains.*

GERMAN BREAD WITH CARAWAY SEEDS

Caraway is a favorite ingredient in German rye breads, adding its unmistakable aniseed flavor. Although often called "German rye with caraway" or "light rye with caraway," the bread does contain a large proportion of wheat flour, giving it a light texture and flavor.

KUGELHOPF

This bread belongs equally to the Alsace region of France and to Vienna in Austria. There are various ways of spelling *kugelhopf* and even more ways for making and baking it. In Alsace it is a savory bread made with bacon, lard and/or fromage blanc and cream cheese. The German and Austrian *kugelhopf,* by contrast, is a yeasted brioche-style bread, made using golden raisins and raisins and enriched with butter and eggs. A good *kugelhopf* has a delicious citrus flavor, provided by lemon rind and juice.

The *kugelhopf* is baked in a fluted mould with a central funnel, and the top billows out like a "kugel," or ball.

MEHRKORN

Mehrkorn means "more grain" and this bread is a multi-grain loaf. The mixture of grains means that the bread is noticeably lighter than many of the principally rye breads.

AUSTRIAN BREADS

As you would expect, a large number of the most popular Austrian breads are similar, if not identical, to those of neighboring Switzerland, Italy, and Germany. However, Austria may well have been responsible for many of the more elaborate continental breads. It was the Austrians who developed the *poolisch* or sponge method of leavening dough, also used in France. This was particularly popular for white breads or those using finer flours, and breads made by this method were noted for their excellent flavor. Not surprisingly, Vienna became the home of fine baking. Croissants are just one among many delicacies that may originally have come from the master bakers of Austria, although any French person will certainly disagree!

BAURNBROT

While Austria is paradise for all those who love rich breads and pastries, there are still country-style loaves to be found. Not least of these is *baurnbrot*, made using buckwheat and wheat flour and molasses, flavored with caraway seeds and leavened using a rye sourdough starter. This makes for a robust and strongly flavored loaf, which tastes best with simple foods, such as country cheeses, sausages and meats, or simply dunked in soup.

DUTCH BREADS

KORNKRACKER

Kornkracker can refer to either loaves or rolls. The bread is popular throughout Germany and Holland. The word means "cracked corn" and the bread is made with cracked whole-grain wheat, together with malted wheat and seeds.

DUTCH FRUIT LOAF

This lightly malted Granary-style loaf rich with fruit and sprinkled with sugar is popular with coffee at any time of the day. It is also a favorite treat for children and is sometimes served with a mild cheese, such as Edam or Gouda.

RIGHT: Kornkracker

FRISIAN SUGAR LOAF

This unusual sweet bread is made using whole sugar lumps that melt as the bread is baked to give delicious pockets of sweetness, which contrast with the cinnamon in the soft white crumb.

DUTCH ROGGEBROOD

Holland also has its own varieties of *kastenbrots* and *krustenbrots*. This box-style bread is similar to the German *roggenbrot*, made with rye flour and leavened using the sourdough method. It often contains molasses and is consequently very dark with a strong malty taste.

Holland even has its own pumpernickel, which like the German variety, contains 100 percent rye flour. The Dutch pumpernickel is a little sweeter than the German version, but with the same strong flavor. It is not for the faint-hearted!

DUTCH CRISPBREADS

The Dutch enjoy crispbreads almost as much as the Scandinavians. They are usually served at breakfast, eaten with cheese or smoked hams, or spread with jam or marmalade. The round breads that are commonly available outside the Netherlands are baked until completely crisp. They have a unique, vaguely sweet flavor, which is surprisingly good with savory foods. Dutch crispbreads come in cylindrical packets and are generally available everywhere.

ABOVE: Dutch fruit bread

RIGHT: Dutch crispbreads — popular everywhere.

SWISS BREADS

One of the least accessible and smallest countries of Western Europe, Switzerland has an extraordinary wealth of unusual and tasty breads. There are probably two explanations for this. First, the mountains that cover 70 percent of Switzerland means that, until quite recently, villages have existed in relative isolation, and rural traditions, such as baking and bread-making have endured, undiluted by commercialization and mass markets. The other significant factor is that four of Switzerland's five neighbors (the fifth is tiny Liechtenstein)—France, Germany, Italy and Austria—are home to most of the best breads in the world.

As well as producing many loaves that are familiar to its neighbors, Switzerland has borrowed some of the best breads to develop its own specialties. These, too, reflect the influence of near neighbors and in common with the pattern elsewhere, rye breads are baked in the north; soft white loaves in the south and east.

BELOW: Crusty bauerruch

APFELNUSSBROT
The name denotes the Germanic origins of this unusual bread, but it seems to be a distillation of a variety of traditions from France as well as Germany. The round, crusty loaf is made from a blend of grains including wheat, rye, barley and spelt, which points to a German influence, yet the apples and walnuts seem typically French, and the bread is not unlike the *pain aux pommes* from France. The best loaves are said to be found in Valais, in the south of the country.

BANGELI
This crusty loaf is a cross between the French baguette and the long white loaves of Germany. It comes from Basel, a Swiss town on the border of France and Germany, which perhaps explains its hybrid appearance. It is a long loaf that looks rather rustic, with seven or eight horizontal slashes and a thick, floury crust. The bread is often cut into chunks to serve with fondue.

BAUERRUCH
Swiss bakers take enormous pride in their work, and some of the Swiss breads are beautifully crafted—for example, the *bauerruch,* which is a rounded crusty loaf shaped in a swirl like a turban or a seashell. It is a fairly dense white bread with a thick, golden crust.

PANIS LUNATIS
This means "moon bread." In Switzerland, some believe it was the precursor to the croissant. Indeed moon bread was baked as long ago as the eighth century. Today, Swiss bakers sell croissants, but they always claim to have invented them.

SAKO
Although some wheat is grown in Switzerland, neither the soil nor the climate favor agriculture, and the little wheat that was coaxed from the land was frequently blended with other grains to make tasty and healthy loaves. The *sako* is a round multi-grain loaf made with eight different cereals. It is usually risen in a floured basket, then turned out for baking. *Sako* is often slashed off-center across the top and is generally sprinkled with cracked wheat

or rolled oats. It is a somewhat dense loaf, excellent for mopping up soups.

SWISS PEASANT LOAF

There are many variations on the theme of a Swiss rustic loaf, but most are round, free-form loaves, made with a blend of wheat and rye flours with cracked rye and chopped walnuts giving the loaves a pleasant texture.

VOGEL LOAF

This is a proprietary Swiss loaf that is renowned for its healthy properties. It was developed over 30 years ago by a Swiss nutritionist, Dr. Alfred Vogel. A multi-grain bread, it contains kibbled wheat, rye grain and bran, giving it a high-fiber

ABOVE: The attractive and simple Swiss peasant loaf.

RIGHT: Healthy Vogel loaf

RIGHT: Zupfe is also known as Swiss braid.

tradition of braiding bread came from is not known, only that it is extremely old. It may have symbolized the braid of hair offered by the wife or widow of a warrior to ensure his safe return from battle. Shaped into a round, it could have represented the course of the sun, while the crescent may have signified the moon. The Swiss braided breads are almost always yeast-leavened, made using white wheat flour, and may be braided with three or more strands of dough. There is really no limit to the baker's art, and the Swiss have a reputation for their skill with shaping bread.

GIPFELTEIG

These are essentially tiny croissants and are the best thing to eat for breakfast if you are visiting Switzerland. They are so small—three or four will fit comfortably in your hand—and so delicious, that it is easy to consume far too many before you decide you have probably had enough! They resemble, and may be identical, to the tiny croissants you will be served in the Alsace area and other parts of western France ,and the bakers use lard as well as butter in the dough to give a texture that is very soft. *Gipfelteig* are best eaten fresh and warm as they are, or spread with a little apricot jam, or some tangy orange marmalade.

WEGGLITAG

These little rolls are often served for breakfast along with *gipfelteig.* The small, oval white rolls are always glazed with beaten egg and notched across the top with scissors to give a crenelated effect and a crunchy crust.

content, which is one of its main selling points. The whole and cracked grain gives the loaf plenty of texture, yet the flavor is not too strong, making it a popular choice for those who like their fiber to be subtle rather than overpowering.

ZUPFE (ZOPF)

Known variously as *zupfe*, *zopf* or Swiss braid, this is a braided loaf made from a rich dough, which typically contains sour cream or milk, eggs and butter. It has a glossy crust and beautifully light crumb. Like its neighbors, Austria and Germany, Switzerland has a great affection for these rich doughs, which are shaped, braided or twisted into spectacular loaves. This is where the tradition of the Jewish *challah* —another braided loaf—is believed to have evolved. Exactly from where the

ABOVE AND BELOW: Wegglitag and gipfelteig are a great way to start the day.

NORDIC BREADS

Rye, oats and barley were once the only crops that would grow in the cooler climate and acidic soils of northern Europe. While wheat was imported for the prosperous, for the majority of people, bread was inevitably made using one type or a blend of these cereals. Rye, which contains gluten, was favored for leavened bread as it would rise and produce a lighter loaf. In Norway, however, where there was a fondness for unleavened bread, oats and barley and sometimes pea-flour were for many centuries the favored ingredients for making their popular *flatbrød*.

Nowadays, wheat can be grown in the more temperate parts of Denmark and Sweden and, of course, being widely imported, white breads are commonly available. Traditionally, the festive breads have always been made from the finest white flours. Scandinavians set great store by their festivals and each year buy or make their Christmas and Easter breads, along with a host of other breads made for celebrations in between.

White breads are particularly popular in the cities, but the Scandinavians continue to love their dark rye breads and visitors will find that there is a wide choice of breads —from the weird and

wonderful breads of Lapland to the *flatbrøds* of Norway, and the rich pumpernickel breads baked in Denmark.

RIGHT: Danish rye bread is lighter in texture and color than German ryes.

DANISH BREADS

RYE BREAD

There are numerous types of Danish rye breads and you will need to sample a few to discover the ones you like best. Danish ryes tend to be lighter and sweeter than most German ryes. Molasses and malt extract are popular ingredients, adding to the dark color, but this is tempered by the greater proportion of white wheat flour. Danish ryes also tend to contain either buttermilk or butter or both. This helps to preserve the loaf and

RIGHT: Rye breads are popular throughout Scandinavia.

RIGHT: The braided tresse

gives a richer and more open-textured bread. Danish ryes are the popular breads for *smørrebrød*, the open sandwiches topped with meats and cheese.

KERNEBROD

A seeded loaf, normally made with a Granary flour, sprinkled liberally with sunflower seeds and linseeds.

TRESSE

This is a braided white loaf, enriched with milk, eggs and butter. It may be scattered freely with poppy or sesame seeds and is popular throughout the year, although at one time this loaf was probably made for special occasions.

DANISH FESTIVE FRUIT LOAF (JULEKAGE)

This is one of the most famous of all the Danish Christmas loaves. Christmas is a hugely important festival in all parts of Scandinavia, not only for its Christian significance, but also because it heralds the end of the long, freezing Danish winter. Similar breads, filled with fruit, nuts and spices, and enriched with butter and eggs, are made all over Scandinavia. *Julekage*

is traditionally spiced with vanilla and cardamom. Crushed sugar is then sprinkled over the top before baking and, finally, confectioners' sugar is sprinkled on the bread when it is cooked.

CARNIVAL BUNS (FASTERLAVNSBOILLER)

Any Dane will be able to tell you about these treats, which they will remember from their childhood and probably now make for their own children. They are traditionally made on the Monday before Shrove Tuesday, which is celebrated not only with breads and cakes but also with some games, including "beating a cat off the barrel," which involves children chasing each other and which thankfully has nothing to do with cats, in spite of its name. The little square or round buns are something like a cross between a bread and an English Yorkshire pudding, made with white flour and yeast and enriched with eggs, butter and milk. Carnival buns are flavored with cardamom and filled

with almond paste and sometimes with chopped peel, and are normally liberally dusted with confectioners' sugar.

SMØRREBRØD

The word simply means "buttered bread" but the famous Danish open sandwiches are so much more than that. Delicious toppings—their ingredients limited only by the imagination of the cook—are laid on thin slices of bread. The aim of the exercise is to produce a snack that is as appealing to the eye as it is to the stomach, and the results are as colorful as they are good to eat. Danish sour rye bread is the preferred base, although for some more delicate toppings, such as smoked salmon, baby shrimp, prawns or lobster, a crusty white bread is sometimes used. Fish and shellfish are favorite toppings, one of the most popular choices being pickled herring with marinated onion rings. Liver paste, salami, cheeses (including the famous blue cheese of Denmark), roast pork, hard-boiled eggs—the list of potential toppings is apparently limitless, as is the Danes' capacity for enjoying their favorite lunchtime snack.

NORWEGIAN AND SWEDISH BREADS

NORWEGIAN FLAT BREAD

Flatbrød is the oldest of all the Norwegian breads and was, until fairly recently, the bread most commonly eaten by the people of Norway. A long time ago these wafer-thin crispbreads would have been made with any cereal that was on hand—mostly oats, rye, barley or pea-flour, or a mixture of all these. The unleavened dough would have been rolled into very thin, large circles and baked on a griddle or on a stone over an open fire. The breads were known to last for months, even up to a year, and would be stored on the beams over the kitchen. These days the breads are factory-baked and sold ready-cut into convenient rectangles. Some bakers, however, continue to make their own, and in parts of Norway the large breads are served at harvest meals, dampened with a little water so they become pliable and can be wrapped around Norwegian sweet cheese or other suitable pieces of food.

NORWEGIAN WHOLE-WHEAT BREAD

This fine bread is made with whole-wheat kernels, skim milk yeast, cottage cheese and whole-wheat flour, and is topped with crushed wheat.

LEFT: Flatbrød

LIMPA

Limpa is a Swedish favorite—a leavened rye loaf, sweetened with molasses or honey, flavored with orange and spiced with cardamom, cumin, fennel and anise seeds. Since wheat flour makes up the greater proportion of flour, the loaf is not as heavy as some rye loaves, although it has the typical dense yet crumbly texture of rye. *Vortlimpa* is a far darker loaf than *limpa*, containing a greater proportion of rye together with the molasses. It, too, contains orange rind, either grated or finely chopped, and can also be made with ground or whole fennel seeds. In spite of the sweet molasses, this dark loaf is intended to be eaten with soft cheese or salted herring.

ROGBRÖD

Røgbröd is the traditional rye bread of Sweden, made in large flat loaves and often containing molasses, an ingredient that has been greatly valued by Sweden and the other Scandinavian countries since it was first imported. Unlike the flat Norwegian ryes, *røgbröd* is leavened, traditionally using a sourdough method, but also using normal yeast. Buttermilk or soured milk is often used instead of ordinary milk, adding to the acidic flavor of the bread, which is also flavored with fennel or caraway seeds.

RIGHT: Lomper is a soft flat bread cooked on a griddle.

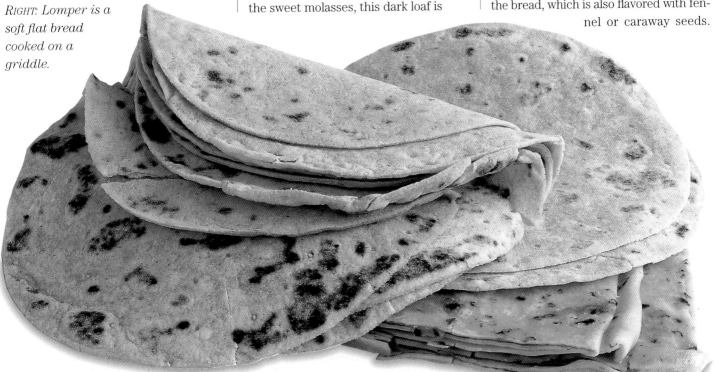

Ragbröd is much the same as *røgbröd*—made of rye and often containing molasses—but is shaped into a ring by being rolled out into a flat round and then having a hole cut in the middle. Traditionally, *ragbröd* would have been looped across the kitchen with string, and even today you may see them displayed in such a way in some bakeries.

LEFT: Swedish krisprolls

SWEDISH CARDAMOM BRAID

This is a delicious sweet fruit bread, made with white flour, enriched with milk, eggs and butter and spiced with the distinctive flavor of cardamom.

SWEDISH CARAWAY BREAD

This is a half-sweet, half-savory white bread, made with a little sugar and butter, yet given a subtle savory flavor by the caraway seeds.

ST. LUCIA BUNS

Throughout Scandinavia, the days leading up to Christmas are as much a time of festivity as Christmas Day itself. St Lucia Day (December 13) is celebrated widely in Sweden. The oldest girl in a family wears a white dress and a crown of glowing candles, symbolizing the light that will come once winter is over. She distributes St Lucia buns, traditionally made with saffron and enriched with eggs, butter and milk. Each bread is shaped like the letter "S" and topped with a raisin.

KNÄCKERBROD

Sweeter than the Finnish *knackebrod*, these Swedish flat breads are made with rolled oats and taste a little like sweet Scottish oatcakes. Unlike Scottish oatcakes, however, they are leavened using baking soda and buttermilk, and are baked in the oven.

SCANDINAVIAN STAR

This unusual and pretty bread is a modern adaptation of some of the best Scandinavian baking traditions. It is made using a blend of white and Granary flours, but its fine flavor is due mainly to the sponge method of making the dough, which allows the flavors to develop, and the longer-than-usual rising. Sunflower seeds and linseeds are added for flavor and the bread is sprinkled liberally with sesame seeds before being stamped into its distinctive star shape. The bread has a good crisp crust, while the crumb is soft with a rich nutty flavor. It makes an excellent breaking bread, which is appropriate as pulling off pieces of bread is preferred in Scandinavia to slicing bread conventionally.

SCANDINAVIAN CRISPBREADS

There are many Scandinavian crispbreads, ranging from crisp rusks to wafer-thin crackers. Norwegian crispbreads are made mainly with whole rye, although there are also many made with a blend of wheat flours. *Krisprolls* are popular in Sweden, eaten at almost any time of the day, but particularly at breakfast. They are baked until entirely crisp and have a noticeably sweet flavor.

LEFT: The Scandinavian star bread, with its liberal sprinkling of sesame seeds, looks attractive and has an excellent flavor.

FINNISH AND ARCTIC BREADS

LEFT: Icelandic bread

FINNISH KNACKEBROD

This thin, cracker-like bread with its characteristic central hole, is made using a blend of rye and corn. Freshly made *knackebrod* are crisp and are delicious with fresh goat cheese or smoked salmon. *Wiborgs kringla* are also from Finland and are similar in many ways to Germany's pretzels: the entwined strands, like a lover's knot, appear on bakery signs in Finland. The enriched yeast bread was traditionally baked on straw, and even today the bread is cooked in a similar way, and it is a feature of the bread that bits of straw need to be pulled off the bottom before it is eaten.

FINNISH EASTER BREAD

For most of Scandinavia, and certainly for those who were better off, most of the original festive breads were made from what was considered the best flour, namely white wheat flour. In the poorer villages and towns, however, most people had to make do with what they could find— usually rye, barley and oatmeal. For festivals, special breads were made to celebrate using only these three cereals. Easter bread was a particular favorite, molded in a traditional round, and made with yogurt and honey or molasses and packed with raisins, golden raisins and nuts. Easter bread is unlikely to be widely available in the cities, but should you travel through villages at the right time of year, you may find these dark specialties with their shiny tops.

HALKAKA

This heavy black rye bread was once the only food for a number of Finnish peasants during the winter. Extremely large loaves were baked and then gradually eaten over the next few months until the bread was finished and it was time to bake again.

RIESKA

Further north in Finland, the leavened breads give way to hard flat loaves. *Rieska* is a Finnish word and comes from Lapland, a region that extends across the northern parts of Norway, Sweden and Finland, and most of which is within the Arctic Circle. *Rieska* are round breads, mostly fairly small and rather flattish. They are normally made with oats or barley, but can also be made with potatoes or any starchy food. Although there is no wheat or rye to raise the dough, they do use a little yeast or baking powder, which makes them slightly less dense.

ICELANDIC BREAD

Most Icelandic breads are based on rye. Various loaves are made, from the crusty loaf with open crumb pictured above to the pancake-like *flatbrauð*, which are enjoyed with *skyr*, a fresh curd cheese that resembles yogurt.

POLAR FLAT BREAD

Called "polar rounds" or "polar thins," these small breads are widely available, sold at many large supermarkets and delicatessens as a style of crispbread. They contain a mixture of rye and wheat flours and have a pleasant, slightly nutty flavor. They go well with strong-flavored cheese, such as goat cheese.

ABOVE: Polar flat breads are now made commercially.

EASTERN EUROPEAN AND RUSSIAN BREADS

In the cool latitudes of northern Europe, rye, buckwheat and barley were the principal cereals for centuries. Large dark breads made from these flours were not only the staple food, but during severe famine were often the only food for all but the most wealthy. "If we have bread and *kvas* (beer) what more do we need?" is a famous Russian saying. Links with southern Europe meant that wheat flour gradually became popular, at first only among the aristocracy but later filtering through to the general population, where the flour was used mostly for festive bread and cakes. Today, thanks to genetic manipulation, wheat is widely grown in Russia, Poland and other parts of eastern Europe, but the fondness for breads made from rye and buckwheat continues to this day, and these traditional breads are still the mainstay for rural communities.

BLINIS

Although not strictly bread, these little buckwheat pancakes were the equivalent of festive sweet breads in a country where buckwheat rather than wheat was the principal crop. Buckwheat was widely cultivated in Russia in the past. At *Maslenitsa*, the week before

RIGHT: Polish rye bread

Lent, large numbers of blinis were consumed. They are just as popular now, eaten at any time of the year, most famously with *smetana* (a sour cream) and caviar, although also delicious with crème fraîche and smoked salmon. In shape and size, blinis resemble a Scotch pancake, but are normally far darker in color, with a savory, slightly bitter flavor from the buckwheat flour. The most authentic blinis are made entirely of buckwheat but many now compromise with a blend of buckwheat and plain flour. The best blinis are yeast-risen, made using buttermilk or yogurt. Store-bought blinis may use baking powder instead, and some contain so little buckwheat flour that they hardly merit the name "blini."

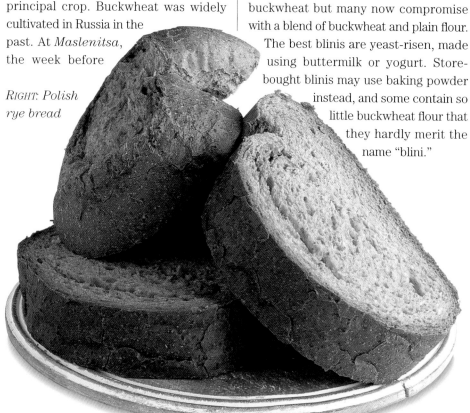

LEFT: Polish whole-wheat rye uses whole-wheat flour with a proportion of rye.

Pre-wrapped bought pancakes are best heated slightly in the microwave or wrapped in a cloth in the oven, so that they warm up without drying out.

BARLEY BREAD

Barley bread has long been baked in regions stretching from Finland to the shores of the Black Sea in the Ukraine. Barley made a change from the dark rye breads although, since it contains no gluten, loaves were consequently dense and heavy. Even today, many of the barley breads from the countries around the Baltic Sea are sturdy loaves, made with a blend of barley and whole-wheat flour. The bread is generally moist and chewy. Cabbage leaves are sometimes used to line the baking pans, a time-honored trick that keeps the crust moist.

POLISH RYE

As the name implies, this is made from rye, although some wheat flour is generally added. This bread, however, is made from refined rye meal, unlike Polish black rye, which uses a coarser rye and wheat meal. Although they might sound not particularly appetizing, both breads are pleasantly flavored.

ABOVE: Once the basic loaf for all poor families, Polish sourdough is now baked by artisan bakers and is enjoyed by all bread enthusiasts.

RIGHT: Caraway seeds give Polish caraway a noticeable anise seed flavor.

POLISH BLACK BREAD

This is a large, flattish, round bread, eaten in Poland, Lithuania and Latvia. Wheat flour is added to give some volume to the loaf, but it is principally made with buckwheat and has a distinctive, rather bitter flavor.

POLISH SOURDOUGH

This is a classic northern peasant-style rye bread. Originally, oats and barley may well have been added to the rye to make a loaf that would feed the family for as long as possible. Each household would take its grain to be milled, and the bread would then be set to rise in proving troughs. The blend of grain plus the use of troughs gave a noticeably different flavor and texture to each loaf, from family to family and even from loaf to loaf.

POLISH CARAWAY BREAD

A traditional Polish medium rye bread, this is made with rye and wheat flour flavored with caraway seeds.

ESTONIAN RYE

This is a sourdough bread made entirely with rye. It is a pan-shaped bread with a distinctive flavor arising from both the rye and the natural leaven.

SWEET PUMPERNICKEL

There are many styles of pumpernickel breads, all made entirely or principally from rye.

RUSSIAN BRAIDED BREAD

Braided yeasted loaves made using white flour are among the most familiar breads of eastern Europe. They are similar, and sometimes identical, to the Jewish *challah*. This part of Europe was home to many Jewish people. Many of these spectacular breads are enriched with milk, eggs and butter and are made as festive breads for special occasions. Others are plainer, sometimes using milk to obtain a softer crust, and are frequently sprinkled with poppy seeds.

RUSSIAN BLACK BREAD

Bread was by far the most important food in Russia until this century. In the nineteenth century, the Russian peasant ate on average 3–3½ pounds of bread a day and even more at harvest time. White breads are now popular in Moscow and other large cities, but it is the ryes that are the best-known and -loved of Russian breads. There are numerous types of black breads, varying in color, density and sour/sweet flavor. Molasses, favored throughout the Baltic States, is frequently added, and originally the breads would have been made on the sourdough principle, although some today are yeast-leavened. Many are similar to German rye breads, since techniques and styles cross borders as easily as weather. A classic Russian black bread, however, is usually made with an equal blend of rye and wheat flour, using a sourdough starter. It

ABOVE: Estonian rye is one of the few pan breads baked in this region.

RIGHT: Russian black bread owes its dark color to molasses and rye.

is spiced and baked on the bottom of the oven. A round loaf, it has an attractive, coarse top. It is normally roughly broken rather than cut and is often eaten with soups and stews. In Ukraine a version of a black rye bread is known as *chenyi khilb*, which is another large round loaf.

ROSSISKY

This is among the better-known Russian rye breads and is now made and sold outside Russia at some supermarkets, delicatessens and healthfood stores. It is 100 percent rye bread, made using a sourdough starter and has a distinctive yet pleasant flavor.

BORODINSKY

This small but compact loaf, traditionally flavored with crushed coriander seeds, is becoming increasingly available outside Russia. Consequently, it represents, for many, the essence of Russian bread.

The story goes that the wife of a Russian general, Marshal Mikhail Kutuzov, made this sweet, aromatic bread for the army, which was defending Borodino, outside Moscow, from the onslaught of Napoleon's army. Although Napoleon then entered Moscow, the French were shortly forced to withdraw, which led to Napoleon's downfall. The Battle of Borodino thus became enshrined in Russian history, and the bread was named

to remember both the eventual victory and the 42,000 men who lost their lives.

The Borodinsky loaf is baked, like the German box breads, in a sealed container; but unlike them it is cooked for only about 2½ hours, and uncovered for the final 15–30 minutes so that the bread is slightly risen with a firm crust. It is made either entirely with dark rye or with a blend of rye and whole-wheat. Barley meal is also often used, giving an earthy flavor, and buttermilk or yogurt is also occasionally added and enhances the natural sourdough flavor. Molasses, however, is traditionally used, and malt extract is frequently added so that the bread acquires a sweet flavor, albeit with distinct sour/savory overtones. Borodinsky is the most expensive and most popular of the Russian rye breads, and is served thinly sliced with strongly flavored fish, such as pickled herring or smoked salmon.

RUSSIAN POTATO BREAD WITH CARAWAY SEEDS

Potatoes were another mainstay for the Russian peasant; breads were often made by using a mixture of a grain and potatoes that had been cooked and mashed. If the mixture included wheat, a flattish but loaf-shaped bread could be made. Caraway seeds were a popular flavoring.

HUNGARIAN CHRISTMAS BREAD

Called *makos es dios kalacs* in Hungarian, this is a popular festive enriched white bread, with the dough rolled around poppy seeds and raisins.

BALABUSKY

These little rolls speckled with caraway seeds are a speciality of Ukraine, a region known for the variety of its breads. The rolls combine rye and wheat flours in varying proportions, but are made with sour cream, which gives a pleasant acidic flavor. Sour cream and cottage cheese are an inheritance from the Tartars who invaded Russia and Ukraine from Asia in the thirteenth century. The liking for sour cream, used in bread making and served with bread, is a feature of much eastern European cooking.

KOLACH (KALACH)

Kolach (kalach) is a sweet yeasted white bread, popular at Christmas in Bulgaria and Russia and especially in St. Petersburg where it was said that it should only be made from the water transported to the city from the Moskva river. It is normally braided, although in Ukraine and Moldova it is often formed into a round, like the sun—a reminder of warmer days to come.

KULICH

Kulich is the traditional Russian Easter bread. Apparently, in Tsarist Russia

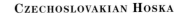

RIGHT: Rossisky (back) and Borodinsky (front) are the cream of Russian breads.

laborers were not permitted to walk through the kitchen in case their heavy steps caused the dough to fall or the bread to collapse in the oven. The bread is similar to a brioche, made with white flour, eggs, butter and milk and rich with raisins, candied peel, angelica and chopped almonds. The tall, round bread is either glazed or iced and then decorated with glacé cherries, angelica or crystallized fruit. It is served, unusually, by slicing off the top and then slicing horizontally again for eating. The top is then replaced to keep the cake fresh for as long as possible.

The cake was also baked for Remembrance Monday, which is the Russian equivalent to All Souls' Day (November 2), when traditionally it would have been taken to the church in order to be blessed by the priest.

KRENDEL

Krendel or *kolindet* is a popular Russian sweet bread. With its intertwining loops, its shape is reminiscent of a pretzel and, similarly, has a significance that has been lost over the years. These breads were popular for birthdays and to celebrate name-days. They were also given to children on Christmas Eve so they may have been connected with the winter solstice. They are yeast-

RIGHT: Ukrainian rye is very popular wherever Slav people have settled.

leavened, made with white flour and enriched with eggs, butter and cream. The breads have a deliciously soft, cake-like consistency and are sometimes served for tea in restaurants or at a *chaikhana* (tea house).

CZECHOSLOVAKIAN HOSKA

Another festive bread, this braided loaf is often decorated with whole almonds and then glazed with egg before and during cooking, so that it bakes to a beautiful golden hue. The bread is quite spectacular and no mean feat for the baker. The three tiers of braids are made successively smaller so that the braids balance on top of each other.

UKRAINIAN RYE

Ukraine is renowned for its huge variety of breads. It is the second largest country in Europe, after Russia, and almost the entire country is one vast plain of extremely fertile black soils. Once known as the bread basket of the U.S.S.R., Ukraine has a rich tradition of bread making. Emigré bakers in Britain and America, as well as European bread specialists, produce some excellent breads. A popular Ukrainian loaf is a sourdough bread made with a half rye, half wheat flour blend. It is baked on the bottom of the oven and has a good chewy crust and a noticeably sour flavor.

THE BREADS OF GREECE, CYPRUS AND TURKEY

Greece has a wonderful array of breads, arising from historical and geographical influences. Here, not only are there the Arabian-style breads of the Ottoman Empire, but also indigenous breads with a long history, which are still baked, particularly on the islands, by people who keep these traditions alive. On some of the Aegean Islands, up until very recently, the wheat and barley harvested by landowners would be carried to the windmill for milling into flour. The dough would then be made and shaped, before being taken to the village oven for baking. Such traditions have now almost entirely died out, and in the cities the bakeries are as sophisticated as those anywhere else in Europe. But in many small villages, on the islands or in the mountains, people still buy the simple but large white crusty bread, which is frequently still baked in an old brick oven, the brushwood being collected by the baker or his family each evening ready for the next day's baking.

Throughout Greece, local bakers produce their own special breads, which necessarily becomes a favorite with their customers. In the cities, the more enterprising bakeries produce a wide range of breads flavored with raisins, olives and herbs, but among the islands and in the mountains, most loaves continue to be of the plain, farmhouse variety—large and crusty and sometimes scattered with sesame seeds. The bread has a slightly coarse texture, which makes it excellent for mopping up sauces and dressings.

Traveling eastward from Greece, the leavened breads of Europe give way to the characteristic flat breads of the Middle East. However, inevitably there are breads that are common to Greece and Turkey, partly because of the crossover of ideas and partly because some breads, such as pita, are so versatile that their popularity endures.

BREADSTICKS

Although similar to Italian *grissini*, Greek and Turkish breadsticks are somewhat chunkier, although just as crunchy. They are mostly sprinkled with sesame or poppy seeds, or may be made using fennel seeds, which gives them a noticeable anise flavor. *Koulouria* are similar, but the bread has been formed into rings, like pretzels. Sold by itinerant street vendors from their large wicker baskets, these too are often liberally sprinkled with sesame seeds, in which case they are referred to as *thessalonikis*.

PAN BREAD

You are only likely to come across this bread, called *tiganópsoma* in Greek, if you visit the delightful Greek island of Santorini, believed by some to be the site of the lost world of Atlantis. It is a simple unleavened bread, mixed to a thick batter and combined with onions and tomatoes before being fried.

GREEK CELEBRATION BREADS

Bread has religious significance all over the world, but nowhere more so than in Greece. Almost all of the important days in the religious calendar have their own specialty bread—some rich with fruit, eggs and butter, others completely plain, depending on the holy day that is being celebrated.

Prosforo (holy bread) is the bread of the Greek Mass, prepared by bakers every Saturday and taken to the church on Sunday by a member of the congregation. The large, round white loaf is stamped with the church seal and is the Host of the Communion, given out by the priest to the faithful during the Mass.

LEFT: Breadsticks

RIGHT: Daktyla is a popular Greek bread.

On Clean Monday, which is the first day of Lent in the Greek Orthodox Church, the *lagana* is the center-piece of a traditional meal of seafood and salads. Clean Monday is so-called because on this day Greek housewives are expected to scrub the kitchens and all utensils, to make sure nothing remains of Celebration—the three-week long festival that precedes the fasting of Lent. Appropriately, the *lagana* is a completely plain unleavened bread, made by local bakers solely for this one day of the year. The dough is formed into a large oval and then sprinkled with sesame seeds before baking.

Tsoureki is the famous Greek Easter bread. The yeasted bread is made from an enriched dough flavored with orange and spices. It can be coiled into a round, but is more frequently made into a long braid and then sprinkled with almonds and sesame or caraway seeds and decorated with the characteristic red hard-boiled eggs. If you visit Greece just before Easter, you will find packets of red-dyed eggs sold everywhere. They symbolize the Resurrection and are knocked together after the Midnight Mass

on Easter Saturday evening with the words, "Christ is Risen." On many of the Greek islands, where old customs still continue, *tsoureki* is the traditional Easter gift from children to their godparents.

Another festive and enriched bread is the *christopsomo*, the Greek Christmas bread. The top is decorated with a large cross, fashioned from the dough, the ends of which encircle cherries or walnuts.

OLIVE BREAD (ELIOTI)

Originally this bread was a Lenten food for the priests of the Eastern Orthodox Church, although now *elioti* is produced all over the country and can be enjoyed at any time of the year. It is generally a white bread, enriched with a little olive oil, flavored with marjoram or oregano and studded with black olives.

DAKTYLA

This unmistakable loaf is a style of bread that belongs equally to Greece, Cyprus and Turkey. Its defining characteristic is the liberal addition of nigella seeds in the bread itself, and the white sesame and black nigella seeds sprinkled

LEFT: There is a rich variety of white bread in Greece, often sprinkled with sesame seeds.

BELOW:
Ekmek

over the top. The bread is oval and is normally large. It has deep slashes along the crust and looks like a large bloomer. It has a slightly peppery flavor thanks to the nigella seeds, and an open, coarse texture.

SILICIAN BREAD

Available now in many countries, these small flat breads sprinkled with cheese and spices are like miniature pizzas.

PITA (PIDE)

Pita breads, or *pide*, to call them by their Turkish name, are probably the best-known Greek and Turkish breads. This style of bread —flat and baked so that it contains

a pocket—is found all over the Middle East, although often in different shapes and by different names. Although pita is a flat bread, it is not an unleavened bread. There is little crumb but the crust is soft and it is leavened with yeast; the flatness and characteristic pocket, called the *mutbag*, are due to the method of baking—ideally in an extremely hot clay oven. Pita breads are widely eaten outside of Greece and Turkey, used as they are intended for stuffing with meats and vegetables. In restaurants in Istanbul, *pide* are served straight from the oven, stuffed with chunks of lamb that has been cooked over hot embers on a nearby spit, and with yogurt and mint. There is a huge

range of different pita bread available— for example whole-wheat pitas, round mini pitas, pitas flavored with herbs or sprinkled with sesame seeds. They are best eaten warm and, when storebought, should be sprinkled with a little water and then placed in a hot oven or under the broiler until they begin to puff up.

EKMEK

This is a large round or oval leavened bread, often dimpled like an Italian focaccia, but made simply with a plain white dough. Like pita bread, the crust is soft and the bread is used either as a pocket for sandwiches or a scoop for picking up food. *Ekmek* can also refer to other breads—the word *ekmek* simply means "bread." In Turkey, you will find numerous longish loaves, sometimes made using whole-wheat, but usually white flour. More elaborate *ekmeks*, baked in rounds or sprinkled with sesame seeds, can be found in bakeries in the large cities.

BELOW: Sutlu ekmek

RIGHT: Pita bread is served almost everywhere in Greece and Turkey.

TURKESTAN BREAD

This is a proprietary loaf sold in Britain but said to be based on the bread made by Turkoman tribes who lived in the Turkestan region around the Caspian Sea.

SIMITS

These little crusty golden bread rings are sold in almost every town in Turkey, and first thing in the

ABOVE: Many Turkish bakers still use wood-burning ovens. Breads, such as pide (right) and tuzsuz (left), cook quickly with a beautifully flavored crust and soft crumb. Hashas (center) is a large loaf that is cooked as the oven begins to cool.

morning the *simit* sellers take their wares down to the harbor and into the market to entice workers and tourists alike. *Simits* are closely related to bagels—they look like them—and in fact an authentic *simit* is made in the same way as a bagel, poached in boiling water before being sprinkled with sesame seeds and baked. Until

LEFT: Simits coated with sesame seeds.

ABOVE: Turkestan bread

quite recently, the *simit* seller would carry the rings piled high on a tray on his head or looped onto long sticks, but nowadays, food regulations mean that *simits* are more likely to be found wheeled around under glass.

THE BREADS OF THE MIDDLE EAST AND NORTH AFRICA

Apart from in Morocco, which abuts Arabia and western Europe, almost all the breads of this enormous region are versions of flat breads. Tradition and culture play a part here. In many of these regions people have always led a nomadic existence, living in tents and moving frequently from place to place. There was never any time or inclination for plates or cutlery and when it came to eating, bread was used both as a food in its own right and as a means of conveying other food to the mouth. In addition, fuel was scarce and bread had to be cooked quickly while the fire was hot. Flat breads that cooked in minutes were a far better option than large, sturdy loaves. Even today, clay ovens almost identical to those depicted on walls of ancient tombs can still be found in some of the smaller villages of Egypt, Iran and Turkey. The ovens are fueled with wood, corn kernels or even camel dung and, when they are hot, the flattened dough is baked against the sides of the walls.

Although the bread is flat, Middle Eastern bread is generally not unleavened, apart from rare exceptions, such as the

BELOW: The flat breads of the Middle East can be indistinguishable from each other. These khoubiz are very similar to the Egyptian aiysh.

Arabian crisp bread *ragayig*. The ancient Egyptians mastered the art of leavening bread, and by the twelfth century B.C., 40 kinds of breads and pastries were available to upper-class Egyptians at their bakeries. Wheat has always been the preferred grain. It is indigenous to Turkey and the Middle East, and the first wheat to be cultivated came from this region.

AIYSH

Aiysh is the Egyptian word for "life," and these flat round loaves must be one of the oldest breads known to mankind. We know that as long ago as 1500 B.C., *aiysh* was made and sold by Egyptian bakers, and the same baking methods are still used today in some parts of the country. The bread is similar to pita bread, but smaller and thicker. It should be made with whole-wheat flour. This same bread is found throughout the Middle East. The shape varies, and the size ranges from 12-inch rounds, or ovals of up to 15 inches. In Yemen, the bread is known as *saluf* in Jordan and Palestine as *shrak* and in Syria as *aiysh shami*. The bread is delicious when freshly cooked, puffing up to leave a hollow center and a soft crust.

KHOUBIZ (KHOBZ)

This word from the Levant and Arabian peninsula, means simply "bread" in Arabian. The bread is virtually identical to Egyptian *aiysh*. Flat and slightly leavened, it is made in rounds varying between 6 inches and 12 inches in diameter. Originally made with a finely ground whole-wheat flour similar to chapati flour, today it is more often made using white flour.

BARBARI

These white breads from Iran can be oval, rectangular or round in shape, varying from small breads, about 4 inches long, to much larger breads measuring up to 12 inches. All are flattish breads, and the loaves are often slashed four or five times like the French *fougasse* to give a fretwork effect. They may be brushed with oil before baking, and spiced versions with cumin or caraway seeds scattered on top are sometimes found.

MANKOUSH (MANNAEESH)

Spelled in many different ways, this is the typical Lebanese version of *khoubiz*. Here, the bread is rolled into 5-inch rounds and indented slightly in the middle so that it is concave. It is then brushed with olive oil and *za'atar*, a blend

RIGHT: Barbari are sometimes called Persian flat breads.

of sesame seeds, thyme, marjoram and *sumac*, a spice made from the dried red berries of a bush native to Sicily and western Asia. This herb and spice blend has an unusual sour flavor, thanks mainly to the *sumac*.

LAVASH

Lavash is one of the largest of the Middle Eastern flat breads. It can be round or oval, is extremely thin and up to 2 feet in diameter. The bread came originally from Armenia and Iran, although its popularity has spread and today it is widely eaten all over the Middle East. The dough is often taken by villagers to the local bakery to be slowly baked in clay ovens called *furunji*. Alternatively, it is baked in a *sorj*, a dome-

BELOW: Flat breads, such as this mankoush from Lebanon, cook quickly and are ideal in lands where fuel is scarce.

covered oven like an inverted wok. Cooked in this way, the bread becomes brittle and crisp and is generally eaten right away, torn in large pieces. *Lavash* can be unleavened or leavened, but its

close relative, *ragayig*, is always unleavened. Like *lavash*, this is a large flat bread, which is quite crisp and brittle when cooked. Almost certainly the most ancient of all breads, predating even *aiysh* and *khoubiz*, *ragayig* is nevertheless still eaten today, cooked in the same way as *lavash* until it is crisp and sometimes dried even more in the sun. *Nane lavash* is oval-shaped with a softer texture and is a cross between *lavash* and an Indian naan.

PIDEH

This is an Armenian version of the Turkish *pide*; it is always made using whole-wheat flour. The rolled-out breads are sprinkled with sesame seeds before being baked.

MOROCCAN AND TUNISIAN BREADS

There are several types of Moroccan bread, mostly variations on the same theme. The wheat flour dough, can be white, whole-wheat or a blend of both, and may be enriched with olive or peanut oil. It may be leavened naturally, although yeasts are more commonly used these days. Either way, the loaf is almost always round and flattish and equally invariably, is made by wives and daughters at home. In the past, and even now among some families, the unbaked loaves are carried to the local bakery to be cooked.

MOROCCAN HOLIDAY BREAD

Cornmeal, together with pumpkin and sunflower seeds, makes this a tasty bread. It is baked for special occasions.

TUNISIAN KESRET

This version of the Arabian bread, *khoubiz*, is mainly distinguished by the fact that it is cooked in a tagine, a North African earthenware cooking pot.

MELLA

This round flat bread, made by Tunisian nomads and sometimes containing caraway seeds, is covered with sand before being placed on the embers of a fire.

MARRAKESH SPICED BREAD

Moroccan cuisine reveals a number of cultural influences. France's short but significant domination with its invasion in the middle of the 19th century is noticeable in a number of spheres. French is still an important language in Morocco and many dishes clearly owe their inspiration to French cuisine, albeit with spicy flavors that are entirely local. Marrakesh spiced bread owes much to the French brioche—made with a yeasted white dough and enriched with butter and sometimes eggs—yet it is very much a product of Morocco. Flower water, either orange or rose, gives it a strongly perfumed taste and it is also sugary sweet, especially when served with honey or jam.

JEWISH BREADS

You do not have to travel far to enjoy traditional Jewish breads. Wherever there is a Jewish community, a wide range of Jewish breads will be produced, both for daily eating and for festivals and celebrations. The other singular aspect of Jewish breads, in contrast to English or French breads, for example, is that by definition, they do not belong to one country or region. Jewish cuisine embraces an enormous spectrum of culinary traditions, ranging across eastern and central Europe, through the Mediterranean, the Middle East, northeast Africa and India.

Visit a Jewish delicatessen and you will find a many loaves bearing a close resemblance to the breads of Germany, Russia and eastern Europe. The harmonization of ideas that occurs when people become neighbors is particularly apparent with age-old traditions such as bread-making, and cultures are decidedly richer for it.

CHALLAH

There are many variations on this spectacular festive bread with its deep brown crust and soft white crumb. Challah is traditionally made for the Sabbath or for other Jewish holidays

ABOVE: Rich challah spirals

and while it is most often seen braided, it can be shaped into spirals or wreaths, or baked in a pan. The dough is made using eggs and vegetable oil, which give it a soft texture somewhere between that of a brioche and a soft white loaf. It is normally slightly sweetened, with either sugar or honey; the sweeter loaves are

also stuffed with raisins. The most popular *challahs*, however, are simply liberally sprinkled with poppy seeds, which is one of their most characteristic features.

In Orthodox Jewish families, two loaves of *challah* are placed on the traditional embroidered tablecloth. A blessing is said over the bread, before it is broken and handed to the other members of the family. The Hebrew word for "blessing" is *brachah*, which derives from the Ashkenazi (eastern European) word for braided bread. The two loaves represent the manna sent down by God to the Israelites after leaving Egypt.

Challah can be braided with three, six or twelve strands of dough. At Rosh Hashanah, it is customary to have round *challahs*, often sweetened with honey and sometimes enriched with raisins or golden raisins. On the eve of Yom Kippur, *challah* is baked in the shape of wings, a ladder or raised arms, symbolizing prayers being made to heaven.

ABOVE: A braided challah

BOULKAS

These are small roll-sized *challahs*, shaped into rounds, braids or spirals and made especially for weddings. However, they are often baked and sold at large bakeries for any occasion.

BAGELS

The bagel—a worldwide favorite —is the customary bread at Bar Mitzvahs, although nowadays they can be bought almost anywhere and enjoyed at any time of the year. Their unique feature, apart from the central hole, is that they are briefly poached in boiling water, or steamed for a minute, before finally being baked. The process means that the dough puffs up in the water but does not rise any

BELOW: Boulkas

more during baking, producing the characteristic dense texture. Even savory-style bagels contain some sugar or malt extract, and a little is also added to the water during boiling. The bagel is then glazed with egg or egg white before being baked to give it a glossy crust, and the result is a noticeably sweet-flavored bread with a compact crumb and a chewy crust.

Bagels are almost always yeast-leavened, but beyond that there are countless variations. They can be made with eggs, may contain cheese and/or butter, or may be made with just water and margarine. Like

BELOW: Assorted bagels

RIGHT: Shabbat bread

small, rather solid roll is basically a small dimpled bun, stuffed with fried onions. The *bialy* earns its name from the city of Bailystok in Poland, which was home to many Jews before they were forced to flee due to persecution.

SUMSUMS

Sumsums are the traditional breads of the Syrian Jews and look similar to bagels, although these little rolls with a hole are not boiled before baking, but go straight into the oven after shaping. *Sumsums* are usually sprinkled with sesame seeds.

SHABBAT BREAKFAST BREAD

Known as *kubaneh*, this unique bread is always cooked overnight so it is ready for the Sabbath breakfast. The bread is from the Yemen, which has its own Jewish cuisine, and is a yeasted white dough, enriched with butter and sweetened with sugar or honey. The rolled-out dough is spread with more butter and then rolled

so many Jewish breads, the bagel seems to have originated in Europe—created, it is said, by a Polish Jew in the Middle Ages to celebrate winning a war. Centuries later, such culinary techniques were taken to New York City where many Jewish immigrants settled at the turn of the twentieth century. The best bagels in the world are considered to be those found in New York City bakeries.

Bagels are mostly eaten sliced into two flat rings. They can be plain or toasted, and are often spread with cream cheese, topped with lox (smoked salmon) and then eaten as a sandwich. There is, of course, no end of other fillings, kosher or not, and similarly there are countless variations. In a Jewish bakery, you are likely to find whole-wheat, rye and multi-grain versions, along with bagels sprinkled with poppy, sesame, caraway and sunflower seeds, sea salt or chopped onion. Among the many sweet

bagels, which are widely available pre-packaged at supermarkets as well as bakeries, are cinnamon and raisin-flavored treats.

BIALYS

These are almost as popular in North America as the bagel, and both come from the same Ashkenazi Jewish culture. The

LEFT: Plain bagels

RIGHT: Matzos

up in a spiral and then steamed in a covered baking dish in a very low oven for up to 12 hours. It can be served with sugar but is also popular Yemeni-style with spicy or garlic chutneys.

MATZO

Matzo is a piece of unleavened bread that is served in Jewish households during Passover, Feast of the Unleavened Bread. The flat, brittle bread is made and baked with great speed and under strict dietary regulations by Jewish bakers to ensure that the flour and water mixture does not start to ferment, even by accident.

Passover is the most important holiday in the Jewish calendar and celebrates the Hebrews' deliverance from slavery in Egypt. *Matzo* is a reminder of how, in their escape from the Egyptians, the Hebrews had no time to let their bread rise. Leavened bread therefore became a prohibited food during the eight days of Passover although, the holiday is otherwise a time to celebrate good food.

Matzo is sometimes served at the table but also ground into meal and used for cakes, cookies and dumplings during Passover (see below).

PASSOVER ROLLS

Since leavened bread is forbidden during Passover, Ashkenazi Jews found intriguing ways of making breads without regular flour, which even without yeast will start a natural fermentation. The trick was to use *matzos*, flat and brittle breads, that have been ground to a fine meal. Passover rolls, which are popular among Jewish communities in Paris and other parts of Europe, are almost identical to little choux buns, made with water, butter, *matzo* meal and eggs, and baked in the oven until golden. They are often split and filled with cream cheese or cream.

LATKES

These small potato pancakes are thought to have originated in Ukraine, where *kartoflani placke* were a popular dish at Christmas, served with goose. The dish was apparently adopted by the large Jewish population of the area, and is now traditionally served on the feast of Chanukah.

JEWISH RYE BREAD

There are many varieties of Jewish rye bread, most of which originated in Eastern Europe, where rye is such a popular grain. The sourdough starter for this well-known rye is made using the crusts of other rye breads. It is then combined with white and rye flour and caraway seeds.

MANDEL BREAD (MANDELBROT)

This is a strange kind of hybrid—part loaf, part teabread and part cookie. The word *mandelbrot* is Yiddish for "almond bread," and the dough is fashioned into a rough loaf shape before being baked. It is not a yeasted bread but is risen using self-rising flour or baking powder and, is enriched with eggs, flavored with lemon and vanilla and studded with almonds. It is more like a cookie than an ordinary bread. After baking, it is cut into thick diagonal slices and baked again, which transforms the loaf/teabread into thick cookies. These cookies were once extremely popular among many Jewish people throughout the world, served with wine or other drinks. However, their popularity has declined over the years and while still baked by some Jewish bakers, they are difficult to find nowadays outside Israel and North America.

RIGHT: Jewish or seeded rye

BREADS OF THE AMERICAS

The United States yields a fabulous potpourri of breads. The thousands of people from Ireland, Italy, Germany and Scandinavia who emigrated to America at the turn of the century had little to take with them save the customs and traditions they held most dear. Baking bread would have been one of the very first tasks for the wife once a home had been established and, understandably, the breads she baked were the breads of her own country—a reminder of home and perhaps a promise of a better future.

Thriving communities were gradually established. Norwegians and other Scandinavians settled in many of the north central states, such as Wisconsin, Minnesota and Iowa; German immigrants settled around the Great Lakes, while in New York and in other large cities along the Eastern Seaboard, Italians and Jews made their homes.

Grain, of course, was no problem in this "Land of Plenty." The United States was already world producers of grain, particularly wheat, but also rye, barley and oats. German and Eastern-European rye breads, country breads from Italy and a vast range of Jewish loaves were produced by the many

RIGHT: Hamburger buns sometimes have a sesame seed topping.

bakeries that sprang up to serve their own communities. Added to this, of course, were the established American loaves, themselves versions of breads brought to the New World by the early settlers, while in the southwest people moving north from Mexico continued to make their customary corn breads and tortillas. If indigenous breads can be said to exist in the United States, they are the breads made by Native Americans—whose bread-making traditions were kept alive by people of Native American descent in North and South Dakota and other central states.

ALL-AMERICAN BREADS

While some breads are mainly popular in, for example, northeastern, southern or southwestern states, certain loaves are extremely well known throughout the whole of the United States. Some of these, such as anadama bread, are best known by reputation. These loaves are sold occasionally at small bakeries as a curiosity, but they are more widely known from

recipe books as the breads handed down by generations. Other breads, however, are the standard loaves, sold in various shapes and sizes at every supermarket and convenience store. The best are, as ever, those made by artisan bakeries.

As a general rule, you will find that standard American loaves—as opposed to those made by local Italian or French bakers, for example—have a more tender and softer crumb. This is because most American loaves contain fat in the form of milk and/or melted butter.

BURGER BUN

Burgers are almost an American way of life, which makes it all the more surprising that store-bought burger buns can be sadly disappointing. While good burger buns do exist, many of the store-bought burger buns are not dissimilar to those found outside America—white, soft squishy and often with a sprinkling of sesame seeds on top. Perhaps their very blandness is considered a necessity to contrast with the beef and relishes inside, but any American burger aficionado will tell you that, on the contrary, the bun is an integral part of the eating experience. The best burger buns are made with a simple dough but, unlike the commercial supermarket variety, do not contain the emulsifiers that give the impression you are eating soft foam. The answer, as with so many breads, is to find a good baker. Some Italian, French and Jewish bakeries are all likely to make their own versions, using the same dough as for their standard country breads and thus producing a bun with a pleasant texture and fine flavor.

GRAHAM BREAD

There is a variety of American whole-wheat loaves, among which graham bread is very well known—the name being synonymous with healthy eating.

RIGHT: Graham bread

The bread is named after a nineteenth-century cleric, Dr. Sylvester W. Graham, who was a keen advocate of using the whole grain for milling flour, recognizing the benefits of bran in the diet. Graham flour, graham bread and graham crackers are all named after him, as the best and most authentic flour is stone-ground and coarsely milled whole-wheat flour.

BASIC WHITE BREAD

This is a simple, well-flavored pan loaf with a slightly chewy crust and a dense but soft texture.

CORNELL BREAD

This light-textured wheat germ bread is mainly of historic interest because, although it is a nutritious loaf, it has less than happy antecedents and is rarely made these days. In the 1930s, Cornell University pioneered a high-protein loaf, made with wheat germ, white and soy flours, sugar and milk for patients who lived in mental hospitals. Gradually, other public institutions, such as schools and hospitals, started producing the loaf. When in the early 1940s, during World War II, meat was either rationed or extremely expensive, people looked for a high-protein alternative, and the Cornell loaf became recommended eating. The bread clearly never recovered from such damning acclaim—even the most wonderful bread is, for most, a poor substitute to meat—and for that war generation, the scarcity and poor food the Cornell loaf represented meant that it became deeply unfashionable.

BROWN AND WHOLE-WHEAT BREAD

There are many variations of whole-wheat bread. Whole-wheat bread is widely available, normally in a loaf shape. There are also variations of brown bread, containing a blend of whole-wheat and white flour. Wheat germ may also be added—you will need to read the side of the package to be sure. Cracked wheat bread has a delicious nutty flavor and crunchy texture and is a good, nutritious loaf. It is usually round, although short batons and loaves are also available. It is made using milk or buttermilk, together with honey, molasses or brown sugar. The most nutritious breads are made with stoneground whole-wheat flour, although white flour with added wheat germ and/or cracked wheat is still a healthy alternative with a good texture

ABOVE: Basic white bread has a soft, close texture.

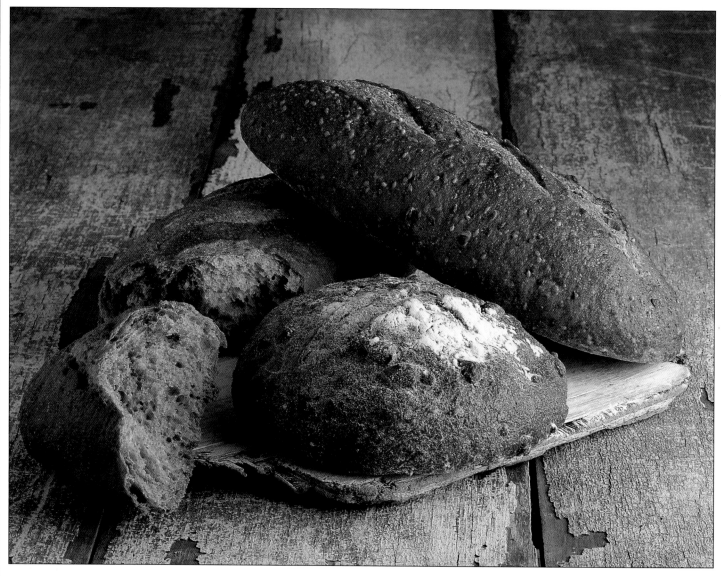

ABOVE: American seven-grain (top), whole-wheat (round) and cracked wheat loaves

and flavor. Seven-grain bread is another healthy loaf. It contains seven grains: normally wheat, rye and corn; and then four of the following – brown rice, buckwheat, soy, oats, barley, millet, sunflower seeds, sesame seeds or flaxseed. As you might expect, it is a dense, sturdy loaf and is popular with healthfood enthusiasts.

PULLMAN LOAF

This white loaf is named after the Pullman railway coach, the box shape of which is exactly that of the bread. The bread is similar to *pain de mie*, the French sandwich loaf. It is made in a rectangular pan, rather longer than a standard loaf pan, sometimes with a sliding lid so that the crust is soft on all sides. Like *pain de mie*, it is used for sandwiches and toasting and is normally white, made American-style with butter or other fat.

SWIRL BREAD

This very attractive loaf is widely available throughout the United States. It is made by using two doughs: one of white flour, the other a whole-wheat flour to which molasses is added. The doughs are rolled out after their first rising and the whole-wheat rectangle is placed on top of the white one. The two are then rolled up together. When cut, each slice of bread has a swirl pattern.

BEER BREAD

Beer and butter are the ingredients that make this a most unusual bread. It comes from Georgia and is raised by

LEFT: The Pullman loaf is used for sandwiches

RIGHT: Swirl bread: molasses gives the dough an intense color.

cheese and has a distinctive and pleasant sour flavor. As the name suggests, it is baked in a casserole. Another dill loaf, but quite unlike the dilly casserole loaf, is the sour dill rye, which is made from a blend of wheat and rye flours, and is strongly flavored with dillweed, caraway seeds and dill pickle brine.

CHOCOLATE BREAD

Chocolate breads are well known in the United States; bakers across the land all make their own favorite. One

using self-rising flour or baking powder. A whole can of beer is poured into the flour mixture to make a thick batter, which is then poured into a round or rectangular loaf pan in which ¼ cup butter has been melted. Once the loaf is cooked, it is turned upside down and the butter trickles through the bread. The result is a moist and beautifully flavored loaf.

DILL BREAD

Dill is a popular ingredient in American breads and there are several well-known dill loaves. The dilly casserole bread is a favorite among home bakers and can sometimes be found at bakeries and specialist shops. As well as dill, it contains cottage

ABOVE: Dill bread

TOMATO BREAD

With bakers from so many nationalities, it is not surprising to find loaves in the United States that are reminiscent of other breads of the world. Tomato bread may remind you of Italian or even some Greek breads, yet here the bread has been thoroughly naturalized, the pretty, pale pink coloring coming from tomato juice, which gives the bread a definite but not overpowering taste of tomato.

SUN-DRIED TOMATO BREAD

Sun-dried tomato bread is similar to tomato bread but contains pieces of sun-dried tomatoes. It has a rustic appearance. The shape is usually a free-form round, which may be slashed across the top and dusted with flour before baking. Sun-dried tomato bread is popular served with pasta or soup.

LEFT: Rustic, Italian-style sun-dried tomato bread

BELOW: Triticale bread

such chocolate loaf is called *babka*. This is a Russian-style bread that has many variations and comes in all sorts of extraordinary shapes. The dough, which is enriched with eggs and butter, can be plain or rich with bittersweet chocolate, and is also sometimes filled with almond paste, raisins, nuts and more roughly chopped chocolate so that the center is moist and soft and deliciously rich.

TRITICALE BREAD

Triticale is a grain that has been developed using modern gene manipulation techniques and is a hybrid of rye, durum and red winter-wheat. This probably sounds more exotic than it is—farmers and agriculturists have been cross-breeding wheat and other cereals for hundreds of years in order to improve both yields and resistance to disease. The triticale grain is particularly high in protein, but low in gluten. When making dough, the flour is blended with at least an equal amount of wheat flour, either white or whole-wheat. The bread has a sweet and nutty flavor that is reminiscent of rye yet without its characteristic density.

OATMEAL BREAD

For the early settlers in America, oats were one of the easier cereals to grow, and oatmeal was used for oatcakes, cooked on a griddle or, if wheat was available, added in varying proportions to flour to make loaves. Since oatmeal contains no gluten, only small quantities can be used if attempting to make anything that resembles a loaf. Wheat flour and occasionally rye flour form the basis of the dough, but oatmeal adds a pleasant flavor and texture.

BANANA BREAD

Teabreads are immensely popular throughout the United States and all kinds of fruits and vegetables are used for flavoring them. The breads call for baking powder, and the batter has the consistency of a cake more than a dough. Consequently, most American teabreads are baked in pans, after which they are turned out and thickly sliced to serve with

OPPOSITE: Babka, a Russian-style chocolate loaf, comes in all shapes and sizes.

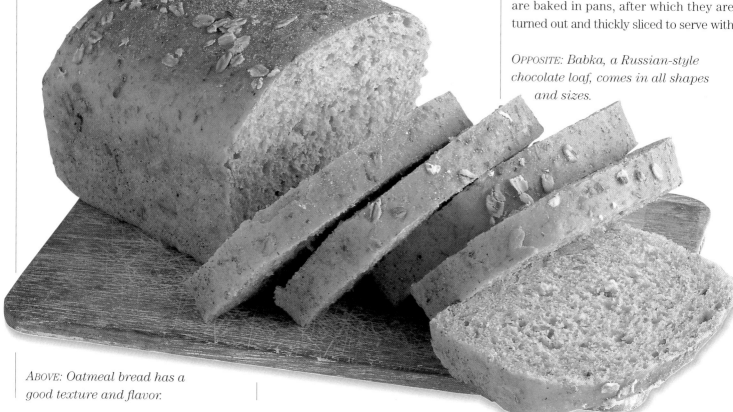

ABOVE: Oatmeal bread has a good texture and flavor.

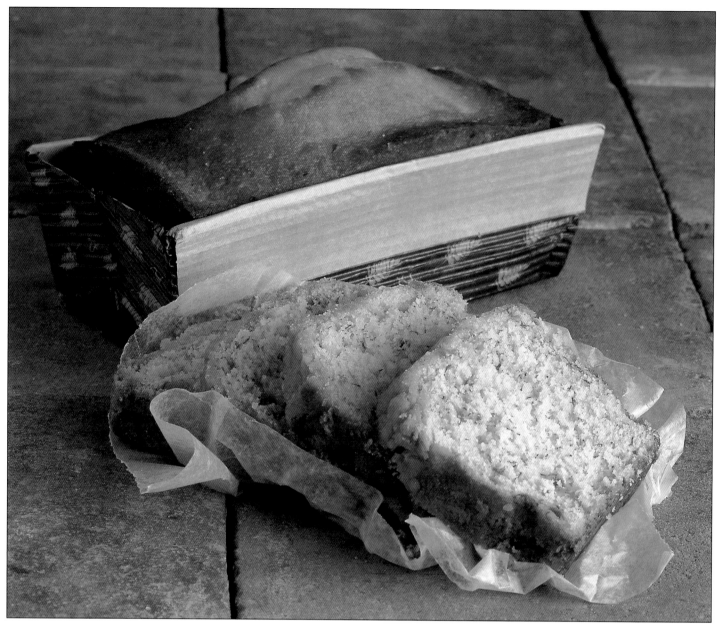

ABOVE: Lemon bread and banana bread

tea or with morning coffee. Bananas are a favorite teabread ingredient.

LEMON BREAD

Lemon bread is as popular as all the other teabreads. It is a finer flavored and more fine-textured loaf than most teabreads. Lemon, in the form of rind or extract, is often added to other teabreads, but is wonderful when given a starring role.

RIGHT: Braided cheddar cheese bread that is flavored with beer.

CHEDDAR CHEESE BREAD

There are all sorts of flavored breads in the United States, and cheese is a favorite ingredient. Grated cheese can be kneaded into the dough to give it a rich, soft flavor, or else sprinkled on top to melt into the crust. Cheddar cheese bread is a simple but tasty yeast-leavened loaf that is almost always made with white flour. It is excellent with soups and barbecue, and is delicious toasted. A braided cheese loaf is sometimes made using beer rather than milk or water.

NORTHEAST AMERICAN BREADS

This is the area of the original 13 colonies, founded by the Pilgrims. The Dutch came, too, as well as other people seeking religious freedom. Among these people were the Amish, whose communities can today be found in Ohio and Indiana but most famously in Pennsylvania. New York City is the food capital of this region, and a breathtaking range of breads from countries all over the world can be found in New York. Some of the most famous include the Italian ciabattas, Irish soda breads, baguettes and *pain de campagne* from France, and Jewish breads such as hearty ryes and what are generally considered to be the best bagels in the world. National breads can be found under their own separate heading, but the following are a selection of breads that have evolved from the recipes settlers adapted to the grains and climate they found in the New World.

ANADAMA BREAD

The story behind this bread is so good that few bread books can resist it, although it is not generally a bread found at most bakeries or supermarkets. The bread dates back to colonial times and is unusual because it is one of the rare cornmeal breads made with yeast. The story goes that an irritable New England woodsman had a wife by the name of Anna, who fed him nothing but a cornmeal and molasses mush for supper. One evening, having had more than he could take, he grabbed some flour and yeast off the shelf, mixed it into the mush and put it in the oven to bake, muttering "Anna, damn her" over and over again. Thus the name "anadama" came about. The loaf is made with yellow cornmeal and wheat flour in varying proportions and is normally baked in a round cake pan.

BOSTON BROWN BREAD

The Pilgrims who arrived in Massachusetts and other New England states must have found quickly that rye, rather than wheat, flourished better in the cold snowy winters and damp summers of their new home. This bread is one of the best known of the old breads—made with rye blended with cornmeal and white flour, which was a common mixture in poor families where corn was readily available but wheat was not. The bread is steamed—these days often in large coffee cans, but presumably originally in ceramic pudding molds. The advantage was that the bread could be made without the need for an oven, another sign that this was a bread of poor people, who strived to make do with the resources they had. The bread is often sweetened with molasses and/or buttermilk, which gives it a distinctive sour/sweet flavor, and is a favorite to eat with Boston baked beans.

BAKED BROWN BREAD/DUTCH OVEN BREAD

This is similar in many ways to Boston brown bread: it is made using rye flour, cornmeal and wheat flour, with molasses and buttermilk. The difference is in the baking. Unlike Boston brown bread, which is steamed, this loaf is baked in the oven. It was originally baked in a Dutch oven, a round type of pot set over a fire. Today, it is cooked in a covered casserole. The bread is placed in a cold oven and then baked until firm.

NEW ENGLAND BUTTERMILK ROLLS

These small, yeast and soda-risen breads are light and flaky with a delightful soft crumb, thanks to the buttermilk from which they are made.

EGG HARBOR BREAD

The bread is made by the Amish, a Mennonite people of Swiss and Dutch origin, who fled their own countries in the eighteenth century due to religious persecution in Europe. They migrated first to Pennsylvania, where their descendants are called Pennsylvania Dutch, and then moved to Ohio and other midwestern states. Everything about their lifestyle is deliberately plain and simple. This white bread from a village on the shores of Lake Michigan is typical—a plain white yeasted dough that is allowed six risings before being baked, which gives a beautifully textured loaf with a soft crumb. Old fashioned Amish bread is made by the families in northern

RIGHT: New England buttermilk rolls are light and flaky.

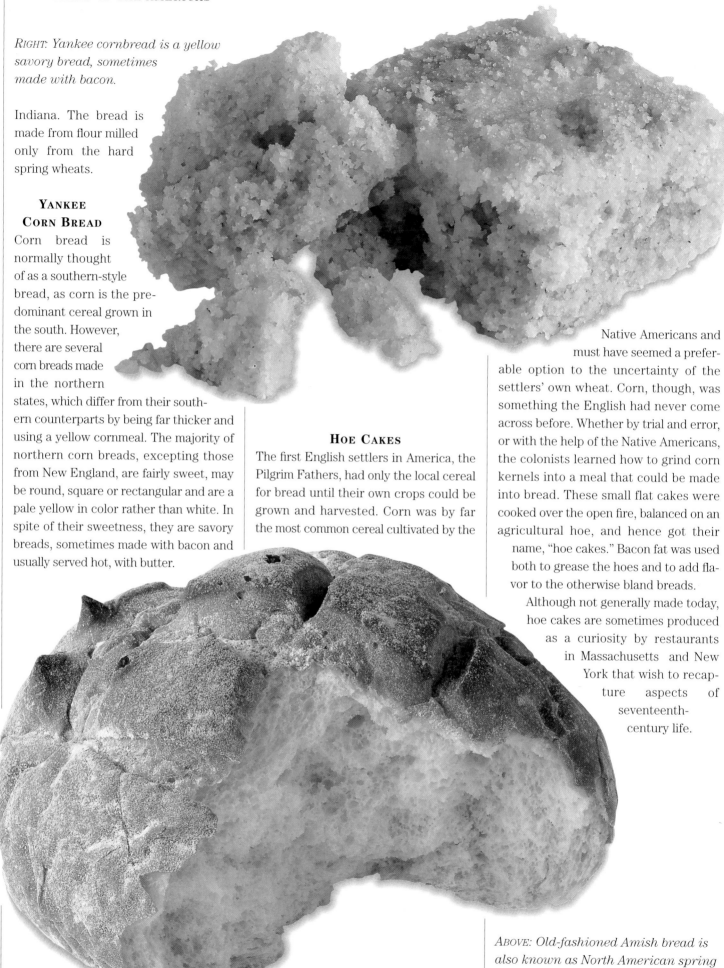

RIGHT: Yankee cornbread is a yellow savory bread, sometimes made with bacon.

Indiana. The bread is made from flour milled only from the hard spring wheats.

YANKEE CORN BREAD

Corn bread is normally thought of as a southern-style bread, as corn is the predominant cereal grown in the south. However, there are several corn breads made in the northern states, which differ from their southern counterparts by being far thicker and using a yellow cornmeal. The majority of northern corn breads, excepting those from New England, are fairly sweet, may be round, square or rectangular and are a pale yellow in color rather than white. In spite of their sweetness, they are savory breads, sometimes made with bacon and usually served hot, with butter.

HOE CAKES

The first English settlers in America, the Pilgrim Fathers, had only the local cereal for bread until their own crops could be grown and harvested. Corn was by far the most common cereal cultivated by the Native Americans and must have seemed a preferable option to the uncertainty of the settlers' own wheat. Corn, though, was something the English had never come across before. Whether by trial and error, or with the help of the Native Americans, the colonists learned how to grind corn kernels into a meal that could be made into bread. These small flat cakes were cooked over the open fire, balanced on an agricultural hoe, and hence got their name, "hoe cakes." Bacon fat was used both to grease the hoes and to add flavor to the otherwise bland breads.

Although not generally made today, hoe cakes are sometimes produced as a curiosity by restaurants in Massachusetts and New York that wish to recapture aspects of seventeenth-century life.

ABOVE: Old-fashioned Amish bread is also known as North American spring loaf. The long fermentation period means that it has an excellent flavor.

MIDWESTERN AND NORTH CENTRAL AMERICAN BREADS

These are the heartlands of America, stretching from the dairy farms of Wisconsin to the prairies of Wyoming. Here in middle America, great store is set by family life, with family meals being a central part. These states were settled mainly by Scandinavians, Germans and Slavs who brought with them the traditions of their homeland. Sourdough ryes and mixed-grain loaves are therefore among the most common breads available.

BELOW: Seeded rye (left) and old Milwaukee rye

SALT-RISING BREAD

There are several recipes in American cookbooks for salt-rising breads, but it is thought that the bread was originally made by pioneers crossing the midwest and western prairies. The starter dough would have been carried in crocks, as the horse- or oxen-drawn wagons made their way across the plains. "Salt-rising" refers to the practice of keeping the active starter in a bowl nestling in a bed of salt, which is easy to warm and retains heat for a long time. The starter would provide the leaven for fresh bread, which would have been made and baked in makeshift ovens each time the wagon train stopped.

Although an authentic bread of the prairies, nowadays this bread is a specialty of some of the East Coast bakers. The nineteenth-century sourdough loaf is known for its delicious and delicate crumb, yet also renowned for the difficulty in actually getting it to work. Several bakeries have succeeded with the bread, but the starter, made from scalded milk, sugar and cornmeal, is notoriously tricky to prepare. Once the starter begins to ferment, milk, white flour, fat, sugar and salt are added to make a sponge. This adds another potential complication, as salt is never usually added to a starter or sponge because it tends to inhibit the yeast. Given the right conditions of warmth and humidity, however, the sponge should rise and fall, after which the remaining flour is added and the dough made into bread in the usual fashion.

LEFT: Heavy sour rye bread

RYE BREAD

There are many rye breads in the midwestern states of Wisconsin, Ohio, Minnesota, Iowa and Nebraska. Pumpernickel is commonly sold, as is a crusty rye bread made using rye and wheat flour and with butter added, which is a feature of many American breads. Like most traditional ryes, Old Milwaukee rye is a sourdough loaf, made with molasses and flavored in typical Germanic-style with caraway seeds. The bread may be shaped into round loaves or fashioned into long, slender ones.

SEEDED RYE

Seeded rye bread is sometimes known as Jewish rye and is popular not only in the midwest, but as far east as New York.

ABOVE: Salt-rising bread

HEAVY SOUR RYE BREAD

This is known as "corn bread" from the cornmeal that is sprinkled on the baking sheet, but is a rye sourdough made with a proportion of wheat flour. It is normally liberally sprinkled with caraway seeds. The bread is frequently sold by weight and can be recognized by its sides, which are liberally sprinkled with cornmeal, and its top, which is sprinkled with caraway seeds.

WEST COAST AMERICAN BREADS

In California, fashions come and go so quickly that it is surprising to find that some of the most traditional American breads are not only still being produced but are even more popular—in the delicatessens, the restaurants and on the dinner party circuit. Many influences have come to play a part. The Pacific Coast was the end of the journey for pioneers hoping to find opportunity and freedom: Hispanics, from the south, gravitated toward the cities of Los Angeles and San Francisco, while Europeans settled all over the region, each culture establishing its own favorite styles of cooking and enthusiastically sampling others.

SAN FRANCISCO SOURDOUGH

San Francisco sourdough is probably the best-known American bread outside the United States and can truly be said to be all-American. It is a round, wheat, oven-baked loaf, with a star slash or a cross-hatched pattern on top. These breads, like the salt-rising breads, were brought to the West Coast by pioneers who crossed the prairies and plains of middle America in search of gold. The trip took the early pioneers five or six months and was extremely hazardous. The Forty-Niners—the men who took part in the 1849 Gold Rush—gave their camps names such as Hell's Half Acre and Hangtown, which gives an idea of what life must have been like. Provisions for the journey included sacks of flour, together with a small piece of leavening saved from the last batch of dough, so that bread could be baked en route. The leavening was stored in a crock inside a sack of flour.

The word "sourdough" refers quite simply to the bread's flavor. The bread has the same sharp/sour taste of yogurt or buttermilk.

It is said that it is impossible to make San Francisco sourdough outside the city itself. The climate of San Francisco, with

LEFT: Perhaps America's best-known bread, the San Francisco sourdough.

its warmth and humidity, is particularly conducive to sourdough breads, and the bacterium, which feeds on the flour and water mixture, is unique to that area. However, home-bakers often attempt approximations, while professional bakeries all over California produce their own versions, including the Berkeley sourdough, which is a baguette-shaped loaf.

MONKEY BREAD

This bread goes under a variety of names, including bubble loaf or poppy seed bubble loaf. The bread normally is made up of seven or eight small dough balls baked in a ring mold, so that when it is baked the bread looks like lots of bubbles. The little balls are dipped into melted butter and then sprinkled with poppy seeds or currants, raisins, nuts and/or sugar and cinnamon before being baked.

SOUTH-WEST AMERICAN BREADS

Texas, New Mexico and Arizona all border Mexico and their cuisine, including the bread, shows all the influences of its southern neighbor. Food can be spicy and very hot, and tortillas and other corn breads are as common as breads made with wheat.

JALAPEÑO CORN BREAD

This is a typical Tex-Mex-style bread, made with a blend of cornmeal and white flour. Hot jalapeño chiles are kneaded into the dough, and some loaves may contain whole corn kernels and cheese, too. The bread can be baked in loaf pans or shaped into rounds and oven bottom-baked and it has a unique, snappy flavor.

SOPAIPILLAS

These small, puffy breads are a speciality of New Mexico. They are made by mixing together flour, baking powder and salt, adding water to make a dough and then incorporating some vegetable fat, as when making puff pastry. The dough is then rolled out extremely thinly and cut into small squares, which are deep fried until puffy. If made professionally in a restaurant or by a baker, the corners can then be snipped off and filled with honey. Otherwise honey or syrup can simply be poured over the breads. A savory alternative uses refried beans.

HOBO BREAD

Hobo bread is so-called, not because it is a favorite among tramps and vagrants, but because it is traditionally eaten outdoors. It is a sweet bread, rich with golden raisins and nuts, that has been baked in a coffee can so that it is shaped like a long cylinder. Its popularity as an outdoor bread is probably due to the fact that the bread keeps well for several months. It is normally stored in the can in which it is cooked.

BREADS OF THE SOUTHERN STATES

This region includes Mississippi, Alabama and Georgia, among others. Corn is cultivated in many of these states and the popularity of corn breads is well known, with many people preferring the flat and rather mealy flavor of the corn to the wheat breads popular in the north.

NEW ORLEANS BREAD

New Orleans has many visible French influences—including its name, after Orleans in France—and not least its excellent breads. *Pain perdu* (French toast) is a favorite breakfast for many New Orleans citizens. New Orleans' French bread is softer than the real French version. It is sometimes known as feather bread and is very light. It has the same open texture as the French baguette, but has added fat and sugar, which makes it slightly richer and sweeter.

SPOON BREAD

This corn confection is known as spoon bread for the simple reason that it has to be eaten with a spoon. It is the consistency of custard and is puffy and creamy inside when cooked. The bread is made with cornmeal, a little white flour, eggs, milk and baking powder. One story suggests that the bread was created when too much liquid was added to a corn bread batter and the baked bread had to be spooned out of the pan. Be that as it may, the Virginians insist that this event happened in one of their kitchens and thus claim spoon bread as their own. In Virginia or neighboring states, you will find this on the menu, occasionally as a dessert but usually in a savory version, made with bacon, cheese and garlic.

SOUTHERN CORN BREAD

There are numerous corn breads in the southern states. Convenience stores and supermarkets sell the more standard-type loaves, but at home, people still make their own breads. As corn bread is best eaten as soon as possible, homemade versions will be the most tasty. Corn breads only rarely use yeast and are relatively quick and easy to make. Southerners like white cornmeal for their breads, rather than the yellow meal preferred in the north, and the breads are generally much thinner. Wheat flour is added to these breads in varying proportions, but in southern corn bread neither wheat flour nor fat is added, so that the corn flavor is predominant. Other breads, such as rich corn bread, are made using cream, milk, butter and eggs. Corn pone is thought to be directly inspired by the Native Americans. It is a small, moist loaf, made from cornmeal along with buttermilk and lard.

NATIVE AMERICAN FRY-BREAD

People have lived in America for thousands of years, developing into various local populations of Native Americans who made bread from both wheat and corn for special occasions and for everyday eating. Hoe cakes made by early English settlers may well be adaptations or even pure copies of the breads made by the local people. Nowadays, there are Native American reservations in various American states such as Oklahoma and several of the more northern states. Traditional breads made on the reservations vary a little in size but are surprisingly similar across the continent, being small flat breads made from a flour and water dough that is rolled thinly and cut into diamonds, circles or squares. In North and South Dakota on the Sioux reservations, the breads are called "frybreads" and are made for powwows—ceremonies or intertribal gatherings featuring much feasting and dancing.

SALLY LUNN

This famous bread from Bath in England is said to have been brought to America by the English settlers. It is known all over the United States but has become a popular specialty bread in the South, where it is served with lunch. The American version was originally made in a Turk's-head mold, but is now less elaborate, baked in a tube pan. There are also miniature versions baked in *petit four* pans, and muffin-size versions made in muffin pans.

CRANBERRY NUT BREAD

This loaf is a bread enriched with eggs and butter, and is distinguished by the bright red berries that speckle the loaf. Cranberries are in season during late fall which is why the bread is often associated with Thanksgiving and Christmas. Cranberry nut bread is commonly given as a gift at this time and is popular for its tart taste, which is often accentuated with the flavor of orange.

ZUCCHINI BREAD

Zucchini is very popular throughout the United States, not only in vegetable dishes, but for use in cakes, muffins and bread. The sweet bread, made with coarsely grated zucchini, sweet spices and sugar, and enriched with eggs and oil, can be iced and served as a dessert cake.

ABOVE: Southern corn bread is made from white cornmeal.

CARIBBEAN AND MEXICAN BREADS

HARD-DOUGH BREAD

This fairly heavy pan or braided white loaf is almost the standard Caribbean bread. It is the most popular bread for the islanders and is becoming increasingly popular in those parts of Britain or the United States with a sizeable Afro-Caribbean population. It has a dense, chewy texture and like many West Indian breads, has a distinctly sweet flavor.

JOHNNY CAKES

Johnny cakes do not seem to have a single origin. There are recipes for them in a number of cookbooks from the United States as well as those from the Caribbean. Most agree however that the word is a corruption of "journey cake"—a bread that can be packed up and given to travelers for their day's journey. In Jamaica, in corroboration of this, johnny cakes can be bought freshly made at roadside stalls all over the island. Just as there is apparently no definitive ancestry, there is equally no single recipe for johnny cakes. Recipes suggest they can be made from cornmeal, wheat flour or a mixture of both. Some contain eggs and milk, while the Jamaican johnny cake is

ABOVE: Johnny cakes are a famous Jamaican bread.

made with butter or lard and coconut oil. In the above photograph the dough has been shaped into balls and fried in oil. Other johnny cakes have a batter-like consistency. Cooked on a griddle or in a pan, they are served as a flat bread.

ABOVE: Hard-dough bread

BULLA BUNS

These are spicy, round discs. They resemble muffins in appearance but are dense, dark and spicy, flavored with allspice and rich with raisins and molasses.

CARIBBEAN BUN

A spicy teabread, this is liberally flavored with allspice and is packed with fruit. The round buns are dark in color and look sticky, thanks to the molasses, which gives them an intense bittersweet flavor. Outside the Caribbean, the buns are often available at ethnic markets and stores in larger cities and come either in small bun sizes or as a larger loaf.

TORTILLAS

Although other wheat loaves are available, tortillas are rightly known as the bread of Mexico. Freshly made and still warm, these flat breads are an essential part of every Mexican meal. Tortillas are also used in an enormous number of Mexican dishes, wrapped around meat, fish, vegetables or cheese and eaten for street food as well as snacks, suppers and elegant dinners.

There are basically two types of tortilla. Maize tortillas are made using a type of cornmeal called *masa harina*, literally meaning dough flour. These are the older of the two, having been made and eaten by native people for literally thousands of years. Until the arrival of the Spanish in the sixteenth century, there was no wheat in Mexico, but in northern parts of the country, where wheat flourished, wheat flour (called just flour) became the preferred choice for tortillas.

HAWAIIAN BREADS

In this delightful tropical paradise, there is a fabulous amalgamation of cultures and cuisines: along with the indigenous Hawaiians, there are Chinese, Japanese, Portuguese and people of Filipino origin.

HAWAIIAN BREAD

This is a perfect tropical bread, made with fresh coconut and macadamia nuts, which give it a delicious crunchy texture. The yeast-leavened white dough is enriched with eggs, butter and milk.

PORTUGUESE SWEET BREAD

Towards the end of the last century, Portuguese immigrants came to Hawaii to work in the sugar fields. Over the years their bread has acquired a character that is part Portuguese and part Hawaiian. The dough is usually yeast-leavened and enriched with eggs and butter. It is also made with condensed rather than fresh milk since the latter was once a scarce commodity on an island given over entirely to fields of sugar cane. Currants and raisins also go into the doughs, as well as being used for decoration. It may be baked in a round in a coil, but is more usually plaited and sprinkled with coarse granulated sugar.

BELOW: Bulla buns

BREAD OF THE DEAD

Should you visit Mexico around November 2, *All Souls' Day*, you may find this famous and traditional bread, called *Pan de Muerto.* It is made as part of the celebrations in memory of the deceased but paradoxically, the holiday is not a sad day, but a fiesta. Everyone visits their relatives' graves, bringing a picnic, wearing bright colorful clothes and carrying candies and flowers along with the special bread. The bread itself comes in various forms but most often is a white, yeast-risen dough, flavored with orange and sometimes with spices. It can be a simple round or a braided loaf coiled into a circle. The bread is then decorated with pieces of dough formed into teardrops, bones or bunches of flowers.

ABOVE: Tortillas

WEST INDIAN ROTIS

West Indian *rotis* are huge and used, as they would be in India, for mopping up stews and curries, such as curried goat. Like Indian *rotis*, they are made with chapati flour, a very fine whole-wheat flour, and are cooked on a griddle. *Rotis* are best eaten warm, and if you do find them at Caribbean stores, they should be sprinkled with a little water, then heated in a hot oven.

ABOVE: Spicy Caribbean bun

INDIAN BREADS

There are principally two types of Indian bread, although all share the characteristic of being flat and oval or round. In Punjab and Kashmir in the northwest and in Pakistan, Afghanistan and Bangladesh there are the naan-style breads. Their defining feature is that naans, unlike the *chapatis* and *parathas* of the south, are leavened and when cooked become light and puffy, unlike the southern breads that are unleavened and much flatter.

The north Indian breads have much in common with many of the Middle Eastern breads—they are large and flat and used as a vehicle for other foods. Recipes for naans and many breads from Syria, Egypt, Iraq and Iran are almost interchangeable. The main difference is the way in which the breads are baked.

BHAKRIS

Bhakris are flat unleavened breads made from *jowar* flour and are sometimes known as *jowar rotis. Jowar* is widely grown in central and southern India. The tiny green seeds from the plant can be roasted and eaten as they are or milled into flour. The dough is molded and patted flat by hand and then baked on a griddle. *Bhakris* can be plain or baked with sesame seeds and are served with butter as a snack.

CHAPATIS

Also unleavened, chapatis are now widely known throughout Britain thanks to the popularity of Indian food. While once a more exotic request from a restaurant menu, chapatis are now almost commonplace, although the commercially available product is a rather poor imitation of the real thing. In India, the chapati is popular in central and southern parts of the country, served with meals and used with the fingers to scoop up food and sauces. These authentic chapatis are made with *atta* (chapati flour), which is a very fine whole-wheat flour.

ROTLAS

There are many variations of chapatis, called *rotlas, rotis,* and *dana rotis* to name but a few. They are all unleavened breads, made using whole-wheat flour, to which ghee, oil, celery seeds and/or fresh cilantro might be added. They are rolled out until thin and cooked like chapatis.

PARATHAS

Parathas are a richer and flakier version of chapatis. The chapati dough is spread with ghee, folded and then cooked over a *tava* (griddle) until puffy.

POORIS (PURIS)

These are puffier still and can be eaten only at a restaurant or in your own kitchen, as they need to be eaten as soon as possible after cooking. They are normally made using chapati dough. Small balls of dough are rolled out into 1-inch rounds and deep-fried on both sides.

NAAN

Naan, unlike the chapatis of the south, is a leavened bread. The leaven varies from region to region and probably from home to home, according to the cook's preferred method. Yeast or a sourdough method can be used; others prefer using a chemical raising agent, such as baking soda or self-rising flour. Yogurt, however, is the main ingredient that differentiates naan from its many Middle Eastern counterparts. It plays a part in fermenting the dough, and some naan are made entirely using a yogurt fermentation. It is this fermentation that gives the bread its characteristic light and puffy texture and soft crust. The flavor comes partly from the sour yogurt and partly, without a doubt, from the

BELOW: Parathas are cooked with ghee and therefore have a golden appearance. Chapatis are cooked without any fat or oil and are flatter. They do not have the golden crust.

LEFT: *Pappadams are popular everywhere with Indian food.*

bakes, it scorches and puffs up to give a bread that is both crisp and soft in parts.

GOAN BATCH BREAD

In Goa, until recently part of Portuguese India, there is a white loaf called *pio*, possibly a corruption of *pao*, the Portuguese word for bread.

PAPPADAMS

These thin crisp discs are widely available outside India, either ready-cooked or ready-to-cook. In India, they are commonly served with vegetarian meals. Pappadams are sold in markets and by street vendors: plain or flavored with spices or seasoned with black or red pepper. The dough is generally made from dried beans, but can also be made from potatoes or sago. It is then rolled thinly and left to dry in the sun. Pappadams can be cooked by either deep-frying or placing under a hot broiler. Either way, they brown in seconds and need close attention while cooking.

tandoor, in which breads are traditionally cooked. A *tandoor* is a clay oven sunk into the ground, and the flattened dough is baked against the blisteringly hot walls of the oven. The pull of gravity produces the teardrop shape. As the dough

RIGHT:
Naan can be plain or stuffed.

AUSTRALIAN BREADS

Australia, like other countries with large immigrant communities, has a wealth of wonderful breads whose origins lie in far-off lands, plus one bread which is indigenous to the country, the famous damper. Once baked in the bush, in the embers of campfires, damper is today a favorite "barbie" food, and is almost as popular outside Australia as it originally was in the Outback.

In recent years there has been something of a revolution in Australian cooking, with some of the world's most innovative chefs producing delicious dishes based on the fine fresh ingredients for which the country is famous. Part of this revolution has been a back-to-basics approach, with more cooks seeking to get away from bland, mass-produced meals in favor of "real" food.

This is certainly true of baked goods. There has been a move away from the handy yet tasteless cottony breads, which once stocked every supermarket bakery shelf, and a return to real bread, with texture and taste.

Australian versions of Italian breads, such as focaccia, ciabatta, olive Toscano, *casalinga* and *bassotto*, and flat, Turkish

Above: The colorful and unusual vegetable il gianfornaio

bread are becoming increasingly popular, as is the brightly colored *il gianfornaio*, which is a mosaic of red, green, yellow and orange doughs, each flavored with a different colored vegetable.

Leading the revolution in Australian bread making are small wood-burning bakeries, such as New Norcia in Western Australia. New Norcia is a monastic town, some 83 miles northeast of Perth. The wood-fired oven that had produced bread for the Benedictine Monks for over a century was shut down in 1989. Four years later it was fired again, and now produces—and sells—a wide range of breads, from a simple old-fashioned white loaf to their popular zucchini bread. The monks also bake their own focaccia, an olive bread and an olive, rosemary and sun-dried tomato bread.

The breads proved so popular that a second wood-fired bakery was opened, this time in the city of Perth. Here the range is even more extensive, and includes several sourdoughs such as raisin and walnut sourdough, San Francisco sourdough and both a light and a dark rye sourdough. Their unusual fig and fennel sourdough is very popular.

Supermarkets, too, have become much more adventurous, and the range of what are loosely termed "Continental breads" includes mixed grain and rye loaves with flavorings as diverse as sunflower seed and pineapple, walnut

RIGHT: Olive Toscano

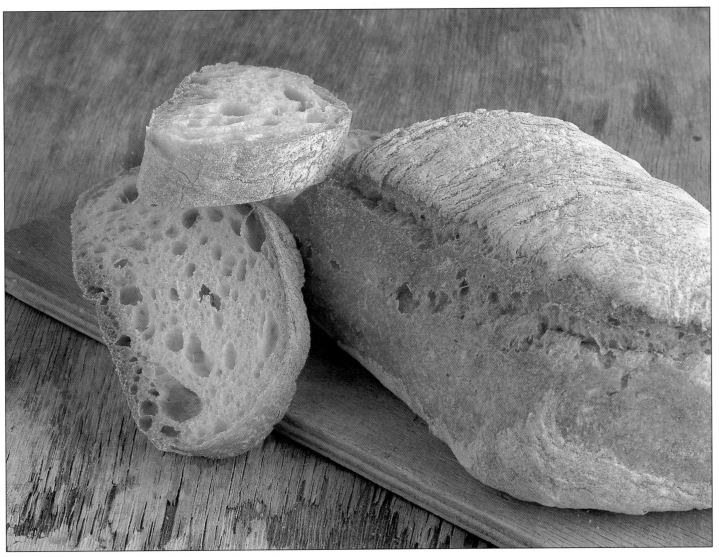

ABOVE: Ciabatta

and fruit, and herb and tomato.

Many Australians bake their own bread, whether in ovens or bread-making machines, and the range of bread mixes available is almost as extensive as the variety of breads on sale at bakeries.

AUSTRALIAN SOURDOUGH

There are a number of sourdoughs made by artisan bakers. Some are made to French recipes, using a similar recipe to that used for the French *pain*

LEFT: Potato sourdough

de campagne. Potato sourdoughs, made with a potato starter, are similar to San Francisco sourdoughs.

OLIVE TOSCANO

Like the Italian *pane Toscano*, this is a crusty, close-textured, and slightly chewy bread, made without any salt. Olive Toscano has green olives added to the dough, which add flavor and contrast well with the salt-free crumb.

DAMPER BREAD

Damper bread is the most famous and probably the only traditional bread of Australia. Like the United States' Native

ABOVE: Bassotto

American bread, it is designed to be made outdoors—in this case, in the bush. The dough, made from wheat flour and water, and sometimes flavored with spices, is patted into cakes and baked either on hot stones or under a pot. The name "damper" comes from the fact that the fire was damped down so that the embers were just the right heat for cooking the

RIGHT: Flat Turkish bread has become one of Australia's favorite breads.

bread. Damper bread was also some-times made by wrapping the dough around sticks and baking it over the fire—the same method as was used for a tradi-tional South African bread called stick bread. The sticks are removed after cooking and the holes in the bread filled with either cheese or butter.

RIGHT: Densely textured red rye bread (left) and farmer rye are generally available at bakeries in the larger Australian cities.

DR. ALLINSON

This bread is based on the original recipe that Dr. Allinson developed in the nine-teenth century. It is a yeast-leavened bread made of organic stoneground whole-wheat flour and canola (a type of cereal) and is rolled in sesame seeds before being baked in a deep-sided loaf pan.

TURKISH BREAD

Turkish bread is one of the most popular breads in Australia, particularly in Sydney. The same as Turkish *ekmet*, it too can come in varying sizes, from small rounds to large ovals. The best breads are made according to traditional Turkish methods, and are baked in wood-burning ovens.

RYE BREAD

There are various rye breads available in the cities; farmer rye is a small dense loaf, while a lite rye has a much lighter flavor and texture with a hint of malt. Black rye is strictly for rye lovers, and is made according to an old European recipe, using a rye sourdough starter, blended with stoneground rye and wheat flour.

LEFT: Dr. Allinson bread is made from organic flour and is rolled in sesame seeds before being baked in a loaf pan.

CHINESE BREADS

While for the people of southern China rice is the staple food, in the wheat-growing region of the north, bread is eaten in lieu of rice.

French-style baked loaves and rolls are becoming increasingly popular throughout the country (especially in the cities), but the traditional breads are almost always steamed. Some *dim sum* breads are fried or baked on a griddle.

MAN TO

Man to are widely eaten throughout the north of China. The small, steaming hot buns are sold everywhere—in restaurants and teahouses, at street stalls and by itinerant sellers. They are eaten sometimes as snacks, but more commonly as the traditional accompaniment to a meal, in the same way as those in the southwest of the country eat rice. They are made from white flour, yeast and sugar and then formed into small balls and steamed in wicker baskets for about 20 minutes. *Man to* have the consistency of many of the steamed *dim sum* dumplings. They can also be added to soups and other dishes.

CHICKEN BUNS (GEE BAO)

These are little steamed buns filled with a mixture of chicken and oyster sauce, and served as *dim sum*.

SCALLION BREAD (CHUNG YAU BENG)

From Hong Kong comes this extraordinary pan-fried bread, made uniquely using a hot roux (a cooked flour and butter paste) that is worked into a similar dough made with cold water. The complicated process involves spreading each piece of dough with a hot oil and flour roux, and then finally rolling it up with scallions. This is not a recipe for the faint hearted, but if you are lucky you may be offered these treats at a restaurant. The ring-shaped breads are fried in oil and have a delicious crisp outside, while inside they have layers of soft dough around the scallions.

SWEET BUNS (HWA JWEN)

These sweet steamed buns are a popular snack food.

PEONY BUNS

These pretty buns are often served as a dessert in Hong Kong. Like *chung yau beng* they are made from two types of dough, the first made by mixing three parts wheat flour with one part root flour, and adding lard, sugar and water. A second dough, made simply from cornstarch and lard, is then prepared. Both doughs are divided into 12 balls and the more elaborate dough is wrapped around the simpler one. Each ball is then rolled out to a round and spread with lotus seed paste before being shaped once more into a ball. A star-shape is cut in the top of each bun, and they are deep-fried until they are crisp. The points of the star on each bun open out to create the peony shape for which the buns are named.

LEFT: Pineapple (left) and cocktail pork man to (steamed buns)

JAPANESE BREADS

There is no tradition of breadmaking in Japan. Rice was, and still is, the staple food and, until relatively recently, bread was completely unknown to all but the most traveled of the Japanese. Japan, unlike other countries in Asia, was virtually untouched by European influences until around the middle of the last century when a new philosophy was adopted and the country began to court the governments of Europe. Many Japanese were sent to France, Britain, Holland and Germany to see what could be learned from the West in terms of seafaring, technology and government. Foodstuffs were probably not high on the agenda, but inevitably these Japanese visitors would have been struck by the concept of baking a food made from the flour of a grain. Recipes were taken back to Japan, and very gradually more and more people acquired a liking for bread. By the middle of this century, a few Japanese bakeries sprang up, making breads often in the

RIGHT: Melon (left) and melon and milk chocolate rolls have a soft crumb.

image of favorite breads from Britain and France but with their own special character.

DOUBLE SOFT WHITE

This is a typical and extremely popular Japanese loaf, which is simply the Japanese version of an English white loaf. Indeed it is often known as "English bread" and in shape is like a pan loaf. However, the flour used by Japanese bakers is particularly soft and dense, and the bread has the texture of a soft milk bread, with a similar soft smooth crust. The bread is cut into

LEFT: Double soft white is about the most popular Japanese bread

thick slices and then lightly toasted and eaten with butter or, more conventionally in Japan, with a spread or fruit preserve.

JAPANESE FRENCH BREAD

This is simply a French baguette, but again made with the very soft Japanese flour, so that the crumb is slightly denser and the crust less fragile than that of an authentic baguette. It can be used for sandwiches or eaten by itself with butter or a spread.

MELON BREAD

A flavored bread, this one is popular in Britain among Japanese expatriates. The breads can be loaf-shaped but are more commonly made as rolls. Melon and milk chocolate rolls contain chunks of chocolate and are a popular snack.

JAPANESE CREAM BREAD

These small soft rolls contain cream and are consequently very soft, not unlike an English bridge roll. Like the soft white bread, these rolls are eaten at tea time with preserves or butter.

RIGHT: Japanese cream bread: these small soft rolls are enriched with cream.

JAPANESE RAISIN BREAD

A simple white fruit bread, this may be pan-baked or baked on a baking sheet.

JAPANESE CREAM FAIRY-TALE ROLLS

These popular tea-time rolls are filled with cream and sometimes with a mixture of chocolate and cream.

RED BEAN ROLLS

Red bean rolls are a delicious combination of ideas and flavors from countries with very different culinary backgrounds. From the outside these little bread rolls look like large English muffins—soft white bread with thin, chewy crusts. Inside though, these little rolls have a delicious sweet filling that is typically Japanese—red bean paste, with its distinctive sweet-and-sour flavor. Red bean rolls are an extremely popular treat.

JAPANESE CURRY BREAD

Like red bean rolls, these are a delicious "East meets West" dish. The breads are deep fried and have a curry-flavored filling of potatoes, with a hint of meat.

SOUTH-EAST ASIAN BREADS

South-east Asia is part of the largest rice growing area of the world and yeast-leavened breads are not typical here. Rice is the staple food and until relatively recently bread was completely unknown. Rice cakes are the nearest thing to the Western idea of bread. Flat and sticky, they are usually sweetened and eaten as delicacies and sweets.

However, bread is not unheard of in South-east Asia. Western influences mean that there is now an established appetite for American and European foods and bread is becoming more popular. In Indonesia, flour mills are now springing up and much of the flour is used for bread making. One favorite white bread is called *roti tawar*. Another bread, *panada*, shows a more adventurous spirit, combining wheat flour with coconut milk. These light, sweet rolls sometimes have vegetable or meat fillings.

LEFT: Japanese Curry bread

BREAD RECIPES OF THE WORLD

There are few things more pleasurable than the aroma and taste of freshly cooked homemade bread. This collection of recipes includes savory and sweet classics from around the world, as well as a good selection of lesser-known specialities. A wide variety of flours, all of which are readily available, has been used to create distinctive breads which reflect the different flavors of the regions. These recipes aim to take the mystery out of bread making and inspire you to try baking many different and delicious breads.

BRITISH BREADS

The range of British breads is extensive and includes a variety of shapes with picturesque names, including the bloomer, cob, split tin, cottage loaf and ornamental harvest loaf. The textures and tastes are influenced by different ingredients and cooking methods. Irish soda bread, as its name suggests, is leavened with bicarbonate of soda instead of yeast, while in Scotland, where bannocks and oatcakes are cooked on a girdle or griddle, grains such as barley and oatmeal contribute to the country-fresh flavors. Doughs enriched with dried fruits, such as Welsh bara brith and Cornish saffron bread, are delicious regional specialities.

GRANARY COB

4 cups Granary or malthouse flour
2 teaspoons salt
½ ounce fresh yeast
1¼ cups lukewarm water or milk and water mixed

FOR THE TOPPING
2 tablespoons water
½ teaspoon salt
wheat germ or cracked wheat, to sprinkle

MAKES 1 ROUND LOAF

Cob is an old word meaning "head." If you make a slash across the top of the dough, the finished loaf, known as a Danish cob, will look like a large roll. A Coburg cob has a cross cut in the top before baking.

1 Lightly flour a baking sheet. Sift the flour and salt together in a large bowl and make a well in the center. Place in a very low oven for 5 minutes to warm.

2 Mix the yeast with a little of the water or milk mixture, then blend in the rest. Add the yeast mixture to the center of the flour and mix to a dough.

3 Turn out onto a lightly floured surface and knead for about 10 minutes, until smooth and elastic. Place in a lightly oiled bowl, cover with lightly oiled plastic wrap and let rise, in a warm place, for 1¼ hours or until doubled in bulk.

4 Turn the dough out onto a lightly floured surface and punch down. Knead for 2–3 minutes, then roll into a ball, making sure the dough looks like a plump round cushion, otherwise it will become too flat. Place in the center of the prepared baking sheet. Cover with an inverted bowl and let rise, in a warm place, for 30–45 minutes.

5 Mix the water and salt and brush over the bread. Sprinkle with wheat germ or cracked wheat.

6 Meanwhile, preheat the oven to 450°F. Bake for 15 minutes, then reduce the oven temperature to 400°F and bake for another 20 minutes or until the loaf is firm to the touch and sounds hollow when tapped on the bottom. Cool on a wire rack.

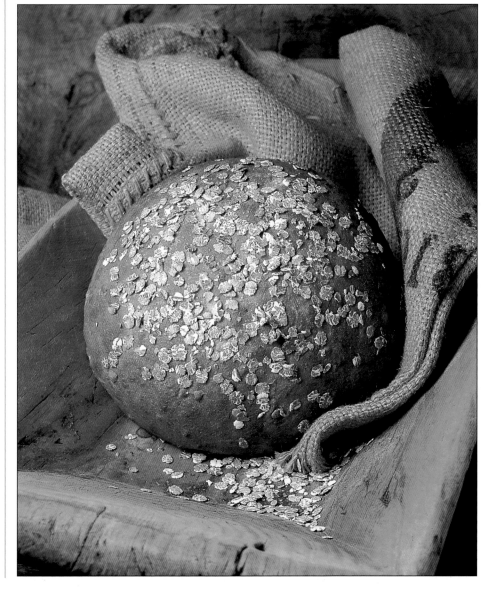

GRANT LOAVES

—

This quick and easy recipe was created by Doris Grant and was included in her cookbook, published in the 1940s—the dough requires no kneading and takes only a minute to mix. The loaves should keep moist for several days.

12 cups whole-wheat flour
1 tablespoon salt
1 tablespoon easy-blend dried yeast
5 cups warm water (95–100°F)
1 tablespoon brown sugar

MAKES 3 LOAVES

1 Thoroughly grease 3 loaf pans, each about 8½ × 4½ × 2½ inches, and set aside in a warm place. Sift the flour and salt together in a large bowl and warm slightly.

2 Sprinkle the dried yeast over ⅔ cup of the water. After a couple of minutes stir in the sugar. Let sit for 10 minutes.

COOK'S TIP
Muscovado sugar gives this bread a rich flavor. An unrefined cane sugar, it is dark and moist.

3 Make a well in the center of the flour and stir in the yeast mixture and remaining water. The dough should be slippery. Mix for about 1 minute, working the sides into the middle.

4 Divide among the prepared pans, cover with oiled plastic wrap and let rise, in a warm place, for 30 minutes or until the dough has risen by about a third to within ½ inch of the top of the pans.

5 Meanwhile, preheat the oven to 400°F. Bake for 40 minutes or until the loaves are crisp and sound hollow when tapped on the bottom. Turn out onto a wire rack to cool.

POPPY-SEEDED BLOOMER

This satisfying white bread, which is the British version of the chunky baton loaf found throughout Europe, is made by a slower rising method and with less yeast than usual. It produces a longer-keeping loaf with a fuller flavor. The dough takes about 8 hours to rise, so you'll need to start this bread early in the morning.

6 cups unbleached white bread flour
2 teaspoons salt
½ ounce fresh yeast
1⅞ cups water

FOR THE TOPPING
½ teaspoon salt
2 tablespoons water
poppy seeds, for sprinkling

MAKES 1 LARGE LOAF

1 Lightly grease a baking sheet. Sift the flour and salt together into a large bowl and make a well in the center.

2 Mix the yeast and ⅔ cup of the water in a cup or bowl. Mix in the remaining water. Add to the center of the flour. Mix, gradually incorporating the surrounding flour, until the mixture forms a firm dough.

COOK'S TIP
The traditional cracked, crusty appearance of this loaf is difficult to achieve in a domestic oven. However, you can get a similar result by spraying the oven with water before baking. If the underneath of the loaf is not very crusty at the end of baking, turn the loaf over on the baking sheet, switch off the heat and leave in the oven for another 5–10 minutes.

VARIATION
For a more rustic loaf, replace up to half the flour with whole-wheat bread flour.

3 Turn out onto a lightly floured surface and knead the dough very well, for at least 10 minutes, until smooth and elastic. Place the dough in a lightly oiled bowl, cover with lightly oiled plastic wrap and let rise, at cool room temperature, about 60–65°F, for 5–6 hours or until doubled in bulk.

4 Punch down the dough, turn out onto a lightly floured surface and knead it thoroughly for about 5 minutes. Return the dough to the bowl, and re-cover. Let rise, at room temperature, for another 2 hours or slightly longer.

5 Punch down again and repeat the thorough kneading. Let the dough rest for 5 minutes, then roll out on a lightly floured surface into a rectangle 1-inch thick. Roll the dough up from one long side and shape it into a square-ended thick baton shape about 13 × 5 inches.

6 Place it seam side up on a lightly floured baking sheet, cover and let rest for 15 minutes. Turn the loaf over and place on the greased baking sheet. Plump up by tucking the dough under the sides and ends. Using a sharp knife, cut 6 diagonal slashes on the top.

7 Let rest, covered, in a warm place, for 10 minutes. Meanwhile, preheat the oven to 450°F.

8 Combine the salt and water and brush this glaze over the bread. Sprinkle with poppy seeds.

9 Spray the oven with water, bake the bread for 20 minutes, then reduce the oven temperature to 400°F; bake for 25 more minutes, or until golden. Transfer to a wire rack to cool.

COTTAGE LOAF

6 cups unbleached white bread flour
2 teaspoons salt
¾ ounce fresh yeast
1⅔ cups lukewarm water

MAKES 1 LARGE ROUND LOAF

COOK'S TIPS
• To ensure a good-shaped cottage loaf the dough needs to be firm enough to support the weight of the top ball.
• Do not over-proof the dough on the second rising or the loaf may topple over—but even if it does it will still taste good.

Snipping the top and bottom sections of the dough at 2-inch intervals not only looks good but also helps the loaf to expand in the oven.

1 Lightly grease 2 baking sheets. Sift the flour and salt together into a large bowl and make a well in the center.

2 Mix the yeast in ⅔ cup of the water until dissolved. Pour into the center of the flour with the remaining water and mix to a firm dough.

3 Knead on a lightly floured surface for 10 minutes until smooth and elastic. Place in a lightly oiled bowl, cover with lightly oiled plastic wrap and let rise, in a warm place, for about 1 hour or until doubled in bulk.

4 Turn out onto a lightly floured surface and punch down. Knead for 2–3 minutes, then divide the dough into two-thirds and one-third; shape each part into a ball.

5 Place the balls of dough on the prepared baking sheets. Cover with inverted bowls and let rise, in a warm place, for about 30 minutes (see Cook's Tips).

6 Gently flatten the top of the larger round of dough and, with a sharp knife, cut a cross in the center, 1½ inches across. Brush with a little water and place the smaller round on top.

7 Carefully press a hole through the middle of the top ball, down into the lower part, using your thumb and first two fingers of one hand. Cover with lightly oiled plastic wrap and let rest in a warm place for about 10 minutes. Preheat the oven to 425°F, and place the bread on the lower shelf. It will finish expanding as the oven heats up. Bake for 35–40 minutes or until golden brown and sounding hollow when tapped. Cool on a wire rack.

CHEESE AND ONION LOAF

Almost a meal in itself, this hearty bread tastes delicious as an accompaniment to salads and cold meats or with soup.

1 onion, finely chopped
3½ tablespoons butter
4 cups unbleached white bread flour
¼ ounce envelope easy-blend
dried yeast
1 teaspoon mustard powder
1½ cups grated aged
cheddar cheese
⅔ cup lukewarm milk
⅔ cup lukewarm water
salt and ground black pepper

MAKES 1 LARGE LOAF

1 Lightly grease a 10 × 4-inch loaf pan. Melt 2 tablespoons of the butter in a heavy frying pan and sauté the onion until it is soft and light golden. Set aside to cool.

2 Sift the flour into a large bowl and stir in the yeast, mustard, salt and pepper. Stir in three-quarters of the grated cheese and the onion. Make a well in the center. Add the milk and water; blend to a soft dough. Turn out onto a lightly floured surface and knead for 10 minutes, until smooth and elastic.

3 Place the dough in a lightly oiled bowl, cover with lightly oiled plastic wrap and let rise, in a warm place, for 45–60 minutes or until doubled in bulk.

4 Turn the dough out onto a lightly floured surface, punch down, and knead gently. Divide into 20 equal pieces and shape into small rounds. Place half in the prepared pan and brush with some melted butter. Top with the remaining rounds of dough and brush with the remaining butter.

5 Cover with oiled plastic wrap and let rise for 45 minutes, until the dough reaches the top of the pan. Meanwhile, preheat the oven to 375°F.

6 Sprinkle the remaining cheese on the top. Bake for 40–45 minutes or until risen and golden brown. Cool on a wire rack.

COOK'S TIP
If you prefer, use ¾ ounce fresh yeast instead of the easy-blend yeast. Mix the fresh yeast with the milk until dissolved, then add to the flour.

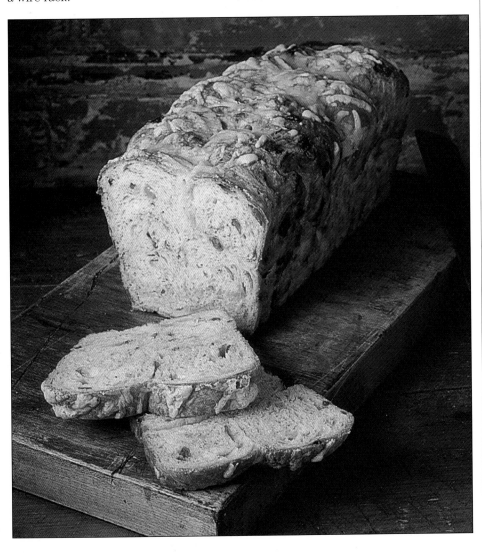

SPLIT PAN

5 cups unbleached white bread flour,
plus extra for dusting
2 teaspoons salt
½ ounce fresh yeast
1¼ cups lukewarm water
4 tablespoons lukewarm milk

MAKES 1 LOAF

As its name suggests, this homey loaf is so called because of the center split.
Some bakers mold the dough in two loaves—they join together while proving
but retain the characteristic crack after baking.

1 Lightly grease a 2-pound loaf pan (7¼ × 4½ inches). Sift the flour and salt together into a large bowl and make a well in the center. Mix the yeast with half the lukewarm water in a bowl, then stir in the remaining water.

2 Pour the yeast mixture into the center of the flour and, using your fingers, mix in a little flour. Gradually mix in more of the flour from around the edge of the bowl to form a thick, smooth batter.

3 Sprinkle a little more flour from around the edge over the batter and leave in a warm place to "sponge." Bubbles will appear in the batter after about 20 minutes. Add the milk and remaining flour; mix to a firm dough.

4 Place on a lightly floured surface and knead for about 10 minutes, until smooth and elastic. Place in a lightly oiled bowl, cover with lightly oiled plastic wrap and let rise, in a warm place, for 1–1¼ hours or until nearly doubled in bulk.

5 Punch down the dough and turn out onto a lightly floured surface. Shape it into a rectangle, the length of the pan. Roll up lengthwise, tuck the ends under and place seam side down in the prepared pan. Cover and let rise, in a warm place, for about 20–30 minutes, or until nearly doubled in bulk.

6 Using a sharp knife, make one deep central slash the length of the bread; dust with flour. Let sit for 10–15 minutes.

7 Meanwhile, preheat the oven to 450°F. Bake for 15 minutes, then reduce the oven temperature to 400°F. Bake for 20–25 more minutes or until the bread is golden and sounds hollow when tapped on the bottom. Turn out onto a wire rack to cool.

WELSH CLAY POT LOAVES

These breads are flavored with chives, sage, parsley and garlic. You can use any selection of your favorite herbs. For even more flavor, try adding a little grated raw onion and grated cheese to the dough.

1 cup whole-wheat bread flour
3 cups unbleached white bread flour
1½ teaspoons salt
½ ounce fresh yeast
⅔ cup lukewarm milk
1½ cups lukewarm water
4 tablespoons butter, melted
1 tablespoon chopped fresh chives
1 tablespoon chopped fresh parsley
1 teaspoon chopped fresh sage
1 garlic clove, crushed
beaten egg, for glazing
fennel seeds, for sprinkling (optional)

MAKES 2 LOAVES

COOK'S TIP
To prepare and seal new clay flower pots, clean them thoroughly, oil them inside and outside and bake them three or four times. Preheat the oven to about 400°F and bake for 30–40 minutes. Try to do this while you are baking other foods.

1 Lightly grease 2 clean 5½-inch diameter, 4½-inch high clay flowerpots. Sift the flours and salt together into a large bowl and make a well in the center. Blend the yeast with a little of the milk until smooth, then stir in the remaining milk. Pour the yeast liquid into the center of the flour and sprinkle over a little of the flour from around the edge. Cover the bowl and let sit in a warm place for 15 minutes.

2 Add the water, melted butter, herbs and garlic to the flour mixture and blend to form a dough. Turn out onto a lightly floured surface and knead for about 10 minutes, until the dough is smooth and elastic.

3 Place in a lightly oiled bowl, cover with lightly oiled plastic wrap and let rise, in a warm place, for 1¼–1½ hours or until doubled in bulk.

4 Turn the dough out onto a lightly floured surface and punch down. Divide in half. Shape and fit into the prepared flower pots. They should about half fill the pots. Cover with oiled plastic wrap and let rise for 30–45 minutes, in a warm place, or until the dough is 1 inch from the tops of the pots.

5 Meanwhile, preheat the oven to 400°F. Brush the tops with beaten egg and sprinkle with fennel seeds, if using. Bake for 35–40 minutes or until golden. Turn out onto a wire rack to cool.

HARVEST FESTIVAL SHEAF

8 cups unbleached white bread flour
1 tablespoon salt
½ ounce fresh yeast
5 tablespoons lukewarm milk
1⅔ cups cold water

FOR THE TOPPING
1 egg
1 tablespoon milk

MAKES 1 LARGE LOAF

This is one of the most visually stunning breads. Celebratory loaves can be seen in various forms in churches and at some bakers throughout Britain around the September harvest.

1 Lightly grease a large baking sheet, at least 15 × 13-inches. Sift the flour and salt together into a large bowl and make a well in the center.

2 Mix the yeast with the milk in a bowl. Add to the center of the flour with the water and mix to a stiff dough. Turn out onto a lightly floured surface and knead for 10–15 minutes, until smooth and elastic.

3 Place in a lightly oiled bowl, cover with lightly oiled plastic wrap and let rise, at room temperature, for about 2 hours or until doubled in bulk.

4 Turn the dough out onto a lightly floured surface, punch down and knead for about 1 minute. Cover and let rest for 10 minutes.

5 Divide the dough in half. Roll out one piece to a 14 × 10-inch oblong. Fold loosely in half lengthwise. Using a sharp knife, cut out a half mushroom shape for the sheaf (leave the folded edge uncut). Make the stalk "base" about 7 inches long.

6 Place the dough on the prepared baking sheet and open out. Prick all over with a fork and brush with water to prevent a skin from forming. Reserve 3 ounces of the trimmings for the tie. Cover and set aside. Divide the remaining dough in two pieces and mix the rest of the trimmings with one half. Cover and set aside. Beat together the egg and milk for the glaze.

7 Roll out the remaining dough on a lightly floured surface to a rectangle, 11 × 7 inches, and cut into 30–35 thin strips 7 inches long. Place side by side lengthwise on the base, as close as possible, to represent wheat stalks. Brush with some glaze.

8 Take the larger piece of reserved dough and divide into four. Divide each piece into about 25, and shape into oblong rolls to make about 100 wheat ears. Make each roll pointed at one end.

9 Holding one roll at a time, snip along each side toward the center, using scissors, to make wheat shapes.

10 Preheat the oven to 425°F. Arrange the ears around the outer edge of the top of the mushroom shape, overlapping them on the baking sheet. Repeat a second row lower down, placing the row between the first ears. Repeat until they are all used. Brush with some glaze as you proceed to prevent the dough from drying out.

11 Divide the smaller piece of reserved dough into 6 pieces and roll each out to a 17-inch strip. Make 2 braids each with 3 strips. Place across the wheat stalks to make a tied bow. Brush with some glaze. Prick between the wheat ears and stalks using a sharp knife, and bake the sheaf for 15 minutes.

12 Reduce the oven temperature to 350°F. Brush the bread with the remaining glaze and bake for another 30–35 minutes or until golden and firm. Let cool on the baking sheet.

COOK'S TIPS
• Check the bread occasionally while baking, and cover the ends with foil after the first 15 minutes if they start to over-brown.
• Harvest loaves are often baked for display, rather than for eating. If you'd like to do this, then leave the baked loaf in the oven, reduce the temperature to very low, 250°F, for several hours until the dough dries out.

SCOTTISH MORNING ROLLS

4 cups unbleached plain white flour,
plus extra for dusting
2 teaspoons salt
¾ ounce fresh yeast
⅔ cup lukewarm milk
⅔ cup lukewarm water
2 tablespoons milk, for glazing

MAKES 10 ROLLS

These rolls are best served warm, as soon as they are baked. In Scotland they are a popular favorite for breakfast with a fried egg and bacon.

1 Grease 2 baking sheets. Sift the flour and salt together into a large bowl and make a well in the center. Mix the yeast with the milk, then mix in the water. Add to the center of the flour and combine together to form a soft dough.

2 Knead the dough lightly in the bowl, then cover with lightly oiled plastic wrap and let rise, in a warm place, for 1 hour, or until doubled in bulk. Turn the dough out onto a lightly floured surface and punch down.

3 Divide the dough into 10 equal pieces. Knead lightly and, using a rolling pin, shape each piece to a flat oval 4 × 3 inches or a flat 3½-inch round.

4 Transfer to the prepared baking sheets, spaced well apart, and cover with oiled plastic wrap. Let rise, in a warm place, for about 30 minutes.

5 Meanwhile, preheat the oven to 400°F. Press each roll in the center with the three middle fingers to equalize the air bubbles and to help prevent blistering. Brush with milk and dust with flour. Bake for 15–20 minutes or until lightly browned. Dust with more flour and cool briefly on a wire rack. Serve warm.

SHAPED DINNER ROLLS

These professional-looking rolls are perfect for entertaining. You can always make double the amount of dough and freeze half, tightly wrapped. Just thaw, glaze and bake as required.

4 cups unbleached white bread flour
2 teaspoons salt
½ teaspoon sugar
¼ ounce envelope
easy-blend dried yeast
¼ cup butter or margarine
1 cup lukewarm milk
1 egg

FOR THE TOPPING
1 egg yolk
1 tablespoon water
poppy seeds and sesame seeds,
for sprinkling

MAKES 12 ROLLS

1 Lightly grease 2 baking sheets. Sift the flour and salt together into a large bowl and stir in the sugar and yeast. Add the butter or margarine and rub in until the mixture resembles fine bread crumbs.

2 Make a well in the center. Add the milk and egg to the well and mix to a dough. Knead on a lightly floured surface for 10 minutes until smooth and elastic. Place in a lightly oiled bowl, cover with lightly oiled plastic wrap and let rise, in a warm place, for 1 hour, or until doubled in bulk.

3 Turn the dough out onto a lightly floured surface, punch down and knead for 2–3 minutes. Divide the dough into 12 equal pieces and shape into rolls as described in steps 4–8.

4 *To make braids:* divide each piece of dough into three equal pieces. Working on a lightly floured surface, roll each piece to a sausage, keeping the lengths and widths even. Pinch 3 strips together at one end, then braid them neatly but not too tightly. Pinch the ends together and tuck under the braid.

5 *To make trefoils:* Divide each piece of dough into three and roll into balls. Place the three balls together in a triangular shape.

6 *To make batons:* Shape each piece of dough into an oblong and slash the surface of each with diagonal cuts just before baking.

7 *To make cottage rolls:* Divide each piece of dough into two-thirds and one-third and shape into rounds. Place the small one on top of the large one and make a hole through the center with the handle of a wooden spoon.

8 *To make knots:* Shape each piece of dough into a long roll and tie a single knot, pulling the ends through.

9 Place the dinner rolls on the prepared baking sheets, spacing them well apart, cover the rolls with oiled plastic wrap and let rise, in a warm place, for about 30 minutes or until doubled in bulk.

10 Meanwhile, preheat the oven to 425°F. Mix the egg yolk and water together for the glaze and brush over the rolls. Sprinkle some with poppy seeds and some with sesame seeds. Bake for 15–18 minutes or until golden. Lift the rolls off the sheet using a spatula and transfer to a wire rack to cool.

IRISH SODA BREAD

Soda bread can be prepared in minutes and is excellent served warm, fresh from the oven. Use all-purpose flour, to create a bread with a finer texture.

2 cups all-purpose flour
2 cups whole-wheat flour, plus extra for dusting
1 teaspoon salt
2 teaspoons baking soda
2 teaspoons cream of tartar
3 tablespoons butter or lard
1 teaspoon sugar
1½–1⅔ cups buttermilk

MAKES 1 ROUND LOAF

VARIATION
Shape into two small loaves and bake for 25–30 minutes.

1 Preheat the oven to 375°F. Lightly grease a baking sheet. Sift the flour and salt into a large bowl.

2 Add the baking soda and cream of tartar, then rub in the butter or lard. Stir in the sugar.

3 Pour in enough buttermilk to mix to a soft dough. Do not over-mix or the bread will be heavy and tough. Shape into a round on a lightly floured surface.

4 Place on the prepared baking sheet and mark a cross using a sharp knife, cutting deep into the dough.

5 Dust lightly with whole-wheat flour and bake for 35–45 minutes or until well risen and the bread sounds hollow when tapped on the bottom. Serve warm.

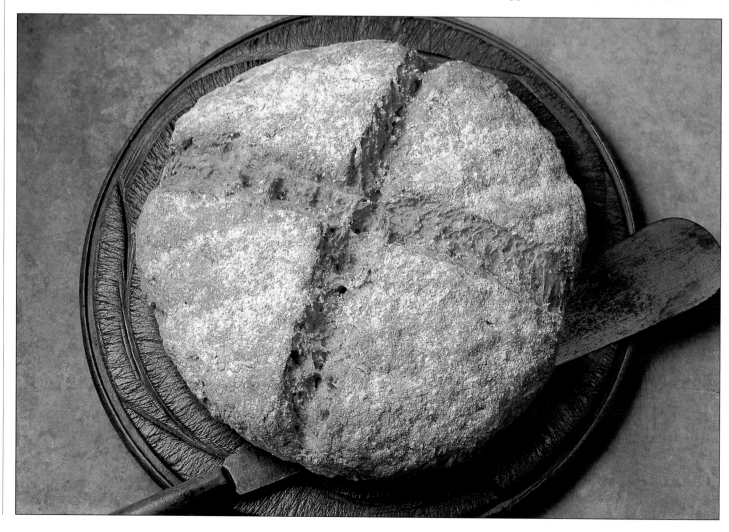

CORNISH SAFFRON BREADS

Often called saffron cake, this light, delicately spiced bread contains strands of saffron and is made in a loaf pan. Whatever the name, the flavor and texture are superb.

1¼ cups milk
½ teaspoon saffron strands
3½ cups all-purpose flour
1 ounce fresh yeast
½ cup ground almonds
½ teaspoon grated nutmeg
½ teaspoon ground cinnamon
¼ cup sugar
½ teaspoon salt
6 tablespoons butter, softened
⅓ cup golden raisins
¼ cup currants

FOR THE GLAZE
2 tablespoons milk
1 tablespoon sugar

MAKES 2 LOAVES

7 Turn the dough out onto a lightly floured surface, punch down, and knead in the golden raisins and currants. Divide in half and shape into two loaves. Place in the prepared pans. Cover with oiled plastic wrap and let rise, in a warm place, for 1½ hours, or until the dough reaches the top of the pans.

1 Lightly grease two 2-pound loaf pans. Heat half the milk until almost boiling.

2 Place the saffron strands in a small heatproof bowl and pour in the milk. Stir gently, then set aside to infuse for 30 minutes.

3 Heat the remaining milk in the same pan until it is just lukewarm.

4 Place ½ cup flour in a small bowl, crumble in the yeast and stir in the lukewarm milk. Mix well, then let sit for about 15 minutes until the yeast starts to ferment.

5 Combine the remaining flour, ground almonds, spices, sugar and salt in a large bowl and make a well in the center. Add the saffron infusion, yeast mixture and softened butter to the center of the flour and mix to a very soft dough.

6 Turn out onto a lightly floured surface and knead for 5 minutes until smooth and elastic. Place in a lightly oiled bowl, cover with lightly oiled plastic wrap and let rise, in a warm place, for 1½–2 hours, or until doubled in bulk.

8 Meanwhile, preheat the oven to 425°F. Bake the loaves for 10 minutes, then reduce the oven temperature to 375°F and bake for 15–20 minutes or until golden.

9 While the loaves are baking, make the glaze. Heat the milk and sugar in a small saucepan, stirring until the sugar has dissolved. As soon as the loaves come out of the oven, brush them with the glaze, let sit in the pans for 5 minutes, then turn out onto a wire rack to cool.

2 cups all-purpose flour
2 cups white bread flour
2 teaspoon salt
2½ cups milk and water mixed
2 tablespoons sunflower oil
1 tablespoon sugar
½ ounce fresh yeast
½ teaspoon baking soda
½ cup lukewarm water

MAKES ABOUT 20 CRUMPETS

COOK'S TIP

If the batter does not produce the characteristic bubbles, add a little more water before cooking the next batch of crumpets.

CRUMPETS

—

Homemade crumpets are less doughy and not as heavy as most supermarket versions. Serve them lightly toasted, oozing with butter.

1 Lightly grease a griddle or heavy frying pan and 4 × 3¼-inch plain cookie cutters or crumpet rings.

2 Sift the flours and salt together into a large bowl and make a well in the center. Heat the milk and water mixture, oil and sugar until lukewarm. Mix the yeast with ⅔ cup of this liquid.

3 Add the yeast mixture and remaining liquid to the center of the flour and beat vigorously for about 5 minutes, until smooth and elastic. Cover with lightly oiled plastic wrap and let rise, in a warm place, for about 1½ hours, or until the mixture is bubbly and about to fall.

4 Dissolve the soda in the lukewarm water and stir into the batter. Re-cover and let rise for 30 minutes.

5 Place the cutters or crumpet rings on the griddle and warm over medium heat. Fill the cutters or rings a generous ½-inch deep. Cook over low heat for 6–7 minutes. The tops should be dry, with a mass of tiny holes.

6 Carefully remove the cutters or rings and turn the crumpets over. Cook for 1–2 minutes or until pale golden. Repeat with remaining batter. Serve warm.

ENGLISH MUFFINS

—

Perfect served warm, split open and buttered for afternoon tea; or try these favorites toasted, split and topped with ham and eggs for brunch.

4 cups white bread flour
1½ teaspoons salt
1½–1⅔ cups lukewarm milk
½ teaspoon sugar
½ ounce fresh yeast
1 tablespoon melted butter or olive oil
rice flour or semolina, for dusting

MAKES 9 MUFFINS

COOK'S TIPS

• Muffins should be cut around the outer edge only using a sharp knife and then torn apart. If toasting, toast the whole muffins first and then split them in half.
• If you'd like to serve the muffins warm, transfer them to a wire rack to cool slightly before serving.

1 Generously flour a non-stick baking sheet. Very lightly grease a griddle. Sift the flour and salt together into a large bowl and make a well in the center. Blend ⅔ cup of the milk, sugar and yeast together. Stir in the remaining milk and butter or oil.

2 Add the yeast mixture to the center of the flour and beat for 4–5 minutes, until smooth and elastic. The dough will be soft but just hold its shape. Cover with lightly oiled plastic wrap and let rise, in a warm place, for 45–60 minutes or until doubled in bulk.

3 Turn out the dough onto a well floured surface and knock back. Roll out to about ½-inch thick. Using a floured 3-inch plain cutter, cut out 9 rounds.

4 Dust with rice flour or semolina and place on the prepared baking sheet. Cover and let to rise, in a warm place, for about 20–30 minutes.

5 Warm the griddle over medium heat. Carefully transfer the muffins in batches to the griddle. Cook slowly for about 7 minutes on each side or until golden brown. Transfer to a wire rack to cool.

LARDY CAKE

4 cups white bread flour
1 teaspoon salt
1 tablespoon lard
2 tablespoons sugar
¾ ounce fresh yeast
1¼ cups lukewarm water

FOR THE FILLING
6 tablespoons lard
6 tablespoons light
brown sugar
½ cup currants, slightly warmed
½ cup golden raisins,
slightly warmed
3 tablespoons mixed chopped peel
1 teaspoon allspice

FOR THE GLAZE
2 teaspoons sunflower oil
1–2 tablespoons sugar

MAKES 1 LARGE LOAF

This special rich fruit bread was originally made throughout many counties of England for celebrating the harvest. Using lard rather than butter or margarine makes an authentic lardy cake.

1 Grease a 10 × 8-inch shallow roasting pan. Sift the flour and salt into a large bowl and rub in the lard. Stir in the sugar and make a well in the center.

2 In a bowl, cream the yeast with half of the water, then blend in the remainder. Add to the center of the flour and mix to a smooth dough.

3 Turn out onto a lightly floured surface and knead for about 10 minutes until smooth and elastic. Place in a lightly oiled bowl, cover with lightly oiled plastic wrap and let rise, in a warm place, for 1 hour, or until doubled in bulk.

4 Turn the dough out onto a lightly floured surface and punch down. Knead for 2–3 minutes. Roll into a rectangle about ¼-inch thick.

5 Using half the lard for the filling, cover the top two-thirds of the dough with flakes of lard. Sprinkle on half the sugar, half the dried fruits and peel and half the allspice. Fold the bottom third up and the top third down, sealing the edges with the rolling pin.

6 Turn the dough by 90 degrees. Repeat the rolling and cover with the remaining lard, fruit and peel and allspice. Fold, seal and turn as before. Roll out the dough to fit the prepared pan. Cover with lightly oiled plastic wrap and let rise, in a warm place, for 30–45 minutes or until doubled in size.

7 Meanwhile, preheat the oven to 400°F. Brush the top of the lardy cake with sunflower oil and sprinkle with sugar.

8 Score a criss-cross pattern on top using a sharp knife, then bake for 30–40 minutes, until golden. Turn out onto a wire rack to cool slightly. Serve warm, cut into slices or squares.

MALTED CURRANT BREAD

This spiced currant bread makes a good tea or breakfast bread, sliced and spread with a generous amount of butter. It also makes superb toast.

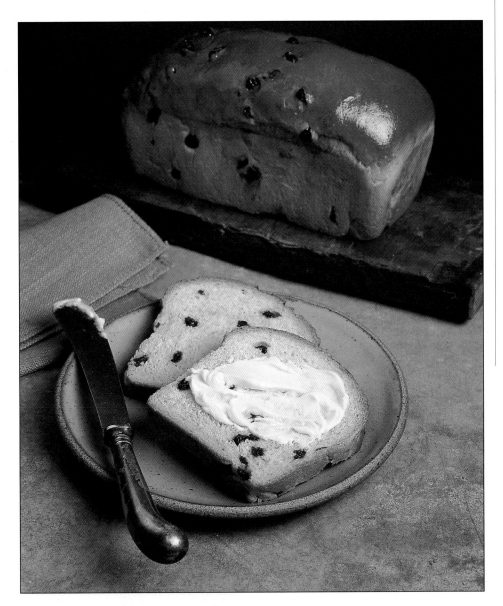

3 tablespoons malt extract
2 tablespoons golden syrup
¼ cup butter
4 cups white bread flour
1 teaspoon allspice
¾ ounce fresh yeast
¾ cup lukewarm milk
¾ cup currants, slightly warmed

FOR THE GLAZE
2 tablespoons milk
2 tablespoons sugar

MAKES 2 LOAVES

COOK'S TIP
When you are making more than one loaf, the easiest way to proof them is to place the pans in a lightly oiled large plastic bag.

4 Turn the dough out onto a lightly floured surface, punch down, then knead in the currants. Divide the dough in half and shape into two loaves. Place in the prepared pans. Cover with oiled plastic wrap and let rise, in a warm place, for 2–3 hours or until the dough reaches the top of the pans.

5 Meanwhile, preheat the oven to 400°F. Bake for 35–40 minutes or until golden. While the loaves are baking, heat the milk and sugar for the glaze in a small saucepan. Turn out the loaves onto a wire rack, then invert them, so that they are the right way up. Immediately brush the glaze evenly over the loaves and let cool.

1 Lightly grease two 1-pound loaf pans. Place the malt extract, golden syrup and butter in a saucepan and heat gently until the butter has melted. Set aside to cool completely.

2 Sift the flour and allspice together into a large bowl and make a well in the center. Mix the yeast with a little of the milk, then blend in the remaining milk. Add the yeast mixture and cooled malt mixture to the center of the flour and blend together to form a dough.

3 Turn out the dough onto a lightly floured surface and knead for about 10 minutes until smooth and elastic. Place in a lightly oiled bowl, cover with lightly oiled plastic wrap and let rise, in a warm place, for 1½–2 hours or until doubled in bulk.

1 cup barley flour
½ cup all-purpose flour or whole-
wheat flour
½ teaspoon salt
½ teaspoon cream of tartar
2 tablespoons butter or margarine
¾ cup buttermilk
½ teaspoon baking soda

MAKES 1 ROUND LOAF

COOK'S TIPS

• If you cannot locate buttermilk,
then use sour milk instead. Stir
1 teaspoon lemon juice into
¾ cup milk and set aside for
an hour to sour.
• If you find the earthy flavor of barley
flour too strong, reduce it to ⅓ cup
and increase the plain white flour to
1 cup. Alternatively, replace half the
barley flour with fine oatmeal.

BARLEY BANNOCK

—

*Bannocks are flat loaves about the size of a dinner plate. They are
traditionally baked on a griddle or girdle (which is the preferred name in
Scotland). Barley flour adds a wonderfully earthy flavor to the bread.*

1 Wipe the surface of a griddle with a
little vegetable oil. Sift the flours, salt
and cream of tartar together into a large
bowl. Add the butter or margarine and
rub into the flour until it resembles fine
bread crumbs.

2 Combine the buttermilk and baking
soda. When the mixture starts to bubble,
add it to the flour. Combine to form a
soft dough. Do not over-mix the dough
or it will toughen.

3 On a floured surface, pat the dough
out to form a round about ¾-inch thick.
Mark the dough into 4 wedges, using a
sharp knife.

4 Heat the griddle until hot. Cook
the bannock on the griddle for
8–10 minutes per side over low heat.
Do not cook too quickly or the outside
will burn before the center is cooked.
Cool the bannock slightly on a wire
rack and eat while still warm.

---

1 cup medium or
fine oatmeal
¼ teaspoon salt
pinch of baking soda
1 tablespoon melted butter
or lard
3–4 tablespoons hot water

MAKES 8 OATCAKES

VARIATIONS

• Oatcakes are traditionally cooked
on the griddle, but they can also
be cooked in the oven at 350°F
for about 20 minutes, or until pale
golden in color.
• Small round oatcakes can be
stamped out using a 3-inch plain
cutter, if preferred.

SCOTTISH OATCAKES

—

*The crunchy texture of these tempting oatcakes makes them difficult to resist.
Serve with butter and slices of a good aged cheese.*

1 Very lightly oil a griddle or heavy
frying pan. Combine the oatmeal, salt
and soda in a bowl.

2 Add the melted butter or lard and
enough hot water to make a dough.
Lightly knead on a surface dusted with
oatmeal until it is smooth. Cut the
dough in half.

3 On an oatmeal-dusted surface roll
each piece of dough out as thinly as
possible into a round about 6 inches
across and ¼ inch thick.

4 Cut each round into 4 quarters or
farls. Heat the griddle over medium
heat, until warm. Transfer 4 farls, using
a spatula, to the griddle and cook over
low heat for 4–5 minutes. The edges
may start to curl.

5 Using the spatula, carefully turn the
farls over and cook for 1–2 minutes. If
preferred, the second side can be cooked
under a preheated broiler until crisp, but
not brown. Transfer to a wire rack to
cool. Repeat with the remaining farls.

WELSH BARA BRITH

This rich, fruity bread—the name literally means "speckled bread"—is a specialty from North Wales. The honey glaze makes a delicious topping.

¾ ounce fresh yeast
scant 1 cup lukewarm milk
4 cups white bread flour
6 tablespoons butter or lard
1 teaspoon allspice
½ teaspoon salt
⅓ cup light brown sugar
1 egg, lightly beaten
⅔ cup raisins, slightly warmed
scant ½ cup currants,
slightly warmed
¼ cup mixed chopped peel
1–2 tablespoons honey,
for glazing

MAKES 1 LARGE ROUND LOAF

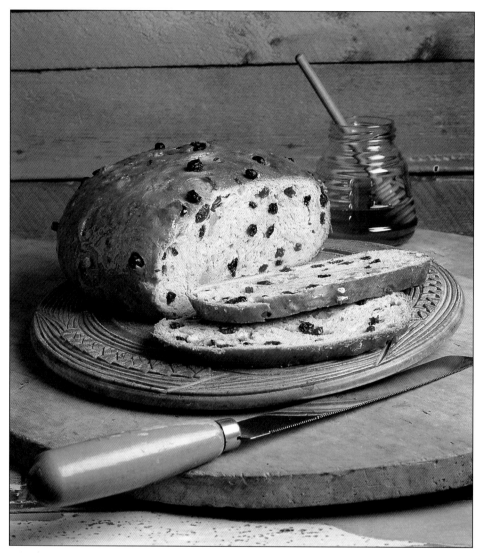

1 Grease a baking sheet. In a bowl, blend the yeast with a little of the milk, then stir in the remainder. Set aside for 10 minutes.

2 Sift the flour into a large bowl and rub in the butter or lard until the mixture resembles bread crumbs. Stir in the allspice, salt and sugar and make a well in the center.

3 Add the yeast mixture and beaten egg to the center of the flour and mix into a rough dough.

4 Turn out the dough onto a lightly floured surface and knead for about 10 minutes until smooth and elastic. Place in a lightly oiled bowl, cover with lightly oiled plastic wrap and let rise, in a warm place, for 1½ hours or until doubled in bulk.

5 Turn out the dough onto a lightly floured surface, punch down, and knead in the dried fruits and peel. Shape into a round and place on the prepared baking sheet. Cover with oiled plastic wrap and let rise, in a warm place, for 1 hour or until the dough doubles in size.

6 Meanwhile, preheat the oven to 400°F. Bake for 30 minutes or until the bread sounds hollow when tapped on the bottom. If the bread starts to over-brown, cover it loosely with foil for the last 10 minutes. Transfer the bread to a wire rack, brush with honey and let cool.

VARIATIONS
• The bara brith can be baked in a 6¼–7½-cup loaf pan or deep round or square cake pan, if you prefer.
• For a more wholesome loaf, replace half the white flour with whole-wheat bread flour.

SALLY LUNN

Sally Lunn is traditionally served warm, sliced into three layers horizontally, spread with clotted cream or butter and re-assembled. It looks fantastic.

2 tablespoons butter
⅔ cup milk or
heavy cream
1 tablespoon sugar
½ ounce fresh yeast
2½ cups white bread flour
½ teaspoon salt
finely grated zest of ½ lemon

FOR THE GLAZE
1 tablespoon milk
1 tablespoon sugar

MAKES 1 ROUND LOAF

1 Lightly butter a 6-inch round cake pan, 3 inches deep. Dust lightly with flour, if the pan is not non-stick. Melt the butter in a small saucepan and then stir in the milk or cream and sugar. The mixture should be tepid. Remove from the heat, add the yeast and blend thoroughly until the yeast has dissolved. Let sit for 10 minutes or until the yeast starts to work.

2 Sift the flour and salt together into a large bowl. Stir in the lemon zest and make a well in the center. Add the yeast mixture to the center of the flour and combine to make a soft dough just stiff enough to form a shape.

3 Turn out the dough onto a lightly floured surface and knead for about 10 minutes until smooth and elastic. Shape into a ball and place in the prepared pan. Cover with lightly oiled plastic wrap and let rise, in a warm place, for 1¼–1½ hours.

4 When the dough has risen to the top of the pan, remove the plastic wrap.

5 Meanwhile, preheat the oven to 425°F. Bake for 15–20 minutes or until light golden. While the loaf is baking, heat the milk and sugar for the glaze in a small saucepan until the sugar has dissolved, then bring to a boil. Brush the glaze over the bread.

6 Let cool in the pan for 10 minutes or until the bread comes away from the side easily, then cool slightly on a wire rack before slicing and filling.

FRENCH BREADS

Although best known for the baguette, France has many more breads to offer, from specialities like fougasse or pain aux noix—which introduce cheese and walnuts—to rustic crusty breads like pain de campagne rustique, pain polka and that old-fashioned rye bread, pain bouillie. Enriched doughs are popular with the French and include the rich, buttery yet light classic breakfast treats of croissants and brioche. Perfect with a cup of coffee!

FRENCH BAGUETTES

5 cups white bread flour
1 cup all-purpose flour
2 teaspoons salt
1/2 ounce fresh yeast
2 1/4 cups lukewarm water

MAKES 3 LOAVES

VARIATION
If you make baguettes regularly you may want to purchase baguette frames to hold and bake the breads in, or long *bannetons* in which to proof this wonderful bread.

Baguettes are difficult to reproduce at home, as they require a very hot oven and steam. However, by using less yeast and a triple fermentation you can produce a bread with a superior taste and far better texture than mass-produced baguettes. These are best eaten on the day of baking.

1 Sift the flours and salt together into a large bowl. Add the yeast to the water in another large bowl and stir to dissolve. Gradually beat in half the flour mixture to form a batter. Cover with plastic wrap and let sit at room temperature for about 3 hours or until nearly tripled in size and starting to collapse.

2 Add the remaining flour a little at a time, beating with your hand. Turn out onto a lightly floured surface and knead for 8–10 minutes to form a moist dough. Place in a lightly oiled bowl, cover with lightly oiled plastic wrap and let rise, in a warm place, for about 1 hour.

3 When the dough has almost doubled in bulk, punch it down, turn out onto a lightly floured surface and divide into 3 equal pieces. Shape each into a ball and then into a rectangle measuring about 6 × 3 inches.

4 Fold the bottom third up lengthwise and the top third down, and press down to make sure the pieces of dough are in contact. Seal the edges. Repeat two or three more times until each loaf is an oblong. Let rest in between folding for a few minutes, if necessary, to avoid tearing the dough.

5 Gently stretch each piece of dough lengthwise into a 13–14-inch long loaf. Pleat a floured dish towel on a baking sheet to make 3 molds for the loaves. Place the breads between the pleats of the towel to help hold their shape while rising. Cover with lightly oiled plastic wrap and let rise, in a warm place, for about 45–60 minutes.

6 Meanwhile, preheat the oven to maximum, at least 450°F. Roll the loaves onto a baking sheet, spaced well apart. Using a sharp knife, slash the top of each loaf several times with long diagonal slits. Place at the top of the oven, spray the inside of the oven with water and bake for 20–25 minutes or until golden. Spray the oven twice more during the first 5 minutes of baking. Transfer to a wire rack to cool.

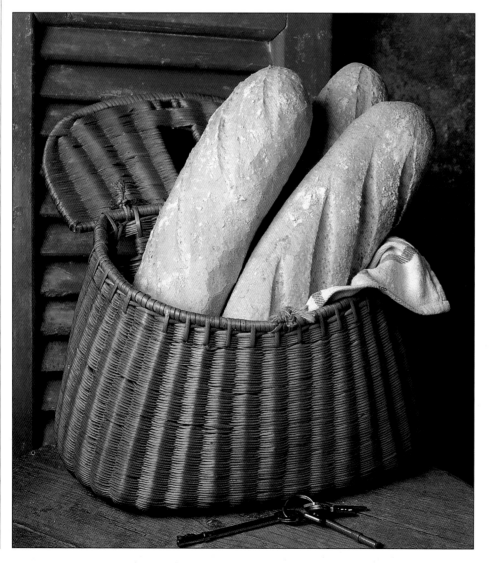

PAIN POLKA

This attractive, deeply cut, crusty bread is made by using a little of the previous day's dough as a starter. However, if you do not have any you can make a starter dough, the details for which are given.

FOR THE STARTER
1 cup 6–15-hours-old French baguette dough
1/4 ounce fresh yeast
1/2 cup lukewarm water
1 cup unbleached all-purpose flour

FOR THE DOUGH
1/4 ounce fresh yeast
scant 1 1/4 cups lukewarm water
4 cups unbleached white bread flour, plus extra for dusting
1 tablespoon salt

MAKES 1 LOAF

COOK'S TIP

The piece of previously made dough can be kept covered in the fridge for up to 2 days, or frozen for up to one month. Just let it come back to room temperature and allow it to rise for an hour before using.

1 Lightly flour a baking sheet. If you have leftover bread dough, proceed to step 3. Make the starter. Mix the yeast with the water, then gradually stir in sufficient flour to form a batter. Beat vigorously, then gradually add the remaining flour and mix to a soft dough.

2 Knead for 5 minutes. Place in a bowl, cover with oiled plastic wrap, and let sit at room temperature for 4–5 hours or until well risen and starting to collapse.

3 In a bowl, mix the yeast for the dough with half of the water, then stir in the remainder. Add the previously made dough or starter (*left*) and knead to dissolve the dough. Gradually add the flour and salt and mix to a dough. Turn out onto a lightly floured surface and knead for 8–10 minutes, until the dough is smooth and elastic.

4 Place the dough in a lightly oiled bowl, cover with lightly oiled plastic wrap and let rise, in a warm place, for about 1 1/2 hours or until doubled in bulk.

5 Turn out the dough onto a lightly floured surface, punch down and shape into a round ball. Flatten slightly and place on the prepared baking sheet.

6 Cover with lightly oiled plastic wrap and let rise, in a warm place, for 1 hour or until almost doubled in size.

7 Dust the top of the loaf with flour and, using a sharp knife, cut the top fairly deeply in a criss-cross pattern. Let rest for 10 minutes. Meanwhile, preheat the oven to 450°F.

8 Bake for 25–30 minutes or until browned. Spray the inside of the oven with water as soon as the bread goes into the oven, and 3 times during the first 10 minutes of baking. Transfer to a wire rack to cool.

CROISSANTS

Golden layers of flaky pastry, puffy, light and flavored with butter is how the best croissants should be. Serve warm on the day of baking.

3 cups white bread flour
1 cup all-purpose flour
1 teaspoon salt
2 tablespoons sugar
½ ounce fresh yeast
scant 1 cup lukewarm milk
1 egg, lightly beaten
1 cup butter

For the Glaze
1 egg yolk
1 tablespoon milk

MAKES 14 CROISSANTS

COOK'S TIP

Make sure that the butter and the dough are about the same temperature when combining to ensure the best results.

1 Sift the flours and salt together into a large bowl. Stir in the sugar. Make a well in the center. Mix the yeast with 3 tablespoons of the milk, then stir in the remainder. Add the yeast mixture to the center of the flour, then add the egg and gradually beat in the flour until it forms a dough.

2 Turn out onto a lightly floured surface and knead for 3–4 minutes. Place in a large lightly oiled bowl, cover with lightly oiled plastic wrap and let rise, in a warm place, for about 45 minutes–1 hour or until doubled in bulk.

3 Punch down, re-cover and chill for 1 hour. Meanwhile, flatten the butter into a block about ¾ inch thick. Punch down the dough and turn out onto a lightly floured surface. Roll out into a rough 10-inch square, rolling the edges thinner than the center.

4 Place the block of butter diagonally in the center and fold the corners of the dough over the butter like an envelope, tucking in the edges to completely enclose the butter.

5 Roll the dough into a rectangle about ¾-inch thick, approximately twice as long as it is wide. Fold the bottom third up and the top third down and seal the edges with a rolling pin. Wrap in plastic wrap and chill for 20 minutes.

6 Repeat the rolling, folding and chilling twice more, turning the dough by 90 degrees each time. Roll out on a floured surface into a 25 × 13-inch rectangle; trim the edges to leave a 24 × 12-inch rectangle. Cut in half lengthwise. Cut crosswise into 14 equal triangles with 6-inch bases.

7 Place the dough triangles on 2 baking sheets, cover with plastic wrap and chill for 10 minutes.

8 To shape the croissants, place each one with the wide end at the top, hold each side and pull gently to stretch the top of the triangle a little, then roll towards the point, finishing with the pointed end tucked underneath. Curve the ends toward the pointed end to make a crescent. Place on two baking sheets, spaced well apart.

9 Combine the egg yolk and milk for the glaze. Lightly brush a little glaze over the croissants, avoiding the cut edges of the dough. Cover the croissants loosely with lightly oiled plastic wrap and let rise, in a warm place, for about 30 minutes or until they are nearly doubled in size.

10 Meanwhile, preheat the oven to 425°F. Brush the croissants with the remaining glaze and bake for 15–20 minutes, or until crisp and golden. Transfer to a wire rack to cool slightly before serving warm.

VARIATION

To make chocolate-filled croissants, place a small square of semi-sweet chocolate or 1 tablespoon coarsely chopped chocolate at the wide end of each triangle before rolling up as in step 8.

PAIN BOUILLIE

This is an old-fashioned style of rye bread, made before sourdough starters were used. Rye flour is mixed with boiling water like a porridge and left overnight to ferment. The finished bread has a rich earthy flavor, with just a hint of caraway.

FOR THE PORRIDGE
2 cups rye flour
1¾ cups boiling water
1 teaspoon honey

FOR THE DOUGH
¼ ounce fresh yeast
2 tablespoons lukewarm water
1 teaspoon caraway seeds, crushed
2 teaspoons salt
3 cups white bread flour
olive oil, for brushing

MAKES 2 LOAVES

1 Lightly grease a 9¼ × 5-inch loaf pan. Place the rye flour for the porridge in a large bowl. Pour in the boiling water and let stand for 5 minutes. Stir in the honey. Cover with plastic wrap and let sit in a warm place for about 12 hours.

2 Make the dough. Put the yeast in a measuring cup and blend in the water. Stir the mixture into the porridge with the crushed caraway seeds and salt. Add the white flour a little at a time, mixing first with a wooden spoon and then with your hands, until the mixture forms a firm dough.

3 Turn out onto a lightly floured surface and knead for 6–8 minutes, until smooth and elastic. Return to the bowl, cover with lightly oiled plastic wrap and let rise, in a warm place, for 1½ hours or until doubled in bulk.

4 Turn out the dough onto a lightly floured surface and knock back. Cut into 2 equal pieces and roll each piece into a rectangle 15 × 4½ inches. Fold the bottom third up and the top third down and seal the edges. Turn over.

5 Brush one side of each piece of folded dough with olive oil and place side by side in the prepared pan, oiled edges next to each other. Cover with lightly oiled plastic wrap and let rise, in a warm place, for 1 hour or until the dough reaches the top of the pan.

6 Meanwhile, preheat the oven to 425°F. Brush the tops of the loaves with olive oil, and using a sharp knife, slash with one or two cuts. Bake for 30 minutes, then reduce the oven temperature to 375°F and bake for another 25–30 minutes. Turn out onto a wire rack to cool.

COOK'S TIP
Serve very thinly sliced, with a little butter, or as an accompaniment to cold meats and cheeses.

EPI

This pretty, wheat shaped crusty loaf makes a good presentation bread. The recipe uses a piece of fermented French baguette dough as a starter, which improves the flavor and texture of the finished bread.

1/4 ounce fresh yeast
generous 1 cup lukewarm water
1/2 cup 6–10-hours-old French baguette dough
2 cups white bread flour
3/4 cup all-purpose flour
1 teaspoon salt

MAKES 2 LOAVES

COOK'S TIP
You can use any amount up to 10 percent of previously made French baguette dough for this recipe. The épi can also be shaped into a circle to make an attractive crown.

5 Let the dough rest between rolling for a few minutes if necessary to avoid tearing. Pleat a floured dish towel on a baking sheet to make 2 molds for the loaves. Place them between the pleats of the towel, cover with lightly oiled plastic wrap and let rise, in a warm place, for 30 minutes.

1 Sprinkle a baking sheet with flour. Mix the yeast with the water in a bowl. Place the French bread dough in a large bowl and break up. Add a little of the yeast water to soften the dough. Mix in a little of the bread flour, then alternate the additions of yeast water and both flours until incorporated. Sprinkle the salt over the dough and knead in. Turn out the dough onto a lightly floured surface and knead for about 5 minutes, until smooth and elastic.

2 Place in a lightly oiled bowl, cover with lightly oiled plastic wrap and let rise, in a warm place, for about 1 hour or until the dough has doubled in bulk.

3 Knock back the dough with your fist, then cover the bowl again with the oiled plastic wrap and let rise, in a warm place, for about 1 hour.

4 Divide the dough into 2 equal pieces, place on a lightly floured surface and stretch each piece into a baguette.

6 Meanwhile, preheat the oven to 450°F. Using scissors, make diagonal cuts halfway through the dough about 2 inches apart, alternating the cuts along the loaf. Gently pull the dough in the opposite direction.

7 Place on the prepared baking sheet and bake for 20 minutes or until golden. Spray the inside of the oven with water 2–3 times during the first 5 minutes of baking. Transfer to a wire rack to cool.

FOR THE CHEF
1/2 cup whole-wheat bread flour
3 tablespoons warm water

FOR THE 1ST REFRESHMENT
4 tablespoons warm water
3/4 cup whole-wheat bread flour

FOR THE 2ND REFRESHMENT
1/2 cup lukewarm water
1 cup white bread flour
1/4 cup whole-wheat bread flour

FOR THE DOUGH
2/3–3/4 cup lukewarm water
3 cups white bread flour
2 teaspoons salt

MAKES 1 LOAF

COOK'S TIPS

• You will need to start making this bread about four days before you'd like to eat it.
• To make another loaf, keep the piece of starter dough (see step 6) in the refrigerator for up to three days. Use the reserved piece of starter dough for the 2nd refreshment in place of the *levain* in step 3, gradually mix in the water, then the flours and let rise as described.

1 To make the *chef*, place the flour in a small bowl, add the water and knead for 3–4 minutes to form a dough. Cover with plastic wrap and let the *chef* sit in a warm place for 2 days.

PAIN DE CAMPAGNE RUSTIQUE

This superb country bread is made using a natural French chef starter to produce a rustic flavor and texture. In France, breads like this are often made three or four times the size of this loaf.

2 Pull off the hardened crust and discard, then remove 2 tablespoons of the moist center. Place in a large bowl and gradually mix in the water for the 1st refreshment. Gradually mix in the flour and knead for 3–4 minutes to form a dough or *levain*, then cover with plastic wrap and let sit in a warm place for 1 day.

3 Discard the crust from the *levain* and gradually mix in the water for the 2nd refreshment. Mix in the flours a little at a time, mixing well after each addition to form a firm dough. Cover with lightly oiled plastic wrap and let rise, in a warm place, for about 10 hours or until doubled in bulk.

4 Lightly flour a baking sheet. For the final stage in the preparation of the dough, gradually mix the water into the *levain* in the bowl, then gradually mix in the flour, then the salt. Turn out the dough onto a lightly floured surface and knead for about 5 minutes, until smooth and elastic.

5 Place the dough in a large lightly oiled bowl, cover with lightly oiled plastic wrap and let rise, in a warm place, for 1½–2 hours or until the dough has almost doubled in bulk.

6 Punch down the dough and cut off ½ cup. Set aside for making the next loaf. Shape the remaining dough into a ball—you should have about 1½ cups.

7 Line a 4 inch high, 9 inch round basket or large bowl with a dish towel and dust with flour.

8 Place the dough ball seam side up in the prepared basket or bowl. Cover with lightly oiled plastic wrap and let rise, in a warm place, for 2–3 hours or until almost doubled in bulk.

9 Preheat the oven to 450°F. Invert the loaf onto the prepared baking sheet and sprinkle with flour.

10 Using a sharp knife, slash the top of the loaf, four times at right angles to each other to form a square pattern.

11 Sprinkle with a little more flour, if desired, then bake for 30–35 minutes or until the loaf has browned and sounds hollow when tapped on the bottom. Transfer to a wire rack to cool.

4 cups white bread flour
1 teaspoon salt
3/4 ounce fresh yeast
generous 1 cup lukewarm water
1 tablespoon extra-virgin olive oil

FOR THE FILLING
1/3 cup Roquefort
cheese, crumbled
1/3 cup walnuts, chopped
2 tablespoons drained, canned
anchovy fillets, soaked in milk,
drained again, and chopped
olive oil, for brushing

MAKES 2 LOAVES

VARIATIONS

• Replace the cheese with
1 tablespoon chopped fresh sage or
thyme or ⅓ cup chopped pitted olives.
• To make a sweet fougasse, replace
1 tablespoon of the water with orange
flower water. Include ⅓ cup chopped
candied orange peel and
2 tablespoons sugar.

1 Lightly grease 2 baking sheets. Sift the
flour and salt together into a large bowl
and make a well in the center. In a
measuring cup, cream the yeast with
4 tablespoons of the water. Pour the
yeast mixture into the center of the
flour with the remaining water and the
olive oil and mix to a soft dough. Turn
out onto a lightly floured surface and
knead the dough for 8–10 minutes, until
smooth and elastic.

FOUGASSE

—

*A fougasse is a lattice-shaped, flattish loaf from the South of France. It can be
cooked as a plain bread or flavored with cheese, anchovies, herbs, nuts or
olives. On Christmas Eve in Provence a fougasse flavored with orange flower
water is part of a table centerpiece of thirteen desserts, used to symbolize
Christ and the Twelve Apostles.*

2 Place the dough in a lightly oiled bowl,
cover with lightly oiled plastic wrap
and let rise, in a warm place, for about
1 hour or until doubled in bulk.

3 Turn out onto a lightly floured surface
and punch down the dough. Divide into
2 equal pieces and flatten one piece of
dough. Sprinkle on the cheese and
walnuts and fold the dough over on
itself 2–3 times to incorporate. Repeat
with the remaining piece of dough, this
time incorporating the anchovies. Shape
each piece of flavored dough into a ball.

4 Flatten each ball of dough and fold the
bottom third up and the top third down,
to make an oblong. Roll the cheese
dough into a rectangle measuring about
11 × 6 inches. Using a sharp knife, make
4 diagonal cuts almost to the edge. Pull
and stretch the dough evenly, so that it
resembles a ladder.

5 Shape the anchovy dough into an oval
with a flat base, about 10 inches long.
Using a sharp knife, make 3 diagonal
slits on each side toward the flat base,
and pull to open the cuts. Transfer to
the prepared baking sheets, cover with
lightly oiled plastic wrap and let rise, in
a warm place, for about 30–45 minutes
or until nearly doubled in bulk.

6 Meanwhile, preheat the oven to 425°F.
Brush both loaves with a little olive oil
and bake for 25 minutes or until golden.
Transfer to a wire rack to cool.

PAIN AUX NOIX

This delicious butter- and milk-enriched whole-wheat bread is filled with walnuts. It is the perfect companion for cheese.

¼ cup butter
3 cups whole-wheat bread flour
1 cup white bread flour
1 tablespoon light brown sugar
1½ teaspoons salt
¾ ounce fresh yeast
generous 1 cup lukewarm milk
1½ cups chopped walnuts

MAKES 2 LOAVES

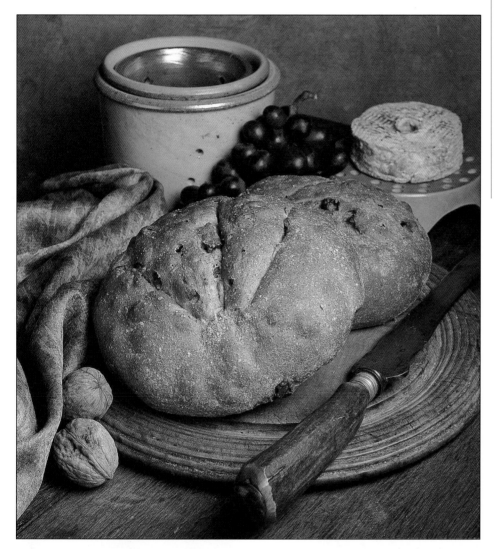

3 Knead on a lightly floured surface for 6–8 minutes. Place in a lightly oiled bowl, cover with lightly oiled plastic wrap and let rise, in a warm place, for 1 hour or until doubled in bulk.

4 Turn out the dough onto a lightly floured surface and gently punch down. Press or roll out to flatten and then sprinkle on the nuts. Gently press the nuts into the dough, then roll it up. Return to the oiled bowl, re-cover and let sit, in a warm place, for 30 minutes.

5 Turn out onto a lightly floured surface, divide in half and shape each piece into a ball. Place on the baking sheets, cover with lightly oiled plastic wrap and let rise, in a warm place, for 45 minutes or until doubled in bulk.

6 Meanwhile, preheat the oven to 425°F. Using a sharp knife, slash the top of each loaf 3 times. Bake for about 35 minutes or until the loaves sound hollow when tapped on the bottom. Transfer to a wire rack to cool.

1 Lightly grease 2 baking sheets. Place the butter in a small saucepan and heat until melted and starting to turn brown, then set aside to cool. Mix the flours, sugar and salt in a large bowl and make a well in the center. Mix the yeast with half the milk. Add to the center of the flour with the remaining milk.

2 Pour the cool melted butter through a fine strainer into the center of the flour so that it joins the liquids already there. Using your hand, combine the liquids in the bowl and gradually mix in small quantities of the flour to make a batter. Continue until the mixture forms a moist dough.

4 cups white bread flour
2 teaspoons salt
1 tablespoon sugar
1/4 cup butter, softened
1/2 ounce fresh yeast
generous 1 cup lukewarm milk, plus
1 tablespoon extra milk, for glazing

MAKES 12 ROLLS

VARIATION
These can also be made into long rolls. To shape, flatten each ball of dough and fold in half. Roll back and forth, using your hand to form a 5-inch long roll, tapered at either end. Just before baking, slash the tops horizontally several times.

3 1/2 cups white bread flour
1 1/2 teaspoons salt
1 teaspoon sugar
1/2 ounce fresh yeast
1/2 cup lukewarm milk
3/4 cup lukewarm water

MAKES 10 ROLLS

1 Lightly grease 2 baking sheets. Sift the flour and salt into a large bowl. Stir in the sugar and make a well in the center.

2 Mix the yeast with the milk until dissolved, then pour into the center of the flour mixture. Sprinkle on a little of the flour from around the edge. Let sit at room temperature for 15–20 minutes or until the mixture starts to bubble.

PETIT PAINS AU LAIT
———
These classic French round milk rolls have a soft crust and a light, slightly sweet crumb. They won't last long!

1 Lightly grease 2 baking sheets. Sift the flour and salt together into a large bowl. Stir in the sugar. Rub the softened butter into the flour.

2 Mix the yeast with 4 tablespoons of the milk. Stir in the remaining milk. Pour into the flour mixture and mix to a soft dough.

3 Turn out onto a lightly floured surface and knead for 8–10 minutes until smooth and elastic. Place in a lightly oiled bowl, cover with lightly oiled plastic wrap and let rise, in a warm place, for 1 hour or until doubled in bulk.

4 Turn out the dough onto a lightly floured surface and gently punch down. Divide into 12 equal pieces. Shape into balls and place on the baking sheets.

5 Using a sharp knife, cut a cross in the top of each roll. Cover with lightly oiled plastic wrap and let rise, in a warm place, for about 20 minutes or until doubled in size.

6 Preheat the oven to 400°F. Brush the rolls with milk and bake for 20–25 minutes or until golden. Transfer to a wire rack to cool.

FRENCH DIMPLED ROLLS
———
A French and Belgian specialty, these attractive rolls are distinguished by the split down the center. They have a crusty finish while remaining soft and light inside—they taste great, too.

3 Add the water and gradually mix in the flour to form a fairly moist, soft dough. Turn out onto a lightly floured surface and knead for 8–10 minutes until smooth and elastic. Place in a lightly oiled bowl, cover with lightly oiled plastic wrap and let rise, at room temperature, for about 1 1/2 hours or until doubled in bulk.

4 Turn out onto a lightly floured surface and punch down. Re-cover and let rest for 5 minutes. Divide the dough into 10 pieces. Shape into balls by rolling the dough under a cupped hand, then roll until oval. Lightly flour the tops. Space apart on the baking sheets, cover with lightly oiled plastic wrap and let rise, at room temperature, for about 30 minutes or until almost doubled in size.

5 Lightly oil the side of your hand and press the center of each roll to make a deep split. Re-cover and let rest for 15 minutes. Meanwhile, place a roasting pan in the bottom of the oven and preheat the oven to 450°F. Pour 1 cup water into the pan and bake the rolls for 15 minutes or until golden. Transfer to a wire rack to cool.

KUGELHOPF

This inviting, fluted ring-shaped bread originates from Alsace, although Germany, Hungary and Austria all have their own variations of this popular recipe. Kugelhopf can be sweet or savory; this version is richly flavored with nuts, onion and bacon.

⅔ cup unsalted butter, softened
12 walnut halves
6 cups white bread flour
1½ teaspoons salt
¾ ounce fresh yeast
1¼ cups milk
4 ounces bacon, diced
1 onion, finely chopped
1 tablespoon vegetable oil
5 eggs, beaten
freshly ground black pepper

MAKES 1 LOAF

VARIATION
If you wish to make a sweet kugelhopf, replace the walnuts with whole almonds and the bacon and onion with 1 cup raisins and ⅓ cup mixed glacé fruits. Add ¼ cup sugar in step 2, and omit the black pepper.

1 Use 2 tablespoons of the butter to grease a 9-inch kugelhopf mold. Place 8 walnut halves around the base and chop the remainder.

2 Sift the flour and salt together into a large bowl and season with pepper. Make a well in the center. In a bowl, cream the yeast with 3 tablespoons of the milk. Pour into the center of the flour with the remaining milk. Mix in a little flour to make a thick batter. Sprinkle a little of the remaining flour on top of the batter, cover with plastic wrap and let sit in a warm place for 20–30 minutes, until the yeast mixture bubbles.

3 Meanwhile, fry the bacon and onion in the oil until the onion is pale golden.

4 Add the eggs to the flour mixture and gradually beat in the flour, using your hands. Gradually beat in the remaining softened butter to form a soft dough. Cover with lightly oiled plastic wrap and let rise, in a warm place, for 45–60 minutes or until almost doubled in bulk. Preheat the oven to 400°F.

5 Punch down the dough and gently knead in the bacon, onion and nuts. Place in the mold, cover with lightly oiled plastic wrap and let rise, in a warm place, for about 1 hour or until it has risen to the top of the mold.

6 Bake for 40–45 minutes or until the loaf has browned and sounds hollow when tapped on the bottom. Cool in the mold for 5 minutes, then on a wire rack.

BRIOCHE

*Rich and buttery yet light and airy, this wonderful loaf captures the essence
of the classic French bread.*

1 Sift the flour and salt together into a
large bowl and make a well in the center.
Put the yeast in a measuring cup and
stir in the milk.

2 Add the yeast mixture to the center of
the flour with the eggs and combine to
form a soft dough.

3 Using your hand, beat the dough for
4–5 minutes, until smooth and elastic.
Cream the butter and sugar together.
Gradually add the butter mixture to the
dough in small amounts, making sure it
is incorporated before adding more.
Beat until smooth, shiny and elastic.

3 cups white bread flour
1/2 teaspoon salt
1/2 ounce fresh yeast
4 tablespoons lukewarm milk
3 eggs, lightly beaten
3/4 cup butter, softened
2 tablespoons sugar

FOR THE GLAZE
1 egg yolk
1 tablespoon milk

MAKES 1 LOAF

4 Cover the bowl with lightly oiled
plastic wrap and let the dough rise, in a
warm place, for 1–2 hours or until
doubled in bulk.

5 Lightly punch down the dough, then
re-cover and place in the refrigerator for
8–10 hours or overnight.

6 Lightly grease a scant 7-cup brioche
mold. Turn the dough out onto a lightly
floured surface. Cut off almost a quarter
and set aside. Shape the rest into a ball
and place in the prepared mold. Shape
the reserved dough into an elongated
egg shape. Using two or three fingers,
make a hole in the center of the large
ball of dough. Gently press the narrow
end of the egg-shaped dough into
the hole.

7 Combine the egg yolk and milk for the
glaze, and brush a little on the brioche.
Cover with lightly oiled plastic wrap and
let rise, in a warm place, for 1½–2 hours
or until the dough nearly reaches the
top of the mold.

8 Meanwhile, preheat the oven to
450°F. Brush the brioche with the
remaining glaze and bake for 10 minutes.
Reduce the oven temperature to 375°F
and bake for another 20–25 minutes or
until golden. Turn out onto a wire rack
to cool.

MEDITERRANEAN BREADS

The warm, rich flavors of the Mediterranean find their way into their breads. Olive oil, sun-dried tomatoes, olives, garlic and fresh herbs are all featured in breads that are so delicious they are now widely enjoyed all over the world. Ciabatta, panini all'olio rolls, focaccia and schiacciata are just a few examples. Spanish, Moroccan and Portuguese breads include local grains like corn and barley, together with seeds such as sesame, sunflower and pumpkin. Elaborate specialty breads are baked for religious festivals, the Greek Easter bread—tsoureki—and the Christmas breads—christopsomo and Twelfth Night bread—being some of the most spectacular.

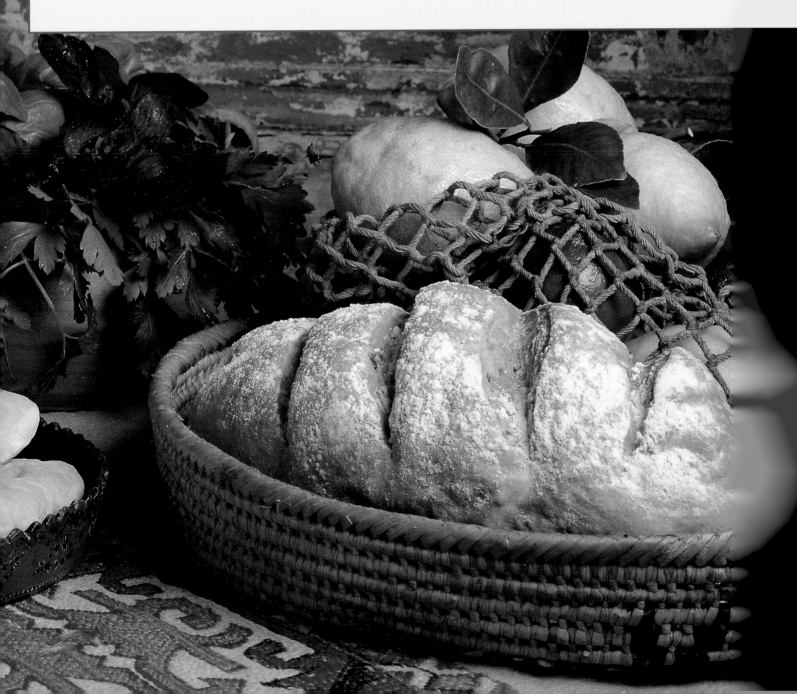

PUGLIESE

This classic Italian open-textured, soft-crumbed bread is moistened and flavored with fruity olive oil. Its floured top gives it a true country look.

FOR THE BIGA STARTER
*1½ cups white
bread flour
¼ ounce fresh yeast
6 tablespoons lukewarm water*

FOR THE DOUGH
*2 cups white bread flour, plus extra
for dusting
2 cups whole-wheat bread flour
1 teaspoon sugar
2 teaspoons salt
½ ounce fresh yeast
generous 1 cup lukewarm water
5 tablespoons extra-virgin olive oil*

MAKES 1 LARGE LOAF

VARIATION
Incorporate 1 cup chopped black olives into the dough at the end of step 5 for extra olive flavor.

1 Sift the flour for the *biga* starter into a large bowl. Make a well in the center. In a small bowl, cream the yeast with the water. Pour the liquid into the center of the flour and gradually mix in the surrounding flour to form a firm dough.

2 Turn the dough out onto a lightly floured surface and knead for 5 minutes until smooth and elastic. Return to the bowl, cover with lightly oiled plastic wrap and let rise, in a warm place, for 8–10 hours or until the dough has risen well and is starting to collapse.

3 Lightly flour a baking sheet. Mix the flours, sugar and salt for the dough in a large bowl. Cream the yeast and the water in another large bowl, then stir in the *biga* and combine.

4 Stir in the flour mixture a little at a time, then add the olive oil in the same way, and mix to a soft dough. Turn out onto a lightly floured surface and knead the dough for 8–10 minutes, until smooth and elastic.

5 Place in a lightly oiled bowl, cover with lightly oiled plastic wrap and let rise, in a warm place, for 1–1½ hours or until doubled in bulk.

6 Turn out onto a lightly floured surface and punch down. Gently pull out the edges and fold under to make a round.

7 Transfer to the prepared baking sheet, cover with lightly oiled plastic wrap and let rise, in a warm place, for 1–1½ hours or until almost doubled in size.

8 Meanwhile, preheat the oven to 450°F. Lightly dust the loaf with flour and bake for 15 minutes. Reduce the oven temperature to 400°F and bake for another 20 minutes or until the loaf sounds hollow when tapped on the bottom. Transfer to a wire rack to cool.

CIABATTA

—

This irregular-shaped Italian bread is so called because it looks like an old shoe or slipper. It is made with a very wet dough flavored with olive oil; baking produces a bread with holes and a wonderfully chewy crust.

1 Cream the yeast for the *biga* starter with a little of the water. Sift the flour into a large bowl. Gradually mix in the yeast mixture and enough of the remaining water to form a firm dough.

2 Turn out the *biga* starter dough onto a lightly floured surface and knead for about 5 minutes, until smooth and elastic. Return the dough to the bowl, cover with lightly oiled plastic wrap and let sit in a warm place for 12–15 hours or until the dough has risen and is starting to collapse.

3 Sprinkle 3 baking sheets with flour. Mix the yeast for the dough with a little of the water until creamy, then mix in the remainder. Add the yeast mixture to the *biga* and gradually mix in.

4 Mix in the milk, beating thoroughly with a wooden spoon. Using your hand, gradually beat in the flour, lifting the dough as you mix. Mixing the dough will take 15 minutes or more and form a very wet dough, impossible to knead on a work surface.

5 Beat in the salt and olive oil. Cover with lightly oiled plastic wrap and let rise, in a warm place, for 1½–2 hours or until doubled in bulk.

6 Using a spoon, carefully transfer one-third of the dough at a time to the prepared baking sheets, trying to avoid punching down the dough in the process.

7 Using floured hands, shape into rough oblong loaf shapes, about 1-inch thick. Flatten slightly with splayed fingers. Sprinkle with flour and let rise in a warm place for 30 minutes.

8 Meanwhile, preheat the oven to 425°F. Bake for 25–30 minutes or until golden brown and hollow-sounding when tapped on the bottom. Transfer to a wire rack to cool.

FOR THE BIGA STARTER
1/4 ounce fresh yeast
3/4–scant 1 cup lukewarm water
3 cups unbleached plain flour, plus extra for dusting

FOR THE DOUGH
1/2 ounce fresh yeast
1 2/3 cups lukewarm water
4 tablespoons lukewarm milk
5 cups unbleached white bread flour
2 teaspoons salt
3 tablespoons extra virgin olive oil

MAKES 3 LOAVES

VARIATION

To make tomato-flavored ciabatta, add 1 cup oil-packed sun-dried tomatoes, drained and chopped. Add with the olive oil in step 5.

4 cups white bread flour
2 teaspoons salt
1/2 ounce fresh yeast
1 cup lukewarm water
4 tablespoons extra-virgin olive oil,
plus extra for brushing

MAKES 16 ROLLS

1 Lightly oil 3 baking sheets. Sift the flour and salt together in a large bowl and make a well in the center.

2 In a small bowl, mix the yeast with half of the water, then stir in the remainder. Add to the center of the flour with the oil and mix to a dough.

3 Turn the dough out onto a lightly floured surface and knead for 8–10 minutes, until smooth and elastic. Place in a lightly oiled bowl, cover with lightly oiled plastic wrap and let rise, in a warm place, for about 1 hour or until the dough has nearly doubled in bulk.

4 Turn onto a lightly floured surface and punch down. Divide into 12 equal pieces and shape into rolls as described in steps 5, 6, 7 and 8.

PANINI ALL'OLIO

The Italians adore interesting and elaborately shaped rolls. This distinctively flavored bread dough, enriched with olive oil, can be used for making rolls or shaped as one large loaf.

5 For *tavalli* (twisted spiral rolls): Roll each piece of dough into a strip about 12 inches long and 1½ inches wide. Twist each strip into a loose spiral and join the ends of dough together to make a circle. Place on the prepared baking sheets, spaced well apart. Brush the *tavalli* lightly with olive oil, cover with lightly oiled plastic wrap and let rise, in a warm place, for 20–30 minutes.

6 For *filoncini* (finger-shaped rolls): Flatten each piece of dough into an oval and roll to about 9 inches in length without changing the basic shape. Make it 2 inches wide at one end and 4 inches wide at the other. Roll up, starting from the wider end. Using your fingers, gently stretch the dough roll to 8–9 inches long. Cut in half. Place on the prepared baking sheets, spaced well apart. Brush the finger shapes with olive oil, cover with lightly oiled plastic wrap and let rise, in a warm place, for 20–30 minutes.

7 For *carciofi* (artichoke-shaped rolls): Shape each piece of dough into a ball and space well apart on the prepared baking sheets. Brush with olive oil, cover with lightly oiled plastic wrap and let rise, in a warm place, for 20–30 minutes. Meanwhile, preheat the oven to 400°F. Using scissors, snip 4–5 ¼-inch deep cuts in a circle on the top of each *carciofo*, then make 5 larger horizontal cuts around the sides. Bake the rolls for 15 minutes. Transfer to a wire rack to cool.

OLIVE BREAD

Black and green olives and good-quality fruity olive oil combine to make this strongly flavored and irresistible Italian bread.

1 Lightly grease a baking sheet. Combine the flours, yeast and salt in a large bowl and make a well in the center.

2 Add the water and oil to the center of the flour and mix to a soft dough. Knead the dough on a lightly floured surface for 8–10 minutes, until smooth and elastic. Place in a lightly oiled bowl, cover with lightly oiled plastic wrap and let rise, in a warm place, for 1 hour or until doubled in bulk.

3 Turn out onto a floured surface and punch down. Flatten out and sprinkle on the olives. Fold up and knead to distribute the olives. Let rest for 5 minutes, then shape into an oval loaf. Place on the prepared baking sheet.

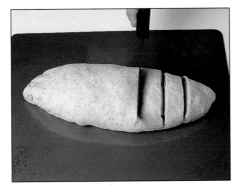

4 Make 6 deep cuts in the top of the loaf, and gently push the sections over. Cover with lightly oiled plastic wrap and let rise, in a warm place, for 30–45 minutes or until doubled in size.

2¹/2 cups white bread flour
1/2 cup whole-wheat flour
1/4 ounce envelope easy-blend dried yeast
1/2 teaspoon salt
scant 1 cup lukewarm water
1 tablespoon extra-virgin olive oil, plus extra, for brushing
1 cup pitted black and green olives, coarsely chopped

MAKES 1 LOAF

VARIATIONS
• Increase the proportion of whole-wheat flour to make the loaf more rustic.
• Add some hazelnuts or pine nuts.

5 Meanwhile, preheat the oven to 400°F. Brush the bread with olive oil and bake for 35 minutes. Transfer to a wire rack to cool.

¾ ounce fresh yeast
1⅓–1½ cups lukewarm water
3 tablespoons extra-virgin olive oil
5 cups white bread flour
2 teaspoons salt
1 tablespoon chopped fresh sage

FOR THE TOPPING
4 tablespoons extra-virgin olive oil
4 garlic cloves, chopped
12 fresh sage leaves

MAKES 2 ROUND LOAVES

FOCACCIA

This simple dimple-topped Italian flat bread is punctuated with olive oil and the aromatic flavors of sage and garlic to produce a truly succulent loaf.

4 Punch down the dough and turn out onto a lightly floured surface. Gently knead in the chopped sage. Divide the dough into 2 equal pieces. Shape each into a ball, roll out into 10-inch circles and place in the prepared pans.

VARIATION
Flavor the bread with other fresh herbs, such as oregano, basil or rosemary, and top with chopped black olives.

1 Lightly oil 2 10-inch shallow round cake pans or pizza pans. Mix the yeast with 4 tablespoons of the water, then stir in the remaining water. Stir in the oil.

2 Sift the flour and salt together into a large bowl and make a well in the center. Pour the yeast mixture into the well in the center of the flour and mix to a soft dough.

3 Turn out the dough onto a lightly floured surface and knead for 8–10 minutes, until smooth and elastic. Place in a lightly oiled bowl, cover with lightly oiled plastic wrap or a large, lightly oiled plastic bag, and let rise, in a warm place, for 1–1½ hours or until the dough has doubled in bulk.

5 Cover with lightly oiled plastic wrap and let rise in a warm place for about 30 minutes. Uncover and, using your fingertips, poke the dough to make deep dimples over the entire surface. Replace the plastic wrap cover and let rise until doubled in bulk.

6 Meanwhile, preheat the oven to 400°F. Drizzle on the olive oil for the topping and sprinkle each focaccia evenly with chopped garlic. Dot the sage leaves on the surface. Bake for 25–30 minutes or until both loaves are golden. Immediately remove the focaccia from the pans and transfer them to a wire rack to cool slightly. These loaves are best served warm.

POLENTA BREAD

Polenta is widely used in Italian cooking. Here it is combined with pine nuts to make a truly Italian bread with a fantastic flavor.

1/2 cup polenta
1 1/4 cups lukewarm water
1/2 ounce fresh yeast
1/2 teaspoon honey
2 cups white bread flour
2 tablespoons butter
3 tablespoons pine nuts
1 1/2 teaspoons salt

FOR THE TOPPING
1 egg yolk
1 tablespoon water
pine nuts, for sprinkling

MAKES 1 LOAF

1 Lightly grease a baking sheet. Combine the polenta and 1 cup of the water in a saucepan and slowly bring to a boil, stirring continuously with a large wooden spoon. Reduce the heat and simmer for 2–3 minutes, stirring occasionally. Set aside to cool for 10 minutes or until just warm.

2 In a small bowl, mix the yeast with the remaining water and honey until creamy. Sift 1 cup of the flour into a large bowl. Gradually beat in the yeast mixture, then gradually stir in the polenta mixture to combine. Turn out onto a lightly floured surface and knead for 5 minutes, until smooth and elastic.

3 Cover the bowl with lightly oiled plastic wrap or a lightly oiled plastic bag. Let the dough rise, in a warm place, for about 2 hours or until it has doubled in bulk.

4 Meanwhile, melt the butter in a small pan, add the pine nuts and cook over medium heat, stirring, until pale golden. Set aside to cool.

5 Add the remaining flour and the salt to the polenta dough and mix to a soft dough. Knead in the pine nuts. Turn out onto a lightly floured surface and knead for 5 minutes, until smooth and elastic.

6 Place in a lightly oiled bowl, cover with lightly oiled plastic wrap and let rise, in a warm place, for 1 hour or until doubled in bulk.

7 Punch down the dough and turn it out onto a lightly floured surface. Cut the dough into 2 equal pieces and roll each piece into a fat sausage about 15 inches long. Braid together and place on the prepared baking sheet. Cover with lightly oiled plastic wrap and let rise, in a warm place, for 45 minutes. Meanwhile, preheat the oven to 400°F.

8 Mix the egg yolk and water and brush over the loaf. Sprinkle with pine nuts and bake for 30 minutes or until golden and sounding hollow when tapped on the bottom. Cool on a wire rack.

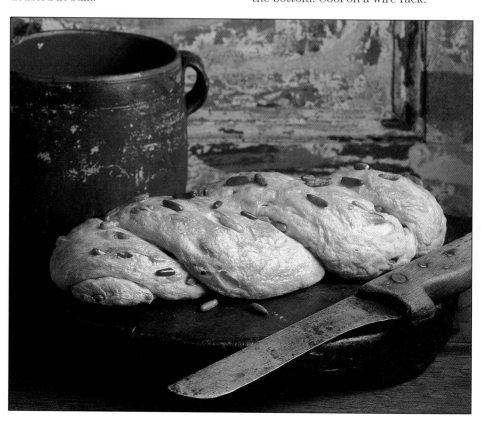

PANE TOSCANO

This bread from Tuscany is made without salt and probably originates from the days when salt was heavily taxed. To compensate for the lack of salt, this bread is usually served with salty foods, such as anchovies and olives.

5 cups white bread flour
1 1/2 cups boiling water
1/2 ounce fresh yeast
4 tablespoons lukewarm water

MAKES 1 LOAF

COOK'S TIP
Salt controls the action of yeast in bread so the leavening action is more noticeable. Don't let this unsalted bread over-rise or it may collapse.

6 Fold the sides of the round into the center and seal. Place seam side up on the prepared baking sheet. Cover with lightly oiled plastic wrap and let rise, in a warm place, for 30–45 minutes or until doubled in size.

7 Flatten the loaf to about half its risen height and flip over. Cover with a large upturned bowl and let rise, in a warm place, for 30 minutes.

1 First, make the starter. Sift 1 1/2 cups of the flour into a large bowl. Pour over the boiling water, let sit for a couple of minutes, then mix well. Cover the bowl with a damp dish towel and let sit for 10 hours.

2 Lightly flour a baking sheet. Cream the yeast with the lukewarm water. Stir into the starter.

3 Gradually add the remaining flour and mix to form a dough. Turn out onto a lightly floured surface and knead for 5–8 minutes, until smooth and elastic.

4 Place in a lightly oiled bowl, cover with lightly oiled plastic wrap and let rise, in a warm place, for 1–1 1/2 hours or until doubled in bulk.

5 Turn out the dough onto a lightly floured surface, punch down, and shape into a round.

8 Meanwhile, preheat the oven to 425°F. Slash the top of the loaf, using a sharp knife, if desired. Bake for 30–35 minutes or until golden. Transfer to a wire rack to cool.

SICILIAN SCROLL

A wonderful pale yellow, crusty-topped loaf, enhanced with a nutty flavor from the sesame seeds. It's perfect for serving with cheese.

4 cups finely ground semolina
1 cup white bread flour
2 teaspoons salt
³/₄ ounce fresh yeast
generous 1¹/₂ cups lukewarm water
2 tablespoons extra-virgin olive oil
sesame seeds, for sprinkling

MAKES 1 LOAF

5 Carefully transfer the dough to the prepared baking sheet, cover with lightly oiled plastic wrap and let rise, in a warm place, for 30–45 minutes or until doubled in size.

6 Meanwhile, preheat the oven to 425°F. Brush the top of the scroll with water and sprinkle with sesame seeds. Bake for 10 minutes. Spray the inside of the oven with water twice during this time. Reduce the oven temperature to 400°F and bake for another 25–30 minutes or until golden. Transfer to a wire rack to cool.

4 Turn out on to a lightly floured surface and punch down. Knead gently, then shape into a fat roll about 20 inches long. Form into an "S" shape.

1 Lightly grease a baking sheet. Combine the semolina, white bread flour and salt in a large bowl and make a well in the center.

2 In a small bowl, mix the yeast with half the water, then stir in the remainder. Add the mixture to the center of the semolina mixture with the olive oil and gradually incorporate the semolina and flour to form a firm dough.

3 Turn out the dough onto a lightly floured surface and knead for 8–10 minutes, until smooth and elastic. Place in a lightly oiled bowl, cover with lightly oiled plastic wrap and let rise, in a warm place, for 1–1¹/₂ hours or until doubled in bulk.

VARIATION
Although sesame seeds are the traditional topping on this delectable Italian bread, poppy seeds, or even crystals of sea salt, could be used instead.

PROSCIUTTO LOAF

*This savory Italian bread from Parma is spiked with the local dried ham.
Just a small amount fills the loaf with delicious flavor.*

1 Lightly grease a baking sheet. Sift the flour and salt together into a large bowl and make a well in the center. In a small bowl, mix the yeast with 2 tablespoons of the water, then gradually mix in the rest. Pour into the center of the flour.

2 Gradually beat in most of the flour with a wooden spoon to make a batter. Beat gently to begin with and then more vigorously as the batter thickens. After most of the flour has been incorporated, beat in the remainder with your hand to form a moist dough.

3 Turn out onto a lightly floured surface and knead for 5 minutes, until smooth and elastic. Place in a lightly oiled bowl, cover with lightly oiled plastic wrap and let rise, in a warm place, for 1½ hours or until doubled in bulk.

4 Turn out the dough onto a lightly floured surface, punch down and then knead for 1 minute. Flatten to a round, then sprinkle with half the prosciutto and pepper. Fold the dough in half and repeat with the remaining ham and pepper. Roll up, tucking in the sides.

*3 cups unbleached white bread flour
1½ teaspoons salt
½ ounce fresh yeast
1 cup lukewarm water
1½ ounces prosciutto, torn into
small pieces
1 teaspoon freshly ground black
pepper*

MAKES 1 LOAF

VARIATIONS
• To make pesto bread, spread 3 tablespoons pesto over the flattened dough in step 6, continue as above.
• For sweet bell pepper bread, add 3 tablespoons finely chopped roasted yellow and red bell peppers instead of the ham in step 4.

5 Place on the prepared baking sheet, cover with lightly oiled plastic wrap and let rise, in a warm place, for about 30 minutes. On a lightly floured surface, roll into an oval, fold in half and seal the edges. Flatten and fold again. Seal and fold again to make a long loaf.

6 Roll into a stubby long loaf. Draw out the edges by rolling the dough under the palms of your hands. Place on the baking sheet, cover with lightly oiled plastic wrap and let rise, in a warm place, for 45 minutes or until the loaf has doubled in size. Meanwhile, preheat the oven to 400°F.

7 Slash the top of the loaf diagonally three or four times, using a sharp knife, and bake for 30 minutes or until golden. Cool on a wire rack.

2 cups white bread flour
1½ teaspoons salt
½ ounce fresh yeast
scant ⅔ cup lukewarm water
2 tablespoons extra-virgin olive oil,
plus extra for brushing
sesame seeds, for coating

MAKES 20 GRISSINI

COOK'S TIP

When baking the grissini turn them
over and reverse the position of the
baking sheets halfway through the
cooking time, so they brown evenly.

SESAME-STUDDED GRISSINI

These crisp, pencil-like breadsticks are easy to make and far more delicious
than the commercially manufactured grissini. Once you start to nibble one, it
will be difficult to stop.

1 Lightly oil 2 baking sheets. Sift the
flour and salt together into a large bowl
and make a well in the center.

2 In a bowl, cream the yeast with the
water. Pour into the center of the flour,
add the olive oil and mix to a soft dough.
Turn out onto a lightly floured surface
and knead for 8–10 minutes, until
smooth and elastic.

3 Roll the dough into a rectangle about
6 × 8 inches. Brush with olive oil, cover
with lightly oiled plastic wrap and let
rise, in a warm place, for about 1 hour or
until doubled in bulk.

4 Preheat the oven to 400°F. Spread out
the sesame seeds. Cut the dough in two
3 x 4-inch rectangles. Cut each piece
into ten 3-inch strips. Stretch each strip
gently until it is about 12 inches long.

5 Roll each grissini, as it is made, in the
sesame seeds. Place the grissini on the
prepared baking sheets, spaced well
apart. Lightly brush with olive oil. let
rise, in a warm place, for 10 minutes,
then bake for 15–20 minutes. Transfer
to a wire rack to cool.

1½ cups unbleached white flour
1 teaspoon salt
1 tablespoon olive oil
7 tablespoons lukewarm water

MAKES 4 PIADINE

COOK'S TIPS

• If you don't have a griddle, a large
heavy frying pan will work
just as well. Keep the cooked
piadine warm while cooking
successive batches.
• Although not traditional in Italy,
these flat breads can also be flavored
with herbs. Add 1 tablespoon of
dried oregano. They also taste
delicious made with garlic—or
chili-flavored olive oil.

PIADINE

These soft unleavened Italian breads, cooked directly on a griddle, were
originally cooked on a hot stone over an open fire. They are best eaten while
still warm. Try them as an accompaniment to soups and dips.

1 Sift the flour and salt together into a
large bowl; make a well in the center.

2 Add the olive oil and water to the
center of the flour and gradually mix in
to form a dough. Knead on a lightly
floured surface for 4–5 minutes, until
smooth and elastic. Place in a lightly
oiled bowl, cover with oiled plastic wrap
and let rest for 20 minutes.

3 Heat a griddle over a medium heat.
Divide the dough into 4 equal pieces and
roll each into an 7-inch round. Cover
until ready to cook.

4 Lightly oil the hot griddle, add 1 or 2
piadine and cook for about 2 minutes
or until they are starting to brown. Turn
the piadine over and cook for another
1–1½ minutes. Serve warm.

PANETTONE

This classic Italian bread can be found throughout Italy around Christmas. It is a surprisingly light bread, even though it is rich with butter and dried fruit.

3½ cups white bread flour
½ teaspoon salt
½ ounce fresh yeast
½ cup lukewarm milk
2 eggs
2 eggs yolks
6 tablespoons sugar
⅔ cup butter, softened
⅔ cup mixed chopped peel
½ cup raisins
melted butter, for brushing

MAKES 1 LOAF

COOK'S TIP
Once the dough has been enriched with butter, do not prove in too warm a place or the loaf will become greasy.

1 Using a double layer of waxed paper, line and butter a 6-inch deep cake pan or soufflé dish. Leave 3 inches of paper above the top of the pan.

2 Sift the flour and salt together into a large bowl. Make a well in the center. Mix the yeast with 4 tablespoons of the milk, then mix in the remainder.

3 Pour the yeast mixture into the center of the flour, add the whole eggs and mix in sufficient flour to make a thick batter. Sprinkle a little of the remaining flour over the top and let "sponge," in a warm place, for 30 minutes.

4 Add the egg yolks and sugar and mix to a soft dough. Work in the softened butter, then turn out on to a lightly floured surface and knead for 5 minutes until smooth and elastic. Place in a lightly oiled bowl, cover with lightly oiled plastic wrap and let rise, in a slightly warm place, for 1½–2 hours, or until doubled in bulk.

5 Punch down the dough and turn out onto a lightly floured surface. Gently knead in the peel and raisins. Shape into a ball and place in the prepared pan. Cover with lightly oiled plastic wrap and let rise, in a slightly warm place, for about 1 hour or until doubled.

6 Meanwhile, preheat the oven to 375°F. Brush the surface with melted butter and cut a cross in the top using a sharp knife. Bake for 20 minutes, then reduce the oven temperature to 350°F. Brush the top with butter again and bake for another 25–30 minutes or until golden. Cool in the pan for 5–10 minutes, then turn out onto a wire rack to cool.

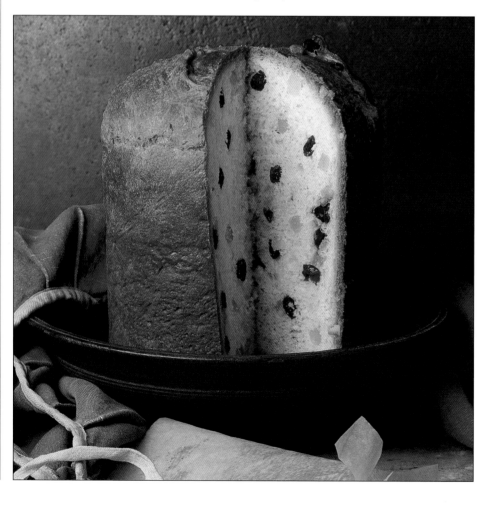

PANE AL CIOCCOLATO

This slightly sweet chocolate bread from Italy is often served with creamy mascarpone cheese as a dessert or snack. The dark chocolate pieces add texture to this light loaf.

3 cups white bread flour
1½ tablespoons cocoa powder
½ teaspoon salt
2 tablespoons sugar
½ ounce fresh yeast
1 cup lukewarm water
2 tablespoons butter, softened
3 ounces semi-sweet chocolate,
coarsely chopped
melted butter, for brushing

MAKES 1 LOAF

1 Lightly grease a 6-inch round deep cake pan. Sift the flour, cocoa powder and salt together into a large bowl. Stir in the sugar. Make a well in the center.

2 In a small bowl, mix the yeast with 4 tablespoons of the water, then stir in the rest. Add to the center of the flour mixture and gradually mix to a dough.

3 Knead in the softened butter, then knead on a floured surface until smooth and elastic. Place in a lightly oiled bowl, cover with lightly oiled plastic wrap and let rise, in a warm place, for about 1 hour or until doubled in bulk.

4 Turn out onto a lightly floured surface and punch down. Gently knead in the chocolate, then cover with lightly oiled plastic wrap; let rest for 5 minutes.

5 Shape the dough into a round and place in the pan. Cover with lightly oiled plastic wrap and let rise, in a warm place, for 45 minutes or until doubled; the dough should reach the top of the pan.

6 Preheat the oven to 425°F. Bake for 10 minutes, then reduce the oven temperature to 375°F and bake for another 25–30 minutes. Brush the top with melted butter and let cool on a wire rack.

VARIATION
You can also shape this bread into one large or two small rounds and bake on a lightly greased baking sheet. Reduce the baking time by about 10 minutes.

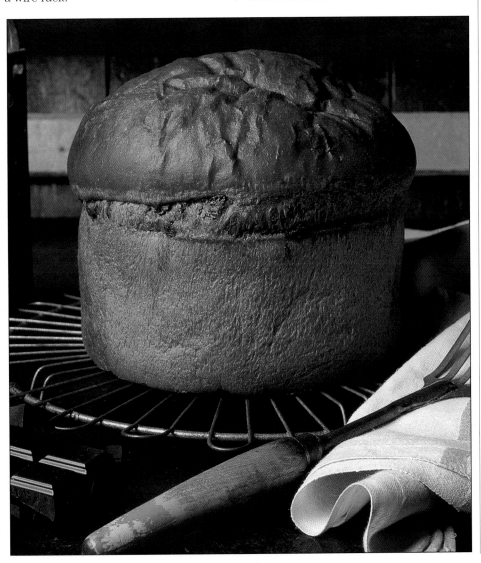

SCHIACCIATA

3 cups white bread flour
½ teaspoon salt
½ ounce fresh yeast
scant 1 cup lukewarm water
4 tablespoons extra-virgin olive oil

FOR THE TOPPING
2 tablespoons extra-virgin olive oil,
for brushing
2 tablespoons fresh rosemary leaves
coarse sea salt, for sprinkling

MAKES 1 LARGE LOAF

This Tuscan version of Italian pizza-style flat bread can be rolled to varying thicknesses to give either a crisp or soft, bread-like finish.

2 Place in a lightly oiled bowl, cover with lightly oiled plastic wrap and let rise, in a warm place, for about 1 hour or until doubled in bulk.

1 Lightly oil a baking sheet. Sift the flour and salt into a large bowl and make a well in the center. Mix the yeast with half the water. Add to the center of the flour with the remaining water and olive oil and mix to a soft dough. Turn out the dough onto a lightly floured surface and knead for 10 minutes, until smooth and elastic.

3 Punch down the dough, turn out onto a lightly floured surface and knead gently. Roll out to a 12 × 8-inch rectangle and place on the prepared baking sheet. Brush with some of the olive oil for the topping and cover with lightly oiled plastic wrap.

4 Let rise, in a warm place, for about 20 minutes, then brush with the remaining oil, prick all over with a fork and sprinkle with rosemary and sea salt. Let rise again in a warm place for 15 minutes.

5 Meanwhile, preheat the oven to 400°F. Bake for 30 minutes or until light golden. Transfer to a wire rack to cool slightly. Serve warm.

PORTUGUESE CORN BREAD

While the Spanish make a corn bread with barley flour, the Portuguese use white flour and cornmeal. This tempting version has a hard crust with a moist, mouthwatering crumb. It slices beautifully and tastes wonderful served simply with butter or olive oil, or with cheese.

¾ ounce fresh yeast
1 cup lukewarm water
2 cups yellow cornmeal
4 cups white bread flour
⅔ cup lukewarm milk
2 tablespoons olive oil
1½ teaspoons salt
polenta, for dusting

MAKES 1 LARGE LOAF

VARIATION
Replace 50 percent of the yellow cornmeal with polenta for a rougher textured, slightly crunchier loaf.

1 Dust a baking sheet with a little cornmeal. Put the yeast in a large bowl and gradually mix in the lukewarm water until smooth. Stir in half the cornmeal and ½ cup of the flour and mix to a batter, with a wooden spoon.

6 Turn out the dough onto a lightly floured surface and punch down. Shape into a round ball, flatten slightly and place on the prepared baking sheet. Dust with polenta, cover with a large upturned bowl and let rise, in a warm place, for about 1 hour or until doubled in size. Meanwhile, preheat the oven to 450°F.

7 Bake for 10 minutes, spraying the inside of the oven with water 2–3 times. Reduce the oven temperature to 375°F and bake for another 20–25 minutes or until golden and hollow sounding when tapped on the bottom. Transfer to a wire rack to cool.

2 Cover the bowl with lightly oiled plastic wrap and let the batter sit undisturbed in a warm place for about 30 minutes or until bubbles start to appear on the surface. Remove the plastic wrap.

3 Stir the milk into the batter, then stir in the olive oil. Gradually mix in the remaining cornmeal, flour and salt to form a pliable dough.

4 Turn out the dough onto a lightly floured surface and knead for about 10 minutes, until smooth and elastic.

5 Place in a lightly oiled bowl, cover with lightly oiled plastic wrap and let rise, in a warm place, for 1½–2 hours or until doubled in bulk.

PAN GALLEGO

Here, a typical round bread with a twisted top from Galicia. The olive oil gives a soft crumb, and the millet, pumpkin and sunflower seeds scattered through the loaf provide an interesting mix of textures.

3 cups white bread flour
1 cup whole-wheat bread flour
2 teaspoons salt
¾ ounce fresh yeast
generous 1 cup lukewarm water
2 tablespoons olive oil or melted lard
2 tablespoons pumpkin seeds
2 tablespoons sunflower seeds
1 tablespoon millet
yellow cornmeal, for dusting

MAKES 1 LARGE LOAF

COOK'S TIP
You can replace the fresh yeast with a ¼ ounce envelope of easy-blend dried yeast. Stir into the flours in step 1. Continue as in the recipe.

1 Sprinkle a baking sheet with cornmeal. Combine the flours and salt in a large bowl.

2 In a small bowl, mix the yeast with the water. Add to the center of the flours with the olive oil or melted lard and mix into a firm dough. Turn out onto a lightly floured surface and knead for about 10 minutes, until smooth and elastic. Place in a lightly oiled bowl, then cover with lightly oiled plastic wrap and let rise, in a warm place, for 1½–2 hours or until doubled in bulk.

3 Punch down the dough and turn out onto a lightly floured surface. Gently knead in the pumpkin seeds, sunflower seeds and millet. Re-cover and let rest for 5 minutes.

4 Shape into a round ball; twist the center to make a cap. Transfer to the prepared baking sheet and dust with cornmeal. Cover with a large upturned bowl and let rise, in a warm place, for 45 minutes or until doubled in bulk.

5 Meanwhile, place an empty roasting pan in the bottom of the oven. Preheat the oven to 425°F. Pour about 1¼ cups cold water into the roasting pan. Lift the bowl off the risen loaf and immediately place the baking sheet in the oven, above the roasting pan. Bake the bread for 10 minutes.

6 Remove the pan of water and bake the bread for another 25–30 minutes or until well browned and hollow-sounding when tapped on the bottom. Transfer to a wire rack to cool.

PAN DE CEBADA

This Spanish country bread has a close, heavy texture and is quite satisfying.
It is richly flavored, incorporating barley flour and yellow cornmeal.

FOR THE SOURDOUGH STARTER
1½ cups cornmeal
scant 2½ cups water
2 cups whole-wheat flour
¾ cup barley flour

FOR THE DOUGH
¾ ounce fresh yeast
3 tablespoons lukewarm water
2 cups whole-wheat flour
1 tablespoon salt
cornmeal, for dusting

MAKES 1 LARGE LOAF

1 In a saucepan, mix the cornmeal for the sourdough starter with half the water, then blend in the remainder. Cook over low heat, stirring continuously, until thickened. Transfer to a large bowl and set aside to cool.

2 Mix in the whole-wheat flour and barley flour. Turn out onto a lightly floured surface and knead for 5 minutes. Return to the bowl, cover with lightly oiled plastic wrap and let the starter sit in a warm place for 36 hours.

5 Punch down the dough and turn out onto a lightly floured surface. Shape into a plump round. Sprinkle with a little cornmeal.

6 Place the shaped bread on the prepared baking sheet. Cover with a large upturned bowl. Let rise, in a warm place, for about 1 hour or until nearly doubled in bulk. Place an empty roasting pan in the bottom of the oven. Preheat the oven to 425°F.

7 Pour 1¼ cups cold water into the roasting pan. Lift the bowl off the risen loaf and immediately place the baking sheet in the oven. Bake the bread for 10 minutes. Remove the pan of water, reduce the oven temperature to 375°F and bake for about 20 minutes. Cool on a wire rack.

3 Dust a baking sheet with cornmeal. In a small bowl, mix the yeast with the water for the dough. Mix the yeast mixture into the starter with the whole-wheat flour and salt and work into a dough. Turn out on to a lightly floured surface and knead for 4–5 minutes, until smooth and elastic.

4 Transfer the dough to a lightly oiled bowl, cover with lightly oiled plastic wrap or an oiled plastic bag and let sit, in a warm place, for 1½–2 hours or until nearly doubled in bulk.

4 cups white bread flour
½ teaspoon salt
1 ounce yeast
*scant ⅔ cup mixed lukewarm milk
and water*
6 tablespoons butter
6 tablespoons sugar
*2 teaspoons finely grated
lemon zest*
*2 teaspoons finely grated
orange zest*
2 eggs
1 tablespoon brandy
1 tablespoon orange flower water
*silver coin or dried bean
(optional)*
*1 egg white, lightly beaten,
for glazing*

FOR THE DECORATION
*a mixture of candied fruit slices
flaked almonds*

MAKES 1 LARGE LOAF

COOK'S TIP

If desired, this bread can be baked
in a lightly greased 9½-inch
ring-shaped cake pan or savarin
mold. Place the dough seam-side
down into the pan or mold and seal
the ends together.

1 Lightly grease a large baking sheet.
Sift the flour and salt together into a
large bowl. Make a well in the center.

TWELFTH NIGHT BREAD

*January 6th, Epiphany or the Day of the Three Kings, is celebrated in
Spain as a time to exchange Christmas presents. Historically this date was
when the Three Wise Men arrived bearing gifts. An ornamental bread ring is
specially baked for the occasion. The traditional version contains a silver
coin, china figure or dried bean hidden inside—the lucky recipient is
declared King of the festival!*

2 In a bowl, mix the yeast with the milk
and water until the yeast has dissolved.
Pour the yeast mixture into the center
of the flour and stir in enough of the
flour from around the sides of the bowl
to make a thick batter.

3 Sprinkle a little of the remaining flour
over the top of the batter and let
"sponge," in a warm place, for about
15 minutes or until frothy.

4 Using an electric whisk or a wooden
spoon, beat the butter and sugar
together in a bowl until soft and creamy,
then set aside.

5 Add the citrus zest, eggs, brandy and
orange flower water to the flour mixture
and use a wooden spoon to mix into a
sticky dough.

6 Using one hand, beat the mixture
until it forms a fairly smooth dough.
Gradually beat in the reserved butter
mixture and beat for a few minutes,
until the dough is smooth and elastic.
Cover with lightly oiled plastic wrap and
let rise, in a warm place, for about
1½ hours or until doubled in bulk.

7 Punch down the dough and turn out
onto a lightly floured surface. Gently
knead for 2 or 3 minutes, incorporating
the lucky coin or bean, if using.

8 Using a rolling pin, roll out the
dough into a long strip measuring
about 26 × 5 inches.

9 Roll up the dough from one long side
like a Swiss roll to make a long sausage
shape. Place seam side down on the
prepared baking sheet and seal the ends
together. Cover with lightly oiled plastic
wrap and let rise, in a warm place, for
1–1½ hours or until doubled in size.

10 Meanwhile, preheat the oven to
350°F. Brush the dough ring with
lightly beaten egg white and decorate
with candied fruit slices, pushing them
slightly into the dough. Sprinkle with
almonds and bake for 30–35 minutes or
until risen and golden. Turn out onto a
wire rack to cool.

MALLORCAN ENSAIMADAS

2 cups white bread flour
½ teaspoon salt
¼ cup sugar
½ ounce fresh yeast
5 tablespoons lukewarm milk
1 egg
2 tablespoons sunflower oil
¼ cup butter, melted
confectioners' sugar, for dusting

MAKES 16 ROLLS

These spiral-or snail-shaped rolls are a popular Spanish breakfast treat. Traditionally, lard or saim was used to brush over the strips of sweetened dough, but nowadays mainly butter is used to add a delicious richness.

1 Lightly grease 2 baking sheets. Sift the flour and salt together into a large mixing bowl. Stir in the sugar and make a well in the center.

2 In a small bowl, mix the yeast with the milk, pour into the center of the flour mixture, then sprinkle a little of the flour mixture evenly on top of the liquid. Let sit in a warm place for about 15 minutes or until frothy.

3 In a small bowl, beat the egg and sunflower oil together. Add to the flour mixture and mix to a smooth dough.

4 Turn out onto a lightly floured surface and knead for 8–10 minutes. until smooth and elastic. Place in a lightly oiled bowl, cover with lightly oiled plastic wrap and let rise, in a warm place, for 1 hour or until doubled in bulk.

5 Turn out the dough onto a lightly floured surface. Punch down and divide the dough into 16 equal pieces. Shape each piece into a thin rope about 15 inches long. Pour the melted butter onto a plate and dip the ropes into the butter to coat.

6 On the baking sheets, curl each rope into a loose spiral, spacing well apart. Tuck the ends under to seal. Cover with lightly oiled plastic wrap and let rise, in a warm place, for about 45 minutes or until doubled in size.

7 Meanwhile, preheat the oven to 375°F. Brush the rolls with water and dust with confectioners' sugar. Bake for 10 minutes or until light golden brown. Cool on a wire rack. Dust again with confectioners' sugar and serve warm.

PITA BREAD

*These Turkish breads are a favorite in both the eastern Mediterranean
and the Middle East, and have are popular in England and the United States.
This versatile soft, flat bread forms a pocket as it cooks,
making it perfect for filling with vegetables, salads or meats.*

*2 cups white bread flour
1 teaspoon salt
1/2 ounce fresh yeast
scant 2/3 cup lukewarm water
2 teaspoons extra-virgin olive oil*

MAKES 6 PITA BREADS

VARIATIONS

To make whole-wheat pita breads,
replace half the white flour
with whole-wheat flour. You
can also make smaller round pita
breads about 4 inches in diameter
to serve as snack breads.

5 Roll out each ball of dough in turn to
an oval about 1/4-inch thick and 6 inches
long. Place on a floured dish towel
and cover with lightly oiled plastic wrap.
Let rise at room temperature for
20–30 minutes.

6 Meanwhile, preheat the oven to 450°F.
Place 3 baking sheets in the oven to
heat at the same time.

7 Place two pita breads on each baking
sheet and bake for 4–6 minutes or until
puffed up; they do not need to brown. If
preferred, cook the pita bread in batches.
It is important that the oven has reached
the recommended temperature before
the pita breads are baked. This ensures
that they will puff up.

8 Transfer the pitas to a wire rack to
cool until warm, then cover with a dish
towel to keep them soft.

1 Sift the flour and salt together into a
bowl. In a small bowl, mix the yeast with
the water until dissolved, then stir in the
olive oil and pour into a large bowl.

2 Gradually beat the flour into the yeast
mixture, then knead the mixture to
make a soft dough.

3 Turn out onto a lightly floured surface
and knead for 5 minutes until smooth
and elastic. Place in a large clean bowl,
cover with lightly oiled plastic wrap
and let rise, in a warm place, for about
1 hour or until doubled in bulk.

4 Punch down the dough. On a lightly
floured surface, divide it into 6 equal
pieces and shape into balls. Cover with
oiled plastic wrap; let rest for 5 minutes.

CHRISTOPSOMO

1/2 ounce fresh yeast
scant 2/3 cup lukewarm milk
4 cups white flour
2 eggs
6 tablespoons sugar
1/2 teaspoon salt
6 tablespoons butter, softened
grated zest of 1/2 orange
1 teaspoon ground cinnamon
1/4 teaspoon ground cloves
pinch of crushed anise seed
8 walnut halves
beaten egg white, for glazing

MAKES 1 LOAF

A Byzantine cross flavored with anise seed tops this Greek Christmas bread, which is also decorated with walnuts for good fortune. The fluffy, light, butter-enriched bread contains orange zest, cinnamon and cloves—all the warm tastes associated with Christmas.

1 Lightly grease a large baking sheet. In a large bowl, mix the yeast with the milk until the yeast is dissolved, then stir in 1 cup of the flour to make a thin batter. Cover with lightly oiled plastic wrap and let "sponge" in a warm place for 30 minutes.

2 Beat the eggs and sugar until light and fluffy. Beat into the yeast mixture. Gradually mix in the remaining flour and salt. Beat in the softened butter and knead to a soft but not sticky dough. Knead on a lightly floured surface for 8–10 minutes, until smooth and elastic. Place in a lightly oiled bowl, cover with lightly oiled plastic wrap and let rise, in a warm place, for 1 1/2 hours or until doubled in bulk.

3 Turn out onto a lightly floured surface and gently punch down. Cut off about 2 ounces of dough; cover and set aside. Gently knead the orange zest, ground cinnamon and cloves into the large piece of dough and shape into a round loaf. Place on the baking sheet.

4 Knead the anise seed into the remaining dough. Cut the dough in half and shape each piece into a 12-inch long rope. Cut through each rope at either end by one-third of its length. Place the two ropes in a cross on top of the loaf, then curl each cut end into a circle, in opposite directions.

5 Place a walnut half inside each circle. Cover the loaf with lightly oiled plastic wrap and let rise for 45 minutes or until doubled in size. Meanwhile, preheat the oven to 375°F. Brush the bread with the egg white and bake for 40–45 minutes or until golden. Cool on a wire rack.

COOK'S TIP
If you do not have any anise seeds, flavor the dough with 1 teaspoon pastis, anisette or ouzo.

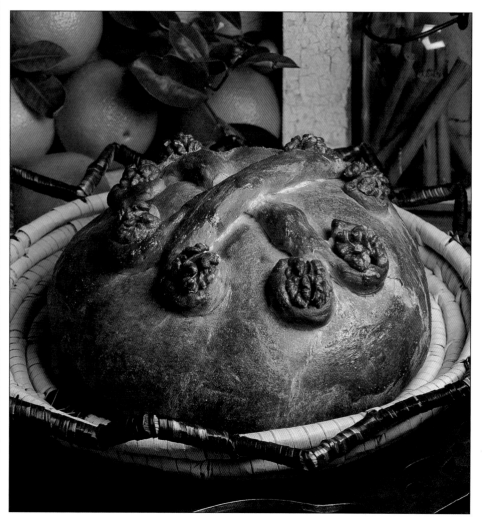

TSOUREKI

Topped with brightly colored eggs, this braided bread is an important part of the Greek Easter celebrations.

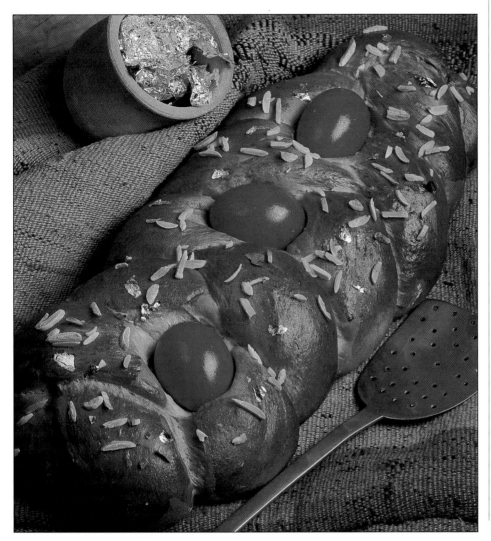

FOR THE EGGS
3 eggs
1/4 teaspoon bright red food coloring
1 tablespoon white wine vinegar
1 teaspoon water
1 teaspoon olive oil

FOR THE DOUGH
4 cups white flour
1/2 teaspoon salt
1 teaspoon ground allspice
1/2 teaspoon ground cinnamon
1/2 teaspoon caraway seeds
3/4 ounce fresh yeast
3/4 cup lukewarm milk
1/4 cup butter
3 tablespoons sugar
2 eggs

FOR THE GLAZE
1 egg yolk
1 teaspoon honey
1 teaspoon water

FOR THE DECORATION
1/2 cup slivered almonds
edible gold leaf, optional

MAKES 1 LOAF

1 Lightly grease a baking sheet. Place the eggs in a pan of water and bring to a boil. Boil gently for 10 minutes. Meanwhile, combine the red food coloring, vinegar and water in a shallow bowl. Remove the eggs from the boiling water, place on a wire rack for a few seconds to dry, then roll in the coloring mixture. Return to the rack to cool and completely dry.

2 When cold, drizzle the olive oil on absorbent paper towels, lift up each egg in turn and rub all over with the oiled paper.

3 To make the dough, sift the flour, salt, allspice and cinnamon into a large bowl. Stir in the caraway seeds.

4 In a bowl, mix the yeast with the milk. In a bowl, cream the butter and sugar, then beat in the eggs. Add the creamed mixture to the flour with the yeast mixture and gradually mix into a dough. Turn out the dough onto a lightly floured surface and knead until smooth and elastic.

5 Place in a lightly oiled bowl, cover with lightly oiled plastic wrap and let rise, in a warm place, for about 2 hours or until doubled in bulk.

6 Punch down the dough and knead for 2–3 minutes. Return to the bowl, re-cover and let rise again, in a warm place, for about 1 hour or until doubled in bulk.

7 Punch down and turn out onto a lightly floured surface. Divide the dough into 3 equal pieces and roll each into a 15–20-inch long rope. Braid these together from the center to the ends.

8 Place on the prepared baking sheet and push the dyed eggs into the loaf. Cover and let rise, in a warm place, for about 1 hour.

9 Meanwhile, preheat the oven to 375°F. Combine the egg yolk, honey and water for the glaze, and brush over the loaf. Sprinkle with almonds and edible gold leaf, if using. Bake for 40–45 minutes or until golden and hollow-sounding when tapped on the bottom. Transfer to a wire rack to cool.

GREEK OLIVE BREAD

The flavors of the Mediterranean simply ooze from this decorative bread, speckled with black olives, red onions and herbs.

*6 cups white flour,
plus extra for dusting
2 teaspoons salt
1 ounce fresh yeast
1½ cups lukewarm water
5 tablespoons olive oil
1½ cups pitted black olives,
roughly chopped
1 red onion, finely chopped
2 tablespoons chopped fresh cilantro
or mint*

MAKES 2 LOAVES

VARIATION
Make one large loaf and increase the baking time by about 15 minutes.

1 Lightly grease 2 baking sheets. Sift the flour and salt together into a large bowl and make a well in the center.

2 In a bowl, blend the yeast with half of the water. Add to the center of the flour with the remaining water and the olive oil; mix to a soft dough.

3 Turn out the dough onto a lightly floured surface and knead for 8–10 minutes, until smooth. Place in a lightly oiled bowl, cover with lightly oiled plastic wrap and let rise, in a warm place, for 1 hour or until doubled in bulk.

4 Turn out onto a lightly floured surface and punch down. Cut off a quarter of the dough, cover with lightly oiled plastic wrap and set aside.

5 Roll out the remaining, large piece of dough to a round. Sprinkle the olives, onion and herbs evenly over the surface, then bring up the sides of the circle and gently knead together. Cut the dough in half and shape each piece into a plump oval loaf, about 8 inches long. Place on the prepared baking sheets.

6 Divide the reserved dough into 4 equal pieces and roll each out into a long strand 24 inches long. Twist together and cut in half. Brush the center of each loaf with water and place two pieces of twisted dough on top of each, tucking the ends underneath the loaves.

7 Cover with lightly oiled plastic wrap and let rise, in a warm place, for about 45 minutes or until the loaves are plump and nearly doubled in size.

8 Meanwhile, preheat the oven to 425°F. Dust the loaves lightly with flour and bake for 35–40 minutes or until golden and hollow-sounding when tapped on the bottom. Transfer to a wire rack to cool.

MOROCCAN HOLIDAY BREAD

*The addition of cornmeal and a cornucopia of seeds gives this superb loaf
an interesting flavor and texture.*

*2½ cups white bread flour
½ cup yellow cornmeal
1 teaspoon salt
¾ ounce fresh yeast
½ cup lukewarm water
½ cup lukewarm milk
1 tablespoon pumpkin seeds
1 tablespoon sesame seeds
2 tablespoons hulled sunflower seeds*

MAKES 1 LOAF

5 Turn out the dough onto a lightly floured surface and punch down. Gently knead the pumpkin and sesame seeds into the dough. Shape into a round ball and flatten slightly.

6 Place on the prepared baking sheet, cover with lightly oiled plastic wrap or slide into a large, lightly oiled plastic bag and let rise, in a warm place, for 45 minutes or until doubled in bulk.

7 Meanwhile, preheat the oven to 400°F. Brush the top of the loaf with water and sprinkle evenly with the sunflower seeds. Bake the loaf for 30–35 minutes or until it is golden and sounds hollow when tapped on the bottom. Transfer the loaf to a wire rack to cool.

1 Lightly grease a baking sheet. Sift the flour, cornmeal and salt into a large bowl.

2 Mix the yeast with a little of the water in a small bowl. Stir in the remainder of the water and the milk. Pour into the center of the flour and mix to a fairly soft dough.

3 Turn out the dough onto a lightly floured surface and knead for about 5 minutes, until smooth and elastic.

4 Place in a lightly oiled bowl, cover with lightly oiled plastic wrap and let rise, in a warm place, for about 1 hour or until doubled in bulk.

VARIATIONS

Incorporate all the seeds in the dough in step 5 and leave the top of the loaf plain. Alternatively, use sesame seeds instead of sunflower seeds for the topping and either incorporate the sunflower seeds in the loaf or leave them out.

NORTH EUROPEAN AND SCANDINAVIAN BREADS

The northern Europeans and Scandinavians make many different breads, from the dense, dark German pumpernickel to a light Polish rye bread. Also, from these northern climes, come the famous Swedish crispbreads, Russian potato bread and blinis, a variety of sweet breads, lightly scented saffron buns and port-flavored rye bread. Christmas breads are enriched with fruit, while Bulgaria has its own poppy-seeded circular bread for religious festivals.

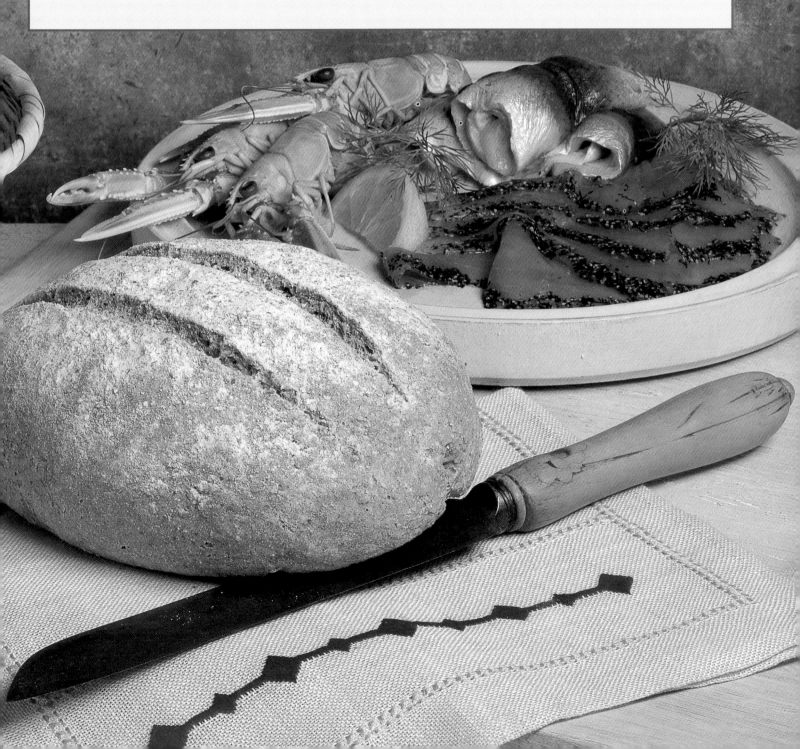

SWISS BRAID

3 cups white flour
1 teaspoon salt
¾ ounce fresh yeast
2 tablespoons lukewarm water
⅔ cup sour cream
1 egg, lightly beaten
¼ cup butter, softened

FOR THE GLAZE
1 egg yolk
1 tablespoon water

MAKES 1 LOAF

COOK'S TIP
If you prefer, use a ¼ ounce envelope
of easy-blend dried yeast.
Add directly to the flour with the salt,
then add the warmed sour cream and
water and combine.

This braided, attractively tapered loaf is known as zupfe *in Switzerland. Often eaten on weekends, it has a glossy crust and a wonderfully light crumb.*

1 Lightly grease a baking sheet. Sift the flour and salt together into a large bowl and make a well in the center. Mix the yeast with the water in a small bowl.

2 Gently warm the sour cream in a small pan until it reaches 98.6°F. Add to the yeast mixture and combine.

3 Add the yeast mixture and egg to the center of the flour and gradually mix into a dough. Beat in the softened butter.

4 Turn out onto a lightly floured surface and knead for 5 minutes, until smooth and elastic. Place in a lightly oiled bowl, cover with lightly oiled plastic wrap and let rise, in a warm place, for about 1½ hours or until doubled in size.

5 Turn out onto a lightly floured surface and punch down. Cut in half and shape each piece of dough into a long rope about 14 inches in length.

6 To make the braid, place the two pieces of dough on top of each other to form a cross. Starting with the bottom rope, fold the top end over and place between the two bottom ropes. Fold the remaining top rope over so that all four ropes are pointing downward. Starting from the left, braid the first rope over the second, and the third rope over the fourth.

7 Continue braiding in this way to form a tapered bread. Tuck the ends underneath and place on the prepared baking sheet. Cover with lightly oiled plastic wrap and let rise, in a warm place, for about 40 minutes.

8 Meanwhile, preheat the oven to 375°F. Mix the egg yolk and water for the glaze, and brush over the loaf. Bake the bread for 30–35 minutes or until golden. Cool on a wire rack.

PRETZELS

*Pretzels, or brezeln, as they are known in Germany, are said to be derived
from the Latin* bracellae *or arms, referring to the crossed "arms" of dough
inside the oval shape. This shape is also used for cookies in Germany and
Austria, and in Alsace the pretzel shape is part of the wrought iron emblem
of quality that bakers display outside their stores.*

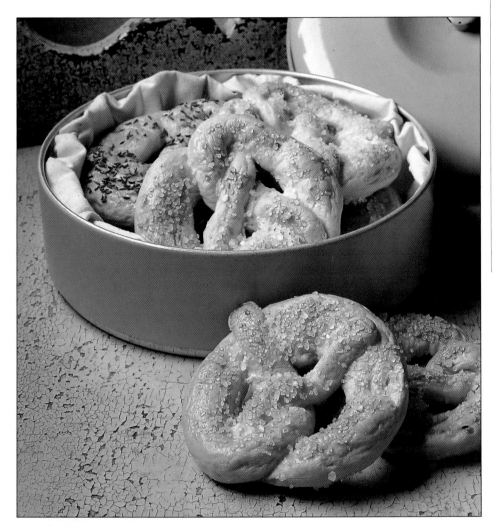

FOR THE YEAST SPONGE
¼ ounce fresh yeast
5 tablespoons water
1 tablespoon white flour

FOR THE DOUGH
¼ ounce fresh yeast
⅔ cup lukewarm water
5 tablespoons lukewarm milk
3½ cups white flour
1½ teaspoons salt
2 tablespoons butter, melted

FOR THE TOPPING
1 egg yolk
1 tablespoon milk
sea salt or caraway seeds, for
sprinkling

MAKES 12 PRETZELS

4 Turn out the dough onto a lightly
floured surface. Divide the dough into
12 equal pieces and form into balls.
Take one ball of dough and cover the
remainder with a dish towel. Roll into a
thin stick 18 inches long and about
½-inch thick in the middle and thinner at
the ends. Bend each end of the dough
sticks into a horseshoe. Cross over and
place the ends on top of the thick part of
the pretzel. Repeat with the remaining
dough balls.

5 Place on the floured baking sheet to
rest for 10 minutes. Meanwhile, preheat
the oven to 375°F. Bring a large
saucepan of water to a boil, then
reduce to a simmer. Add the pretzels
to the simmering water in batches,
about 2–3 at a time, and poach for
about 1 minute. Drain the pretzels on
a dish towel and place on the greased
baking sheets, spaced well apart.

1 Lightly flour a baking sheet. Also
grease 2 baking sheets. In a small bowl,
mix the yeast for the yeast sponge with
the water, then mix in the flour, cover
with plastic wrap and let stand at room
temperature for 2 hours.

2 Mix the yeast for the dough with the
water until dissolved, then stir in the milk.
Sift 3 cups of the flour and the salt into a
large bowl. Add the yeast sponge mixture
and the butter; mix for 3–4 minutes.
Turn out onto a lightly floured surface
and knead in the remaining flour to
make a medium firm dough. Place in a
lightly oiled bowl, cover with lightly oiled
plastic wrap and let rise, in a warm
place, for 30 minutes or until almost
doubled in bulk.

3 Turn out onto a lightly floured surface
and punch down the dough. Knead into
a ball, return to the bowl, re-cover and
let rise for 30 minutes.

6 Combine the egg yolk and milk and
brush this glaze over the pretzels.
Sprinkle with sea salt or caraway seeds
and bake the pretzels for 25 minutes or
until they are deep golden. Transfer to a
wire rack to cool.

PUMPERNICKEL

*This famous German bread is extremely dense and dark,
with an intense flavor. It is baked very slowly and is more like a
steamed bread than a baked one.*

*4 cups rye flour
2 cups whole-wheat flour
⅔ cup bulgur wheat
2 teaspoons salt
2 tablespoons molasses
3½ cups warm water
1 tablespoon vegetable oil*

MAKES 2 LOAVES

COOK'S TIP

This bread improves over time. Keep
for at least 24 hours double-wrapped
inside a plastic bag or waxed paper
and foil before slicing.

1 Lightly grease two 7 × 3½-inch loaf
pans. Combine the rye flour, whole-
wheat flour, bulgur wheat and salt in a
large bowl.

2 Mix the molasses with the warm water
and add to the flours with the vegetable
oil. Combine to form a dense mass.

3 Place in the prepared pans, pressing
well into the corners. Cover with lightly
oiled plastic wrap and let sit in a warm
place for 18–24 hours.

4 Preheat the oven to 225°F. Cover
the pans tightly with foil. Fill a roasting
pan with boiling water and place a rack
on top.

5 Place the pans on top of the rack and
transfer very carefully to the oven. Bake
the loaves for 4 hours. Increase the oven
temperature to 325°F. Top up the water
in the roasting pan if necessary, uncover
the loaves and bake for another
30–45 minutes or until the loaves
feel firm and the tops are crusty.

6 Let cool in the pans for 5 minutes,
then turn out onto a wire rack to cool
completely. Serve cold, very thinly
sliced, with cold meats.

GERMAN SOURDOUGH BREAD

This bread includes rye, whole-wheat and all-purpose flours for a superb depth of flavor. Serve it cut in thick slices, with creamy butter or a sharp cheese.

FOR THE SOURDOUGH STARTER
3/4 cup rye flour
1/3 cup warm water
pinch caraway seeds

FOR THE DOUGH
1/2 ounce fresh yeast
1 1/3 cups lukewarm water
2 1/2 cups rye flour
1 1/4 cups whole-wheat flour
1 1/4 cups all-purpose flour
2 teaspoons salt

MAKES 1 LOAF

1 Combine the rye flour, warm water and caraway for the starter in a large bowl with your fingertips, to make a soft paste. Cover with a damp dish towel and let sit in a warm place for about 36 hours. Stir after 24 hours.

2 Lightly grease a baking sheet. In a measuring cup, blend the yeast for the dough with the lukewarm water. Add to the starter and mix thoroughly.

5 Turn out onto a lightly floured surface, punch down and knead gently. Shape into a round and place in a floured basket, or *couronne*, with the seam up. Cover with lightly oiled plastic wrap and let rise, in a warm place, for 2–3 hours.

6 Meanwhile, preheat the oven to 400°F. Turn out the loaf onto the prepared baking sheet and bake for 35–40 minutes. Cool on a wire rack.

COOK'S TIP
Proofing the dough in a floured basket or *couronne* gives it its characteristic patterned crust, but is not essential. Make sure that you flour the basket well, otherwise the dough may stick.

3 Mix the rye flour, whole-wheat bread flour and all-purpose flour for the dough with the salt in a large bowl; make a well in the center. Pour in the yeast liquid and gradually incorporate the surrounding flour to make a smooth dough.

4 Turn out the dough on to a lightly floured surface and knead for 8–10 minutes until smooth and elastic. Place in a lightly oiled bowl, cover with lightly oiled plastic wrap and let rise, in a warm place, for 1 1/2 hours, or until nearly doubled in bulk.

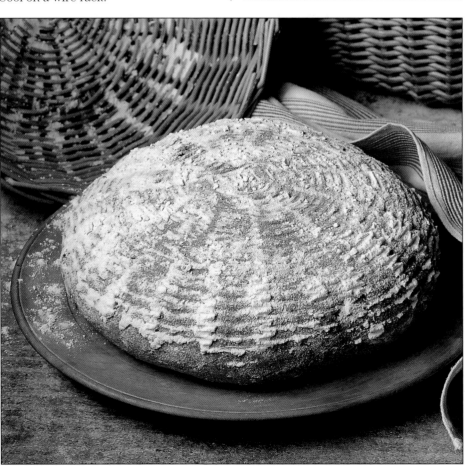

STOLLEN

This German specialty bread, made for the Christmas season, is rich with rum-soaked fruits and is wrapped around a moist almond filling. The folded shape of the dough over the filling represents the baby Jesus wrapped in swaddling clothes.

1/2 cup golden raisins
1/4 cup currants
3 tablespoons rum
3 1/4 cups white flour
1/2 teaspoon salt
1/4 cup sugar
1/4 teaspoon ground cardamom
1/2 teaspoon ground cinnamon
1 1/2 ounces fresh yeast
1/2 cup lukewarm milk
1/4 cup butter, melted
1 egg, lightly beaten
1/3 cup mixed chopped peel
1/3 cup blanched whole
almonds, chopped
melted butter, for brushing
confectioners' sugar, for dusting

FOR THE ALMOND FILLING
1 cup ground almonds
1/4 cup sugar
1/2 cup confectioners' sugar
1/2 teaspoon fresh lemon juice
1/2 egg, lightly beaten

MAKES 1 LARGE LOAF

COOK'S TIP
You can dust the cooled stollen with confectioners' sugar and cinnamon, or drizzle over a thin glacé icing.

3 In a small bowl, mix the yeast with the milk until creamy. Pour into the flour and mix a little of the flour from around the edge into the milk mixture to make a thick batter. Sprinkle some of the remaining flour on top of the batter, then cover with plastic wrap and let sit in a warm place for 30 minutes.

4 Add the melted butter and egg and mix into a soft dough. Turn out the dough onto a lightly floured surface and knead for 8–10 minutes, until smooth and elastic. Place in a lightly oiled bowl, cover with lightly oiled plastic wrap and let rise, in a warm place, for 2–3 hours or until doubled in bulk.

1 Lightly grease a baking sheet. Preheat the oven to 350°F. Put the golden raisins and currants in a heatproof bowl and warm for 3–4 minutes. Pour in the rum and set aside.

2 Sift the flour and salt together into a large bowl. Stir in the sugar and spices.

5 Combine the ground almonds and sugars for the filling. Add the lemon juice and enough egg to knead to a smooth paste. Shape into an 8-inch long sausage, cover and set aside.

6 Turn out the dough onto a lightly floured surface and punch down.

7 Pat out the dough into a rectangle about 1 inch thick and sprinkle on the golden raisins, currants, mixed chopped peel and almonds. Fold and knead the dough to incorporate the fruit and nuts.

8 Roll out the dough into an oval about 12 × 9 inches. Roll the center slightly thinner than the edges. Place the almond paste filling along the center and fold over the dough to enclose it, making sure that the top of the dough doesn't completely cover the base. The top edge should be slightly in from the bottom edge. Press down to seal.

9 Place the loaf on the prepared baking sheet, cover with lightly oiled plastic wrap and let rise, in a warm place, for 45–60 minutes or until doubled in size.

10 Meanwhile, preheat the oven to 400°F. Bake the loaf for about 30 minutes or until it sounds hollow when tapped on the bottom. Brush the top with melted butter and transfer to a wire rack to cool. Dust with confectioners' sugar just before serving.

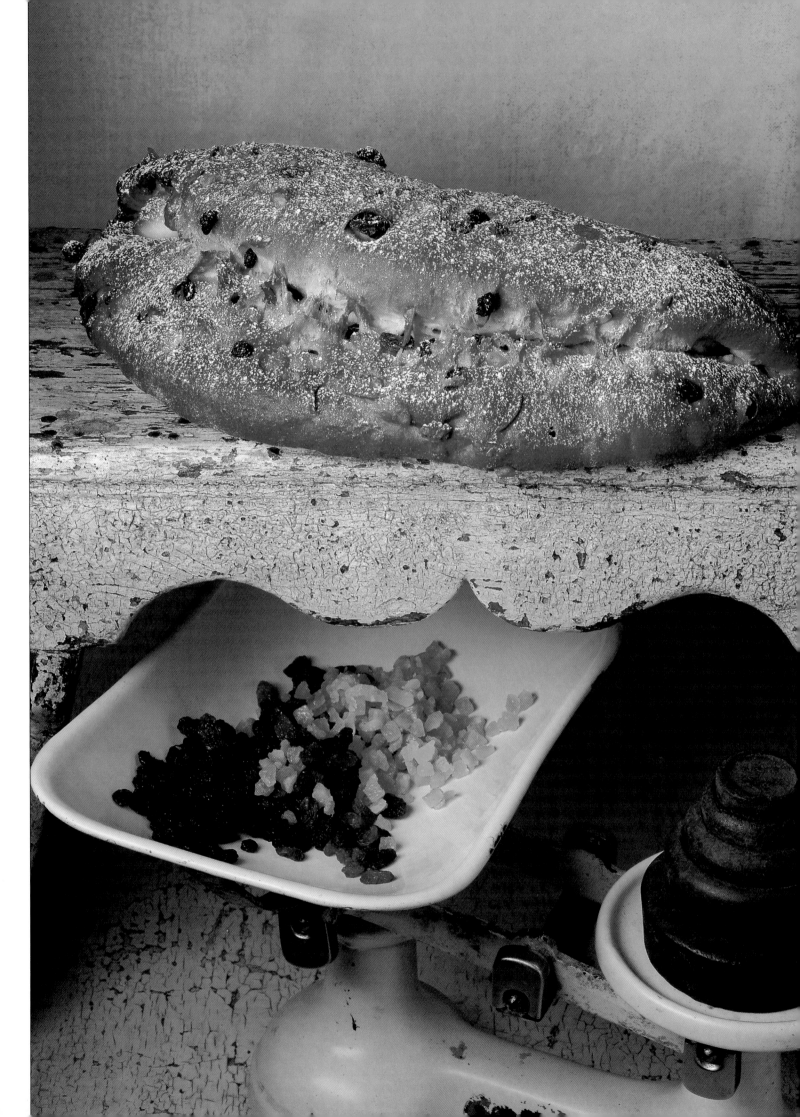

BUCHTY

*Popular in both Poland and Germany as breakfast treats, these are also
excellent split and toasted, and served with cured meats.*

4 cups white flour
1 teaspoon salt
¼ cup sugar
scant ½ cup butter
½ cup milk
¾ ounce fresh yeast
3 eggs, lightly beaten
3 tablespoons butter, melted
confectioners' sugar, for dusting
(optional)

MAKES 16 ROLLS

COOK'S TIP
If you do not have a square pan use a
round one. Place 2 rolls in the center
and the rest around the edge.

1 Grease an 8-inch square pan, (preferably
with a removable bottom). Sift the flour
and salt together into a large bowl and stir
in the sugar. Make a well in the center.

2 Melt ¼ cup of the butter in a small
pan, then remove from the heat and stir
in the milk. Let cool until lukewarm. Stir
the yeast into the milk mixture until it
has dissolved.

3 Pour into the center of the flour and
stir in enough flour to form a thick
batter. Sprinkle with a little of the
surrounding flour, cover and let sit in a
warm place for 30 minutes.

4 Gradually beat in the eggs and
remaining flour to form a soft, smooth
dough. This will take about 10 minutes.
Cover with lightly oiled plastic wrap
and let rise, in a warm place, for about
1½ hours or until doubled in bulk.

5 Turn out the dough onto a lightly
floured surface and punch down. Divide
into 16 equal pieces and shape into
rounds. Melt the remaining butter, roll
the rounds in it to coat, then place,
slightly apart, in the pan. Cover with lightly
oiled plastic wrap and let rise, in a warm
place, for about 1 hour or until doubled.

6 Meanwhile, preheat the oven to
375°F. Spoon any remaining melted
butter evenly over the rolls and bake
for 25 minutes or until golden brown.
Turn out onto a wire rack to cool. If
serving buchty as a breakfast bread,
dust the loaf with confectioners' sugar
before separating it into rolls.

POLISH RYE BREAD

This rye bread is made with half white flour, which gives it a lighter, more open texture than a traditional rye loaf. Served thinly sliced, it is the perfect accompaniment for cold meats and fish.

*2 cups rye flour
2 cups white flour
2 teaspoons caraway seeds
2 teaspoons salt
¾ ounce fresh yeast
scant ⅔ cup lukewarm milk
1 teaspoon honey
scant ⅔ cup lukewarm water
whole-wheat flour, for dusting*

MAKES 1 LOAF

1 Lightly grease a baking sheet. Mix the flours, caraway seeds and salt in a large bowl and make a well in the center.

2 In a small bowl or measuring cup, mix the yeast with the milk and honey. Pour into the center of the flour, add the water and gradually incorporate the surrounding flour and caraway mixture until a dough forms.

3 Turn out the dough onto a lightly floured surface and knead for 8–10 minutes, until smooth, elastic and firm. Place in a large, lightly oiled bowl, cover with lightly oiled plastic wrap and let rise, in a warm place, for about 3 hours or until doubled in bulk.

4 Turn out the dough onto a lightly floured surface and punch down. Shape into an oval loaf and place on the prepared baking sheet.

5 Dust with whole-wheat flour, cover with lightly oiled plastic wrap and let rise, in a warm place, for 1–1½ hours or until doubled in size. Meanwhile, preheat the oven to 425°F.

6 Using a sharp knife, slash the loaf with two long cuts about 1 inch apart. Bake for 30–35 minutes or until the loaf sounds hollow when tapped on the bottom. Transfer the loaf to a wire rack and set aside to cool.

HUNGARIAN SPLIT FARMHOUSE LOAF

A golden, fennel seed-encrusted loaf with a moist white crumb. It is equally delicious made into rolls — just reduce the baking time to 15–20 minutes.

4 cups white flour
2 teaspoon salt
½ teaspoon fennel seeds, crushed
1 tablespoon sugar
¾ ounce fresh yeast
1⅛ cups lukewarm water
2 tablespoons butter, melted

FOR THE TOPPING
1 egg white
pinch of salt
2 teaspoons fennel seeds, for sprinkling

MAKES 1 LOAF

1 Lightly grease a baking sheet. Sift the white flour and salt together into a large bowl and stir in the crushed fennel seeds and sugar. Make a well in the center.

2 In a small bowl, mix the yeast with a little water, stir in the rest, then pour into the center of the flour. Stir in enough flour to make a runny batter. Sprinkle more of the flour on top, cover and let sit in a warm place for 30 minutes or until the sponge starts to bubble and rise.

3 Add the melted butter and gradually mix in with the remaining flour to form a dough. Turn out onto a lightly floured surface and knead for 8–10 minutes, until smooth and elastic. Place in a lightly oiled bowl, cover with lightly oiled plastic wrap and let rise, in a warm place, for 45–60 minutes or until doubled in bulk.

4 Turn out onto a lightly floured surface and punch down. Shape into an oval and place on the prepared baking sheet. Cover with lightly oiled plastic wrap and let rise, in a warm place, for 30–40 minutes or until doubled in size.

5 Meanwhile, preheat the oven to 425°F. Combine the egg white and salt and brush this glaze over the loaf. Sprinkle with fennel seeds and then, using a sharp knife, slash along its length. Bake for 20 minutes, then reduce the oven temperature to 350°F and bake for 10 more minutes or until it sounds hollow when tapped on the bottom. Transfer to a wire rack to cool.

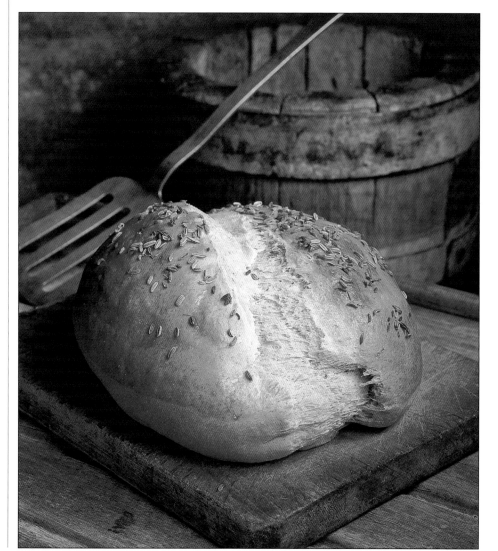

GEORGIAN KHACHAPURI

*These savory buns are sold from street stalls as warm snacks. The sealed
bread parcels envelop a meltingly delicious cheese filling;
goat cheese is typically used in Georgia.*

*2 cups white flour
1 teaspoon salt
½ ounce fresh yeast
⅔ cup lukewarm milk
2 tablespoons butter, softened*

*FOR THE FILLING
2 cups grated sharp cheddar cheese
8 ounces Munster or Taleggio cheese,
cut into small cubes
1 egg, lightly beaten
1 tablespoon butter, softened
salt and freshly ground black pepper*

*FOR THE GLAZE
1 egg yolk
1 tablespoon water*

MAKES 4 BUNS

3 Turn the dough out onto a lightly
floured surface and knead for
2–3 minutes. Divide into 4 equal pieces
and roll each out into a 8-inch circle.

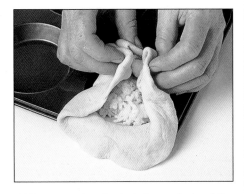

4 Place one dough circle in one hole of the
Yorkshire pudding (or popover) pan and
fill with a quarter of the cheese filling.
Gather the overhanging dough into the
center and twist to form a topknot. Repeat
with the remaining dough and filling.
Cover with lightly oiled plastic wrap and let
rise, in a warm place, for 20–30 minutes.

1 Lightly grease a Yorkshire pudding
(or popover) pan with four 4-inch holes.
Sift the flour and salt into a large bowl.
Mix the yeast with the milk, add to the
flour and mix into a dough. Knead in
the butter, then knead on a lightly
floured surface until smooth and elastic.
Place in a lightly oiled bowl, cover with
lightly oiled plastic wrap and let rise, in
a warm place, for 1–1½ hours or until
doubled in bulk.

2 Meanwhile, put the cheeses in a bowl
and stir in the egg and softened butter
for the filling. Season with plenty of salt
and pepper.

VARIATIONS
• Use Red Leicester or Parmesan
instead of the cheddar.
• Make one large bread instead of the
buns. Bake for 50–55 minutes.

5 Meanwhile, preheat the oven to 350°F.
Mix the egg yolk and water, and brush
over the dough. Bake for 25–30 minutes
or until light golden. Cool for 2–3 minutes
in the pan, then turn out onto a wire
rack. Serve warm.

POPPY SEED ROLL

A favorite sweet yeast bread in both Poland and Hungary, this has an unusual filling of poppy seeds, almonds, raisins and glacé fruit spiraling through the dough.

3 cups white flour
½ teaspoon salt
2 tablespoons sugar
¾ ounce fresh yeast
½ cup lukewarm milk
1 egg, lightly beaten
¼ cup butter, melted
1 tablespoon toasted sliced almonds

FOR THE FILLING
⅔ cup poppy seeds
¼ cup butter
6 tablespoons sugar
½ cup raisins
½ cup ground almonds
⅓ cup mixed chopped glacé fruit, finely chopped
½ teaspoon ground cinnamon

FOR THE ICING
1 cup confectioners' sugar
1 tablespoon fresh lemon juice
2–3 teaspoons water

MAKES 1 LARGE LOAF

1 Lightly grease a baking sheet. Sift the flour and salt together into a large bowl. Stir in the sugar. Mix the yeast with the milk. Add to the flour with the egg and melted butter and mix into a dough.

2 Turn out onto a lightly floured surface and knead for 8–10 minutes, until smooth and elastic. Place in a lightly oiled bowl, cover with lightly oiled plastic wrap and let rise, in a warm place, for 1–1½ hours or until doubled in size.

3 Meanwhile, pour boiling water over the poppy seeds for the filling, then let cool. Drain thoroughly in a fine sieve. Melt the butter in a small pan, add the poppy seeds and cook, stirring, for 1–2 minutes. Remove from the heat and stir in the sugar, raisins, ground almonds, glacé fruit and cinnamon. Set aside to cool.

4 Turn the dough out onto a lightly floured surface, punch down and knead lightly. Roll out into a rectangle 14 × 10 inches. Spread the filling to within ¾ inch of the edges.

5 Roll up the dough, starting from one long edge, like a Swiss roll, tucking in the edges to seal. Place seam side down on the prepared baking sheet. Cover with lightly oiled plastic wrap and let rise, in a warm place, for 30 minutes or until doubled in size.

6 Meanwhile, preheat the oven to 375°F. Bake for 30 minutes or until golden brown. Transfer to a wire rack to cool until just warm.

7 In a small saucepan, combine the confectioners' sugar, lemon juice and enough water to make an icing stiff enough to coat the back of a spoon. Heat gently, stirring, until warm. Drizzle the icing on the loaf and sprinkle the sliced almonds on. Let cool completely, then serve sliced.

RUSSIAN POTATO BREAD

*In Russia, potatoes are often used to replace some of the flour in bread
recipes. They endow the bread with excellent keeping qualities.*

8 ounces potatoes, peeled
and diced
¼ ounce envelope easy-blend
dried yeast
3 cups white flour
1 cup whole-wheat flour,
plus extra for sprinkling
½ teaspoon caraway
seeds, crushed
2 teaspoons salt
2 tablespoons butter

MAKES 1 LOAF

1 Lightly grease a baking sheet. Add the
potatoes to a saucepan of boiling water
and cook until tender. Drain and reserve
⅔ cup of the cooking water. Mash and
sieve the potatoes and let cool.

2 Combine the yeast, flours, caraway
seeds and salt in a large bowl. Add the
butter and rub in. Combine the reserved
potato water and sieved potatoes.
Gradually work this mixture into the
flour mixture to form a soft dough.

3 Turn out onto a lightly floured surface
and knead for 8–10 minutes until smooth
and elastic. Place in a lightly oiled bowl,
cover with lightly oiled plastic wrap and
let rise, in a warm place, for 1 hour or
until doubled in bulk.

4 Turn out onto a lightly floured surface,
punch down and knead gently. Shape
into a plump oval loaf, about 7 inches
long. Place on the prepared baking
sheet and sprinkle with a little whole-
wheat flour.

5 Cover the dough with lightly
oiled plastic wrap and let rise, in a
warm place, for 30 minutes or until
doubled in size. Meanwhile, preheat
the oven to 400°F.

6 Using a sharp knife, slash the top with
3–4 diagonal cuts to make a criss-cross
effect. Bake for 30–35 minutes or until
golden and sounding hollow when
tapped on the bottom. Transfer to a wire
rack to cool.

VARIATION
To make a cheese-flavored
potato bread, omit the caraway
seeds and knead 1 cup grated
cheddar, Red Leicester or a crumbled
blue cheese, such as Stilton, into
the dough before shaping.

6 cups white flour
2 teaspoons salt
1 ounce fresh yeast
½ cup lukewarm milk
1 teaspoon honey
2 eggs
⅔ cup plain yogurt
¼ cup butter, melted
beaten egg, for glazing
poppy seeds, for sprinkling

MAKES 1 LARGE LOAF

VARIATION
For a special finish, divide the dough
into 3 equal pieces, roll into long thin
strips and braid together, starting with
the center of the strips. Once braided,
shape into a circle and seal the ends
together. Make sure that the hole in
the center is quite large, otherwise the
hole will fill in as the bread rises.

KOLACH

*Often prepared for religious celebrations and family feasts, this Bulgarian
bread gets its name from its circular shape—kolo, which means circle. It has a
golden crust sprinkled with poppy seeds and a moist crumb, which makes
this loaf a very good keeper.*

1 Grease a large baking sheet. Sift the
flour and salt together into a large bowl
and make a well in the center.

2 In a small bowl, mix the yeast with the
milk and honey. Add to the center of the
flour with the eggs, yogurt and melted
butter. Gradually mix into the flour to
form a firm dough.

3 Turn out onto a lightly floured surface
and knead for 8–10 minutes, until
smooth and elastic. Place in a lightly
oiled bowl, cover with lightly oiled plastic
wrap or slip into an oiled plastic bag. let
rise, in a warm place, for 1½ hours or
until doubled in bulk.

4 Punch down the dough and turn out
onto a lightly floured surface. Knead
lightly and shape into a ball. Place seam
side down and make a hole in the center
with your fingers.

5 Gradually enlarge the cavity, turning
the dough to make a 10-inch circle.
Transfer to the baking sheet, cover with
lightly oiled plastic wrap and let rise, in
a warm place, for 30–45 minutes or
until doubled in size.

6 Meanwhile, preheat the oven to
400°F. Brush the loaf with beaten egg
and sprinkle with poppy seeds. Bake
for 35 minutes or until golden. Cool on a
wire rack.

BLINIS

*Blinis are the celebrated leavened Russian pancakes. Traditionally served
with sour cream and caviar, they have a very distinctive flavor and a fluffy,
light texture.*

½ cup buckwheat flour
½ cup all-purpose flour
*½ teaspoon freshly ground
black pepper*
1 teaspoon salt
½ ounce fresh yeast
scant 1 cup lukewarm milk
1 egg, separated

MAKES ABOUT 10 BLINIS

VARIATION
You can use all buckwheat flour,
which will give the blinis a
stronger flavor.

1 Combine the buckwheat flour, plain
flour, pepper and salt in a large bowl.

2 In a small bowl, mix the yeast with
4 tablespoons of the milk, then mix in
the remaining milk.

3 Add the egg yolk to the flour mixture
and gradually whisk in the yeast mixture
to form a smooth batter. Cover with
plastic wrap and let stand in a warm
place for 1 hour.

4 Whisk the egg white until it forms soft
peaks and fold into the batter. Lightly oil
a heavy frying pan and heat it.

5 Add about 3 tablespoons of the batter
to make a 4-inch round pancake. Cook
until the surface begins to dry out, then
turn the pancake over using a spatula
and cook for 1–2 minutes. Repeat with
the remaining batter. Serve warm.

SUNSHINE LOAF

*Scandinavia, Land of the Midnight Sun, has numerous breads based on rye.
This splendid table centerpiece is made with a blend of rye and white flours,
the latter helping to lighten the bread.*

FOR THE STARTER
4 tablespoons lukewarm milk
4 tablespoons lukewarm water
1/4 ounce fresh yeast
scant 1 cup white flour

FOR THE DOUGH
1/2 ounce fresh yeast
generous 2 cups lukewarm water
4 cups rye flour
2 cups white flour
1 tablespoon salt
milk, for glazing
caraway seeds, for sprinkling

MAKES 1 LARGE LOAF

VARIATION
This bread can be shaped into one
large round or oval loaf, if preferred.

1 Combine the milk and water for the
starter in a large bowl. Mix in the yeast
until dissolved. Gradually add the bread
flour, stirring it with a metal spoon.

2 Cover the bowl with plastic wrap and
let the mixture sit in a warm place for
3–4 hours or until well risen, bubbly and
starting to collapse.

3 Mix the yeast for the dough with
4 tablespoons of the water until creamy,
then stir in the remaining water.
Gradually mix into the starter to dilute
it, and then add the rye flour to form a
smooth batter. Cover with lightly oiled
plastic wrap and let sit in a warm place,
for 3–4 hours or until well risen.

4 Stir the bread flour and salt into the
batter to form a dough. Turn onto a
lightly floured surface and knead for
5 minutes, until smooth and elastic.
Place in a lightly oiled bowl, cover with
lightly oiled plastic wrap and let rise, in
a warm place, for about 1 hour or until
doubled in bulk.

5 Punch down on a lightly floured
surface. Cut the dough into 5 equal
pieces. Roll one piece into a 20-inch
"sausage" and roll up into a spiral shape.

6 Cut the remaining pieces of dough in
half and shape each one into an 8-inch
rope. Place in a circle on a large baking
sheet, spaced equally apart, like rays of
the sun, and curl the ends around,
leaving a small gap in the center. Place
the spiral shape on top. Cover with
lightly oiled plastic wrap and let rise, in
a warm place, for 30 minutes.

7 Meanwhile, preheat the oven to 450°F.
Brush the bread with milk, sprinkle with
caraway seeds and bake for 30 minutes
or until lightly browned. Transfer to a
wire rack to cool.

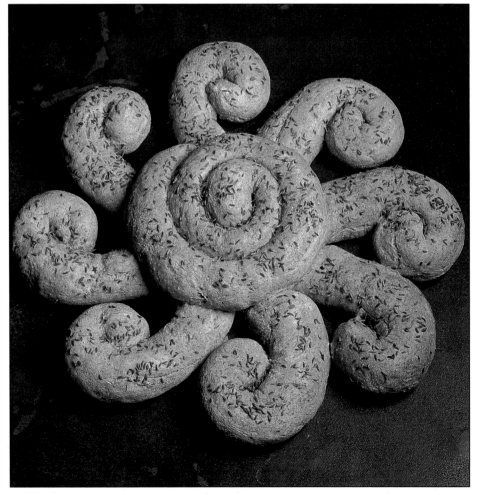

SAVORY DANISH CROWN

Filled with golden onions and cheese, this butter-rich bread ring is quite irresistible and needs no accompaniment.

1 Lightly grease a baking sheet. Sift the flour and salt together into a large bowl. Rub in 3 tablespoons of the butter. In a small bowl, mix the yeast with the milk and water. Add to the flour with the egg and mix into a soft dough.

2 Turn out onto a lightly floured surface and knead for 10 minutes, until smooth and elastic. Place in a lightly oiled bowl, cover with lightly oiled plastic wrap or slide into an oiled plastic bag and let rise, in a warm place, for about 1 hour or until doubled in bulk.

3 Punch down and turn out onto a lightly floured surface. Roll out into an oblong about ½-inch thick.

4 Dot half the remaining butter over the top two-thirds of the dough. Fold the bottom third up and the top third down and seal the edges. Turn by 90 degrees and repeat with the remaining butter. Fold and seal as before. Cover the dough with lightly oiled plastic wrap and let rest for about 15 minutes.

5 Turn by another 90 degrees. Roll and fold again without any butter. Repeat once more. Wrap in lightly oiled plastic wrap and let rest in the refrigerator for 30 minutes.

6 Meanwhile, heat the oil for the filling. Add the onions and cook for 10 minutes until soft and golden. Remove from the heat and stir in the bread crumbs, almonds, Parmesan, salt and pepper.

7 Add half the beaten egg to the bread crumb mixture and bind together.

8 Roll out the dough on a lightly floured surface into a rectangle measuring 22 × 9 inches. Spread with the filling to within ¾ inch of the edges, then roll up like a Swiss roll from one long side. Using a very sharp knife, cut in half lengthwise. Braid together with the cut sides up and shape into a ring. Place on the prepared baking sheet, cover with lightly oiled plastic wrap and let rise, in a warm place, for 30 minutes.

9 Meanwhile, preheat the oven to 400°F. Brush the remaining beaten egg over the dough. Sprinkle with sesame seeds and Parmesan cheese and bake for 40–50 minutes or until golden. Transfer to a wire rack to cool slightly if serving warm, or cool completely to serve cold, cut into slices.

3 cups white flour
1 teaspoon salt
generous ¾ cup butter, softened
¾ ounce fresh yeast
scant 1 cup mixed lukewarm milk and water
1 egg, lightly beaten

FOR THE FILLING
2 tablespoons sunflower oil
2 onions, finely chopped
¾ cup fresh bread crumbs
¼ cup ground almonds
½ cup freshly grated Parmesan cheese
1 egg, lightly beaten
salt and freshly ground black pepper

FOR THE TOPPING
1 tablespoon sesame seeds
1 tablespoon freshly grated Parmesan cheese

MAKES 1 LARGE LOAF

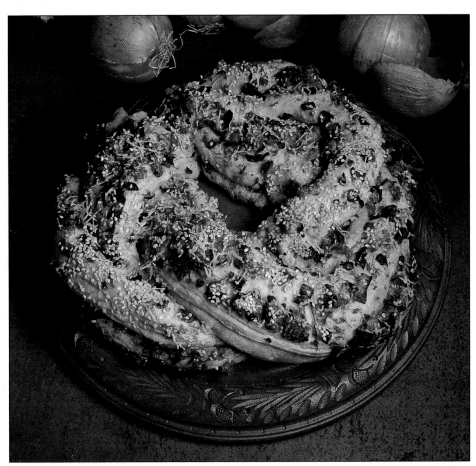

1 ounce fresh yeast
5 tablespoons lukewarm milk
4 cups white flour
2 teaspoons salt
6 tablespoons butter
15 whole cardamom pods
½ teaspoon vanilla extract
⅓ cup light brown sugar
grated zest of ½ lemon
2 eggs, lightly beaten
¼ cup dried apricots, chopped
¼ cup candied pineapple, chopped
*¼ cup red and green candied
cherries, chopped*
*3 tablespoons pitted,
dried dates, chopped*
*2 tablespoons crystallized
ginger, chopped*

FOR THE GLAZE
1 egg white
2 teaspoons water

FOR THE DECORATION
1 tablespoon sugar
½ teaspoon ground cinnamon
*8 pecans or whole
blanched almonds*

MAKES 1 LOAF

VARIATIONS
• You can vary the fruits for this loaf.
Try candied peaches, yellow candied
cherries, golden raisins, raisins,
candied angelica, dried mango or
dried pears and use in place of some
or all of the fruits in the recipe. Use a
mixture of colors and make sure that
the total weight is the same as above.
• Use walnuts instead of the pecans
or almonds.

DANISH JULEKAGE

*In Scandinavia special slightly sweet holiday breads containing fragrant
cardamom seeds are common. This exotic bread, enriched with butter and a
selection of candied and dried fruits or "jewels", is traditionally served over
the Christmas period with hot spiced punch.*

1 Lightly grease a 9 × 5-inch loaf pan.
In a small bowl, mix the yeast with
the milk.

2 Sift the flour and salt together into a
large bowl. Add the butter and rub in.
Make a well in the center. Add the yeast
mixture to the center of the flour and
butter mixture and stir in enough flour
to form a thick batter. Sprinkle on a
little of the remaining flour and set aside
in a warm place for 15 minutes.

3 Remove the seeds from the cardamom
pods. Put them in a mortar or strong
bowl and crush with a pestle or the end
of a rolling pin. Add the crushed seeds
to the flour with the vanilla extract,
sugar, lemon rind and eggs, then mix
into a soft dough.

4 Turn out onto a lightly floured surface
and knead for 8–10 minutes, until
smooth and elastic. Place in a lightly
oiled bowl, cover with lightly oiled plastic
wrap and let rise, in a warm place, for
1–1½ hours or until doubled in bulk.

5 Punch down the dough and turn it out
on to a lightly floured surface. Flatten
into a rectangle and sprinkle on half of
the apricots, pineapple, cherries, dates
and ginger. Fold the sides into the
center and then fold in half to contain
the fruit. Flatten into a rectangle again
and sprinkle on the remaining fruit. Fold
and knead gently to distribute the fruit.
Cover the fruited dough with lightly
oiled plastic wrap and let rest for 10
minutes.

6 Roll the fruited dough into a rectangle
15 × 10 inches. With a short side
facing you, fold the bottom third up
lengthwise and the top third down,
tucking in the sides, to form a 9 × 5-inch
loaf. Place in the prepared pan, seam
side down. Cover with lightly oiled
plastic wrap and let rise, in a warm
place, for 1 hour or until the dough has
reached the top of the pan.

7 Meanwhile, preheat the oven to 350°F.
Using a sharp knife, slash the top of the
loaf lengthwise and then make diagonal
slits on either side.

8 Combine the egg white and water for
the glaze, and brush on top. Mix the
sugar and cinnamon in a bowl, then
sprinkle on top. Decorate with pecans or
almonds. Bake for 45–50 minutes or
until risen and browned. Transfer to a
wire rack to cool.

COOK'S TIP
Keep a close watch on the bread,
especially during the final 15 minutes
of cooking. If the top of the loaf starts
to brown too quickly, cover loosely
with foil.

4 cups rye flour
1 teaspoon salt
¼ cup butter
¾ ounce fresh yeast
generous 1 cup lukewarm water
2 cups wheat bran

MAKES 8 CRISPBREADS

COOK'S TIP
The hole in the center of these
crispbreads is a reminder of the days
when breads were strung on a pole,
which was hung across the rafters to
dry. Make smaller crispbreads, if
desired, and tie them together with
bright red ribbon for an unusual
Christmas gift.

KNÄCKERBRÖD

A very traditional Swedish crispbread with a lovely rye flavor.

1 Lightly grease 2 baking sheets.
Preheat the oven to 450°F. Mix the rye
flour and salt in a large bowl. Rub in the
butter, then make a well in the center.

2 In a small bowl, mix the yeast with a
little water, then stir in the remainder.
Pour into the center of the flour, mix
into a dough, then mix in the bran.
Knead on a lightly floured surface for
5 minutes, until smooth and elastic.

3 Divide the dough into 8 equal pieces
and roll each one out on a lightly floured
surface to an 8-inch round.

4 Place 2 rounds on the prepared baking
sheets and prick all over with a fork. Cut
a hole in the center of each round, using
a 1½-inch cutter.

5 Bake for 15–20 minutes or until the
crispbreads are golden and crisp.
Transfer to a wire rack to cool. Repeat
with the remaining crispbreads.

FINNISH BARLEY BREAD

*In Northern Europe breads are often made using cereals such as barley and
rye, which produce very satisfying, tasty breads. This quick-to-prepare flat
bread is best served warm with butter.*

2 cups barley flour
1 teaspoon salt
2 teaspoons baking powder
2 tablespoons butter, melted
½ cup light cream
4 tablespoons milk

MAKES 1 SMALL LOAF

1 Lightly grease a baking sheet. Preheat
the oven to 400°F. Sift the dry
ingredients into a bowl. Add the butter,
cream and milk. Mix into a dough.

2 Turn out the dough onto a lightly
floured surface and shape into a flat
round about ½-inch thick.

3 Transfer to the prepared baking sheet
and, using a sharp knife, lightly mark
the top into 6 sections.

4 Prick the surface of the round evenly
with a fork. Bake for 15–18 minutes or
until pale golden. Cut into wedges and
serve warm.

COOK'S TIPS
• This flat bread tastes very good
with cottage cheese, especially
cottage cheese with chives.
• For a citrusy tang, add
2–3 teaspoons finely grated lemon,
lime or orange zest to the flour
mixture in step 1.

LUSSE BRÖD

½ cup milk
pinch of saffron threads
3½ cups white flour
½ cup ground almonds
½ teaspoon salt
6 tablespoons sugar
1 ounce fresh yeast
½ cup lukewarm water
few drops of almond extract
¼ cup butter, softened

FOR THE GLAZE
1 egg
1 tablespoon water

MAKES 12 BUNS

VARIATION
Gently knead in 3 tablespoons
currants after punching down the
dough in step 4.

Saint Lucia Day, December 13th, marks the beginning of Christmas in Sweden. As part of the celebrations, girls dressed in white robes wear crowns of lighted candles and walk through the village streets offering these saffron buns to the townspeople.

1 Lightly grease 2 baking sheets. Place the milk in a small saucepan and bring to a boil. Add the saffron, remove from the heat and let infuse for about 15 minutes. Meanwhile combine the flour, ground almonds, salt and sugar in a large bowl.

2 In a small bowl, mix the yeast with the water. Add the saffron liquid, yeast mixture and almond extract to the flour mixture and mix into a dough. Gradually beat in the softened butter.

3 Turn out onto a lightly floured surface and knead for 5 minutes, until smooth and elastic. Place in a lightly oiled bowl, cover with lightly oiled plastic wrap and let rise, in a warm place, for about 1 hour or until doubled in bulk.

4 Turn out onto a lightly floured surface and punch down. Divide into 12 equal pieces and make into different shapes: roll into a long rope and shape into an "S" shape; to make a star, cut a dough piece in half and roll into two ropes, cross one over the other and coil the ends; make an upturned "U" shape and coil the ends to represent curled hair; divide a dough piece in half, roll into two thin ropes and twist together.

5 Place on the prepared baking sheets, spaced well apart, cover with lightly oiled plastic wrap and let rise, in a warm place, for about 30 minutes.

6 Meanwhile, preheat the oven to 400°F. Beat the egg with the water for the glaze, and brush onto the rolls. Bake for 15 minutes or until golden. Transfer to a wire rack to cool slightly to serve warm, or cool completely to serve cold.

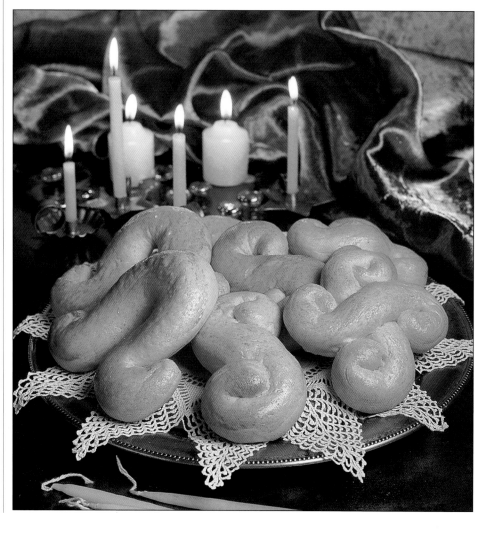

VÖRT LIMPA

*This festive Swedish bread is flavored with warm spices and fresh orange.
The beer and port work nicely to soften the rye taste. The added sugars also
give the yeast a little extra to feed on and help aerate and lighten the bread.
It is traditionally served with cheese.*

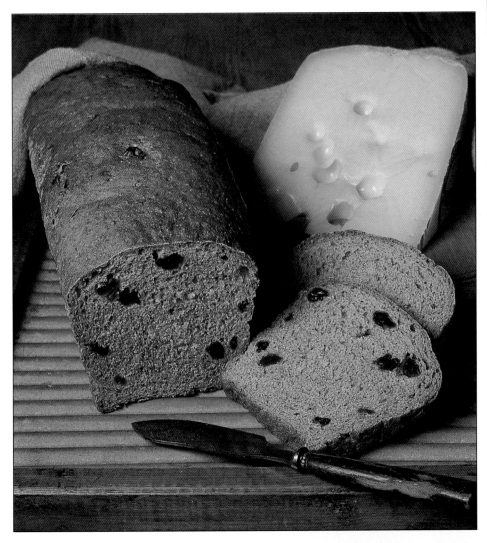

3 cups rye flour
3 cups white flour
½ teaspoon salt
2 tablespoons sugar
1 teaspoon grated nutmeg
1 teaspoon ground cloves
1 teaspoon ground ginger
1½ ounces fresh yeast
1¼ cups light ale
½ cup port
1 tablespoon molasses
2 tablespoons butter, melted
1 tablespoon grated orange zest
½ cup raisins
1 tablespoon malt extract, for glazing

MAKES 1 LARGE LOAF

VARIATION
This bread can be shaped into a
round or oval and baked on a baking
sheet, if preferred.

5 Turn out the dough onto a lightly
floured surface and punch down. Gently
knead in the orange zest and raisins.
Roll into a 12-inch square.

6 Fold the bottom third of the dough
up and the top third down, sealing the
edges. Place in the prepared pan, cover
with lightly oiled plastic wrap and let rise,
in a warm place, for 1 hour or until the
dough reaches the top of the pan.

7 Meanwhile, preheat the oven to
375°F. Bake for 35–40 minutes or
until browned. Turn out onto a wire
rack, brush with malt extract and
let cool.

1 Lightly grease a 12 × 4-inch loaf pan.
Combine the rye and white flours, salt,
sugar, nutmeg, cloves and ginger in a
large bowl.

2 In another large bowl, using a wooden
spoon, blend the yeast into the ale until
dissolved, then stir in the port, molasses
and melted butter.

3 Gradually add the flour mixture to the
yeast liquid, beating to make a smooth
batter. Continue adding the flour a little
at a time and mixing until the mixture
forms a soft dough.

4 Turn out onto a lightly floured surface
and knead for 8–10 minutes, until smooth
and elastic. Place in a lightly oiled bowl,
cover with lightly oiled plastic wrap and
let rise, in a warm place, for 1 hour or
until doubled in size.

BREADS OF THE AMERICAS

Yeast breads, quick breads based on baking powder, Mexican flat breads and sweet breads are all part of the diverse range found in the Americas. Traditional American ingredients such as cornmeal, molasses, corn and pumpkin provide the distinctive flavors associated with Boston brown bread, Anadama bread, corn bread, Virginia spoon bread and pumpkin and walnut bread. Universally popular breads include Jewish challah, which is traditionally baked to celebrate religious holidays, and the ubiquitous bagel.

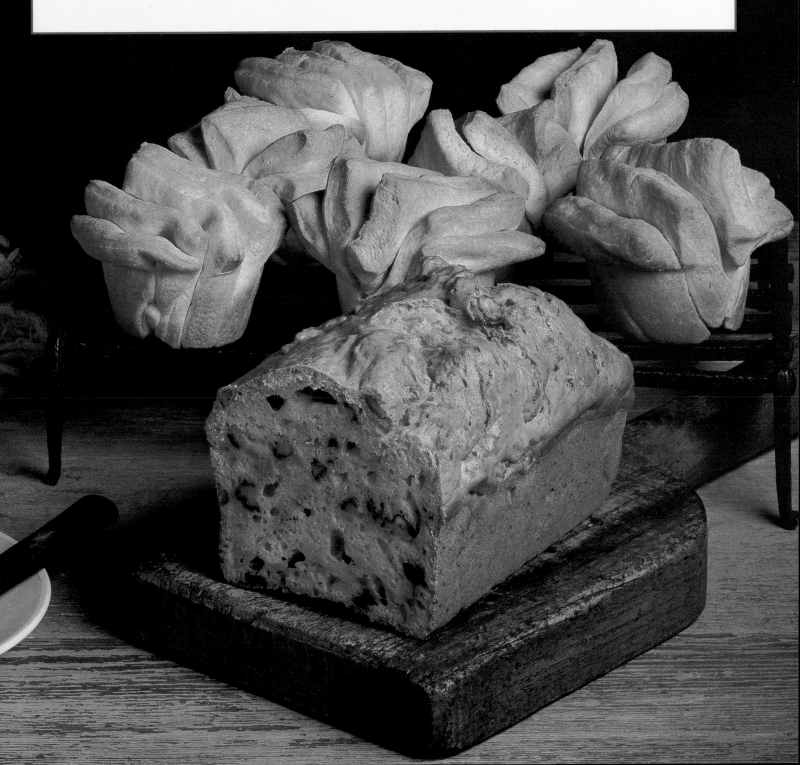

SAN FRANCISCO SOURDOUGH BREAD

In San Francisco this bread is leavened using a flour and water paste, which is left to ferment with the aid of airborn yeast. The finished loaves have a moist crumb and crispy crust, and will keep for several days.

FOR THE STARTER
1/2 cup whole-wheat flour
pinch of ground cumin
1 tablespoon milk
1–2 tablespoons water
1ST REFRESHMENT
2 tablespoons water
1 cup whole-wheat flour
2ND REFRESHMENT
4 tablespoons water
1 cup white flour

FOR THE BREAD
1ST REFRESHMENT
5 tablespoons very warm water
3/4 cup all-purpose flour
2ND REFRESHMENT
3/4 cup lukewarm water
1³/4–2 cups all-purpose flour

FOR THE SOURDOUGH
1¹/4 cups warm water
5 cups white flour
1 tablespoon salt
flour, for dusting
ice cubes, for baking

MAKES 2 ROUND LOAVES

1 Sift the flour and cumin for the starter into a bowl. Add the milk and enough water to make a firm but moist dough. Knead for 6–8 minutes to form a firm dough. Return the dough to the bowl, cover with a damp dish towel and let sit in a warm place, 75–80°F, for about 2 days. When it is ready the starter will appear moist and wrinkled and will have developed a crust.

2 Pull off the hardened crust and discard. Scoop out the moist center (about the size of a hazelnut), which will be aerated and sweet smelling, and place in a clean bowl. Mix in the water for the 1st refreshment. Gradually add the whole-wheat flour and mix into a dough.

3 Cover with plastic wrap and set in a warm place for 1–2 days. Discard the crust and gradually mix in the water for the 2nd refreshment to the starter, which by now will have a slightly sharper smell. Mix in the white flour, cover and let sit in a warm place for 8–10 hours.

4 For the bread, mix the sourdough starter with the water for the 1st refreshment. Gradually mix in the flour to form a firm dough. Knead for 6–8 minutes, until firm. Cover with a damp dish towel and let sit in a warm place for 8–12 hours or until doubled in bulk.

5 Gradually mix in the water for the 2nd refreshment, then add enough flour to form a soft, smooth elastic dough. Re-cover and let sit in a warm place for 8–12 hours. Gradually stir in the water for the sourdough, then work in the flour and salt. This will take 10–15 minutes. Turn out onto a lightly floured surface and knead until smooth and very elastic. Place in a large lightly oiled bowl, cover with lightly oiled plastic wrap and let rise, in a warm place, for 8–12 hours.

6 Divide the dough in half and shape into 2 round loaves by folding the sides over to the center and sealing.

7 Place seam side up in flour-dusted *couronnes*, bowls or baskets lined with flour-dusted dish towels. Re-cover and let rise in a warm place for 4 hours.

8 Preheat the oven to 425°F. Place an empty roasting pan in the bottom of the oven. Dust 2 baking sheets with flour. Turn out the loaves seam side down on the prepared baking sheets. Using a sharp knife, cut a criss-cross pattern by slashing the top of the loaves 4–5 times in each direction.

9 Place the baking sheets in the oven and immediately drop the ice cubes into the hot roasting pan to create steam. Bake the bread for 25 minutes, then reduce the oven temperature to 400°F and bake for another 15–20 minutes or until it sounds hollow when tapped on the bottom. Transfer to wire racks to cool.

COOK'S TIP
If you want to make sourdough bread regularly, keep a small amount of the starter covered in the refrigerator. It will keep for several days. Use the starter for the 2nd refreshment, then continue as directed.

MONKEY BREAD

This American favorite is also called bubble bread—because of the "bubbles" of dough. The pieces of dough are tossed in a heavenly coating of butter, nuts, cinnamon and rum-soaked fruit.

1/4 ounce envelope easy-blend dried yeast
4 cups white flour
1/2 teaspoon salt
1 tablespoon sugar
1/2 cup lukewarm milk
1/2 cup lukewarm water
1 egg, lightly beaten

FOR THE COATING
1/2 cup golden raisins
3 tablespoons rum or brandy
1 cup walnuts, finely chopped
2 teaspoons ground cinnamon
2/3 cup light brown sugar
1/4 cup butter, melted

MAKES 1 LOAF

1 Lightly grease a 9-inch springform cake pan. Combine the dried yeast, flour, salt and sugar in a large bowl and make a well in the center.

2 Add the milk, water and egg to the center of the flour and combine into a soft dough. Turn out onto a lightly floured surface and knead for about 10 minutes, until smooth and elastic. Place in a lightly oiled bowl, cover with lightly oiled plastic wrap and let rise, in a warm place, for 45–60 minutes or until doubled in bulk.

3 Place the golden raisins in a small saucepan, pour in the rum or brandy and heat for 1–2 minutes or until warm. Take care not to overheat. Remove from the heat and set aside. Mix the walnuts, cinnamon and sugar in a small bowl.

4 Turn out the dough onto a lightly floured surface and knead gently. Divide into 30 equal pieces and shape into small balls. Dip the balls, one at a time, into the melted butter, then roll them in the walnut mixture. Place half in the prepared pan, spaced slightly apart. Sprinkle on all the soaked raisins.

VARIATION
Replace the easy-blend dried yeast with 3/4 ounce fresh yeast. Mix with the liquid until creamy before adding to the flour.

5 Top with the remaining dough balls, dipping and coating as before. Sprinkle on any remaining walnut mixture and melted butter. Cover with lightly oiled plastic wrap or slide the pan into a lightly oiled large plastic bag and let rise, in a warm place, for about 45 minutes or until the dough reaches the top of the pan.

6 Meanwhile, preheat the oven to 375°F. Bake for 35–40 minutes or until well risen and golden. Turn out onto a wire rack to cool.

PUMPKIN AND WALNUT BREAD

Pumpkin, nutmeg and walnuts combine to yield a moist, tangy and slightly sweet bread with an indescribably good flavor. Serve partnered with meats or cheese, or simply lightly buttered.

1 Grease and neatly line a 8½ × 4½ inch loaf pan with parchment paper. Preheat the oven to 350°F.

2 Place the pumpkin in a saucepan, add water to cover by about 2 inches, then bring to a boil. Cover, lower the heat and simmer for 20 minutes, or until the pumpkin is very tender. Drain well, then purée in a food processor or blender. Let cool.

3 Place 1¼ cups of the purée in a large bowl. Add the sugar, nutmeg, melted butter and eggs to the purée and mix together. Sift the flour, baking powder and salt together into a large bowl and make a well in the center.

4 Add the pumpkin mixture to the center of the flour and stir until smooth. Mix in the walnuts.

1¼ pounds pumpkin, peeled, seeded and cut into chunks
6 tablespoons sugar
1 teaspoon grated nutmeg
¼ cup butter, melted
3 eggs, lightly beaten
3 cups white flour
2 teaspoons baking powder
½ teaspoon salt
¾ cup walnuts, chopped

MAKES 1 LOAF

COOK'S TIP
If fresh pumpkin is not in season, canned puréed pumpkin in the same quantity makes a fine substitute.

5 Transfer to the prepared pan and bake for 1 hour, or until golden and starting to shrink from the sides of the pan. Turn out on to a wire rack to cool.

scant 1 cup yellow cornmeal
scant 1 cup white flour or
whole-wheat flour
scant 1 cup rye flour
1/2 teaspoon salt
1 teaspoon baking soda
generous 1/2 cup raisins
1/2 cup milk
1/2 cup water
1/2 cup molasses

MAKES 1 OR 2 LOAVES

COOK'S TIP
If you do not have empty coffee cans,
or similar molds, cook the bread in
one or two heatproof bowls of
equivalent capacity.

1 Line the base of one 5-cup cylindrical
metal or glass container, with greased
waxed paper. Alternatively, remove the
lids from two 1-pound coffee cans, wash
and dry the cans thoroughly, then line
with greased waxed paper.

2 Combine the cornmeal, white or
whole-wheat flour, rye flour, salt, baking
soda and raisins in a large bowl. Warm
the milk and water in a small saucepan
and stir in the molasses.

3 Add the molasses mixture to the dry
ingredients and combine using a spoon
until it just forms a moist dough. Do not
overmix.

BOSTON BROWN BREAD

*Rich, moist and dark, this bread is flavored with molasses and can include
raisins. In Boston it is often served with savory baked beans.*

4 Fill the container or cans with the
dough; they should be about two-thirds
full. Cover neatly with foil or greased
waxed paper and tie securely.

5 Bring water to a depth of 2 inches
to a boil in a deep, heavy saucepan large
enough to accommodate the container
or cans. Place a trivet in the pan, stand
the container or cans on top, cover the
pan and steam for 1½ hours, adding
more boiling water to maintain the
required level as necessary.

6 Cool the loaves for a few minutes in
the container or cans, then turn them on
their sides and the loaves should slip
out. Serve warm, with savory dishes or
Boston baked beans.

ANADAMA BREAD

A traditional bread from Massachusetts, made with molasses, cornmeal, whole-wheat and white flour. According to legend, it was created by the husband of a woman called Anna, who had left a cornmeal mush and some molasses in the kitchen. On finding only these ingredients for supper, her husband mixed them with some flour, water and yeast to make this bread, while muttering "Anna, damn her!"

3 tablespoons butter
1/2 cup molasses
scant 2 1/2 cups water
1/2 cup cornmeal
2 teaspoons salt
1 ounce fresh yeast
2 tablespoons lukewarm water
2 1/2 cups whole-wheat flour
4 cups white flour

MAKES 2 LOAVES

1 Grease two 6-cup loaf pans. Heat the butter, molasses and measured water in a pan until the butter has melted. Add the cornmeal and salt and stir over low heat until boiling. Cool until lukewarm.

2 In a small bowl, mix the yeast with the lukewarm water, then set aside for 5 minutes.

3 Combine the cornmeal mixture and the yeast mixture in a large bowl. Fold in the whole-wheat flour and then the white flour to form a sticky dough. Turn out onto a lightly floured surface and knead for 10–15 minutes, until the dough is smooth and elastic. Add a little more flour if needed.

4 Place in a lightly oiled bowl, cover with lightly oiled plastic wrap and let rise, in a warm place, for about 1 hour or until doubled in bulk.

VARIATION

Use a 1/4 ounce envelope of easy-blend dried yeast instead of fresh. Mix it with the whole-wheat flour. Add to the cornmeal mixture, then add the lukewarm water, which would conventionally be blended with the fresh yeast.

5 Knead the dough lightly on a well floured surface, shape into 2 loaves and place in the prepared pans. Cover with lightly oiled plastic wrap and let rise, in a warm place, for 35–45 minutes or until doubled in size and the dough reaches the top of the pans.

6 Meanwhile, preheat the oven to 400°F. Using a sharp knife, slash the tops of the loaves 3–4 times. Bake for 15 minutes, then reduce the oven temperature to 350°F and bake for another 35–40 minutes or until it sounds hollow when tapped on the bottom. Turn out on to a wire rack to cool slightly. Serve warm.

CHALLAH

Challah is an egg-rich, light-textured bread baked for the Jewish Sabbath and to celebrate religious holidays. It is usually braided with 3 or 4 strands of dough, but 8 strands or more may be used to create especially festive loaves.

5 cups white flour
2 teaspoons salt
¾ ounce fresh yeast
scant 1 cup lukewarm water
2 tablespoons sugar
2 eggs
6 tablespoons butter or margarine, melted

FOR THE GLAZE
1 egg yolk
1 tablespoon water
2 teaspoons poppy seeds, for sprinkling

MAKES 1 LARGE LOAF

COOK'S TIP
If desired, divide the dough in half and make two small challahs, keeping the braids quite simple. Decorate with the poppy seeds or leave plain. Reduce the baking time by about 10 minutes.

1 Lightly grease a baking sheet. Sift the flour and salt together into a large bowl and make a well in the center. In a small bowl, mix the yeast with the water and sugar, add to the center of the flour with the eggs and melted butter or margarine and gradually mix in the surrounding flour to form a soft dough.

2 Turn out onto a lightly floured surface and knead for 10 minutes, until smooth and elastic. Place in a lightly oiled bowl, cover with lightly oiled plastic wrap and let rise, in a warm place, for 1 hour or until doubled in bulk.

3 Punch down, re-cover and let rise again in a warm place for about 1 hour. punch down, turn out onto a lightly floured surface and knead gently. Divide into 4 equal pieces. Roll each piece into a rope about 18 inches long. Line up next to each other. Pinch the ends together at one end.

4 Starting from the right, lift the first rope over the second and the third rope over the fourth. Take the fourth rope and place it between the first and second ropes. Repeat, starting from the right, and continue until braided.

5 Tuck the ends under and place the loaf on the prepared baking sheet. Cover with lightly oiled plastic wrap and let rise in a warm place, for about 30–45 minutes or until doubled in size. Meanwhile, preheat the oven to 400°F. Beat the egg yolk and water for the glaze together.

6 Brush the egg glaze gently over the loaf. Sprinkle evenly with the poppy seeds and bake for 35–40 minutes or until the challah is a deep golden brown. Transfer to a wire rack and let cool before slicing.

BAGELS

Bagels are eaten in many countries, and are very popular in the United States. They can be made from white, whole-wheat or rye flour and finished with a variety of toppings, including caraway, poppy or sesame seeds and onion.

3 cups white flour
2 teaspoons salt
1/4 ounce envelope easy-blend dried yeast
1 teaspoon malt extract
scant 1 cup lukewarm water

FOR POACHING
2 1/2 quarts water
1 tablespoon malt extract

FOR THE TOPPING
1 egg white
2 teaspoons cold water
2 tablespoons poppy, sesame or caraway seeds

MAKES 10 BAGELS

5 Meanwhile, preheat the oven to 425°F. Place the water and malt extract for poaching in a large saucepan, bring to a boil, then reduce to a simmer. Place the bagels in the water 2 or 3 at a time and poach for about 1 minute. They will sink and then rise again when first added to the pan. Using a large draining spoon, turn over and cook for 30 seconds. Remove and drain on a dish towel. Repeat with the remaining bagels.

1 Grease 2 baking sheets. Sift the flour and salt together into a large bowl. Stir in the dried yeast. Make a well in the center. Combine the malt extract and water, add to the center of the flour and mix into a dough. Knead on a floured surface until elastic.

2 Place in a lightly oiled bowl, cover with lightly oiled plastic wrap and let rise, in a warm place, for about 1 hour or until doubled in bulk.

3 Turn out onto a lightly floured surface and punch down. Knead for 1 minute, then divide into 10 equal pieces. Shape into balls, cover with plastic wrap and let rest for 5 minutes.

4 Gently flatten each ball and make a hole through the center with your thumb. Enlarge the hole slightly by turning your thumb around. Place on a floured tray; re-cover and let sit in a warm place, for 10–20 minutes or until they begin to rise.

6 Place five bagels on each prepared baking sheet, spacing them well apart. Beat the egg white with the water for the topping, brush the mixture on top of each bagel and sprinkle with poppy, sesame or caraway seeds. Bake for 20–25 minutes or until golden brown. Transfer to a wire rack to cool.

2 cups all-purpose flour
1 teaspoon salt
3/4 teaspoon baking powder
3 tablespoons lard or
solid vegetable shortening
2/3 cup warm water

MAKES 12 TORTILLAS

3/4 cup white flour
1 1/2 cups yellow cornmeal
1 teaspoon salt
1 1/2 tablespoons baking powder
1 tablespoon sugar
4 tablespoons butter, melted
1 cup milk
3 eggs
scant 1 1/4 cups canned corn, drained

MAKES 1 LARGE LOAF

WHEAT TORTILLAS

Tortillas are the staple flat bread in Mexico, where they are often made from masa harina, a flour milled from corn. These soft wheat tortillas are also popular in the southwestern part of the United States.

1 Mix the flour, salt and baking powder in a bowl. Rub in the fat, stir in the water and knead lightly until you have a soft dough. Cover with plastic wrap and let rest for 15 minutes. Divide into 12 equal pieces and shape into balls. Roll out on a lightly floured surface into 6–7-inch rounds. Re-cover to keep moist.

2 Heat a heavy frying pan or griddle, add one tortilla and cook for 1 1/2–2 minutes, turning over as soon as the surface starts to bubble. It should stay flexible. Remove from the pan and wrap in a dish towel to keep warm while cooking the remaining tortillas in the same way.

DOUBLE CORN BREAD

In the American South, corn bread is made with white cornmeal and is fairly flat, while in the North it is thicker and made with yellow cornmeal. Whatever the version, it's delicious—this recipe combines yellow cornmeal with sweet corn. It is great served warm, cut into wedges and buttered.

1 Preheat the oven to 400°F. Grease and line an 8 1/2-inch round cake pan with baking parchment. Sift the flour, cornmeal, salt and baking powder together into a large bowl. Stir in the sugar and make a well in the center.

2 Combine the melted butter, milk and eggs. Add to the center of the flour mixture and beat until just combined.

3 Using a wooden spoon, stir the corn quickly into the mixture. Pour into the prepared pan and bake for 20–25 minutes or until a metal skewer inserted into the center comes out clean.

4 Invert the bread onto a wire rack and lift off the lining paper. Cool slightly. Serve warm, cut into wedges.

VIRGINIA SPOON BREAD

1³/4 cups milk
²/3 cup cornmeal
1 tablespoon butter
³/4 cup grated sharp cheddar cheese
1 garlic clove
3 eggs, separated
¹/2 cup corn
kernels (optional)
salt and freshly ground black pepper

MAKES 1 LARGE LOAF

Spoon bread is a traditional dish from the southern United States which, according to legend, originated when too much water was added to a corn bread batter and the baked bread had to be spooned out of the pan. Served hot from the oven, this ethereally light offering—enhanced with cheddar cheese and a hint of garlic—is delicious.

VARIATIONS
Add 4 ounces fried chopped bacon or 1–2 teaspoons finely chopped green chili for different flavored spoon breads.

2 Place the milk in a large heavy saucepan. Heat gently, then gradually add the cornmeal, stirring. Add salt and slowly bring to a boil, stirring constantly. Cook for 5–10 minutes, stirring frequently, until thick and smooth.

3 Remove from the heat and stir in the butter, cheddar cheese, garlic and egg yolks. Season to taste.

1 Preheat the oven to 350°F. Grease a 6-cup soufflé dish.

4 In a bowl, whisk the egg whites until they form soft peaks. Stir one-quarter into the cornmeal mixture and then gently fold in the remainder. Fold in the well-drained corn, if using.

5 Spoon the mixture into the prepared soufflé dish and bake for 45–50 minutes or until puffed and beginning to brown. Serve immediately.

COOK'S TIPS
• Use a perfectly clean bowl and whisk for whisking the egg whites, and make sure it is free of grease by washing and drying thoroughly, then wiping out with a little lemon juice.
• If any shell drops in with the egg, scoop it out with another, larger piece of shell.

NEW ENGLAND FANTANS

These fantail rolls look stylish and are so versatile that they are equally suitable for a simple snack or a gourmet dinner party!

1/2 ounce fresh yeast
5 tablespoons buttermilk, at room temperature
2 teaspoons sugar
5 tablespoons milk
5 tablespoons butter
3 1/4 cups white flour
1 teaspoon salt
1 egg, lightly beaten

MAKES 9 ROLLS

1 Grease a muffin sheet with 3-inch cups or foil cases. Mix the yeast with the buttermilk and sugar and then let stand for 15 minutes.

2 In a saucepan, heat the milk with 3 tablespoons of the butter until the butter has melted. Cool until lukewarm.

3 Sift the flour and salt together into a large bowl. Add the yeast mixture, milk mixture and egg and mix into a soft dough. Turn out onto a lightly floured surface and knead for 5–8 minutes, until smooth and elastic. Place in a lightly oiled bowl, cover with lightly oiled plastic wrap and let rise, in a warm place, for about 1 hour, until doubled in size.

4 Turn out onto a lightly floured surface, punch down and knead until smooth and elastic. Roll into an oblong measuring 18 × 12 inches and about 1/4-inch thick. Melt the remaining butter, brush it over the dough and cut it lengthwise into 5 equal strips. Stack on top of each other and cut across into 9 equal 2-inch strips.

5 Pinch one side of each layered strip together, then place pinched side down into a prepared muffin cup or foil case. Cover with lightly oiled plastic wrap and let rise, in a warm place, for 30–40 minutes or until the fantans have almost doubled in size. Meanwhile, preheat the oven to 400°F. Bake for 20 minutes or until golden. Turn out onto a wire rack to cool.

VARIATION
To make cinnamon-spiced Fantans, add 1 teaspoon ground cinnamon to the remaining butter in step 4 before brushing over the dough strips. Sprinkle the rolls with a little confectioners' sugar as soon as they come out of the oven, then let cool before serving.

MEXICAN "BREAD OF THE DEAD"

A celebratory loaf made for the Day of the Dead. Even though the name of this bread suggests otherwise, this holiday is actually a very happy day when Mexicans pay their respects to the souls of their dead. Traditionally the bread is decorated with a dough skull, bones and tears.

3 star anise
6 tablespoons cold water
6 cups white flour
1 teaspoon salt
1/2 cup sugar
1 ounce fresh yeast
3/4 cup lukewarm water
3 eggs
4 tablespoons orange liqueur
1/2 cup butter, melted
grated zest of 1 orange
confectioners' sugar, for dusting

MAKES 1 LARGE LOAF

VARIATION
Top the baked bread with orange icing. Blend 1/2 cup confectioners' sugar and 1–2 tablespoons orange liqueur. Pour the icing over the bread and let it dribble down the sides.

1 Grease a 10½-inch fluted round cake pan. Place the star anise in a small saucepan and add the cold water. Bring to a boil and boil for 3–4 minutes or until the liquid has reduced to 3 tablespoons. Discard the star anise and let the liquid cool.

2 Sift the flour and salt together into a large bowl. Stir in the sugar and make a well in the center.

3 In a small bowl, dissolve the yeast in the lukewarm water. Pour into the center of the flour and mix in a little flour, using your fingers, until a smooth, thick batter forms. Sprinkle on a little of the remaining flour, cover with plastic wrap and let the batter sit in a warm place for 30 minutes or until the mixture starts to bubble.

4 Beat the eggs, the reserved liquid flavored with star anise, orange liqueur and melted butter together. Gradually incorporate into the flour mixture to form a smooth dough.

5 Turn out the dough onto a lightly floured surface and gently knead in the orange zest. Knead for 5–6 minutes, until smooth and elastic. Shape into a 10½-inch round and place in the prepared pan. Cover with lightly oiled plastic wrap and let rise, in a warm place, for 2–3 hours or until almost at the top of the pan and doubled in bulk.

6 Meanwhile, preheat the oven to 375°F. Bake the loaf for 45–50 minutes or until golden. Turn out onto a wire rack to cool. Dust with confectioners' sugar to serve.

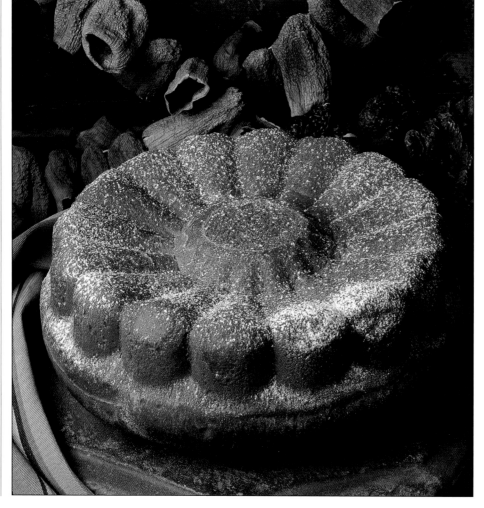

WEST INDIAN ROTIS

Caribbean food is based on cuisines from many areas of the world, influenced by a wide range of cultures. It is the Anglo-Indian connection that brought the Indian flat bread called roti to Trinidad in the West Indies.

1 Combine the flour, baking powder and salt in a large bowl, and make a well in the center. Gradually mix in the water to make a firm dough.

2 Knead on a lightly floured surface until smooth. Place in a lightly oiled bowl, and cover with lightly oiled plastic wrap. Let stand for 20 minutes.

3 Divide the dough into 8 equal pieces and roll each one on a lightly floured surface into an 7-inch round. Brush the surface of each round with a little of the clarified butter or ghee, fold in half and half again. Cover the folded rounds with lightly oiled plastic wrap and set aside for 10 minutes.

4 cups atta *or whole-wheat flour*
1 teaspoon baking powder
1 teaspoon salt
1¹/₄ cups water
8–10 tablespoons clarified butter or ghee

MAKES 8 ROTIS

4 Take one roti and roll out on a lightly floured surface into a round about 8–9 inches in diameter. Brush both sides with some clarified butter or ghee.

5 Heat a griddle or heavy frying pan, add the roti and cook for about 1 minute. Turn over and cook for 2 minutes, then turn over again and cook for 1 minute. Wrap in a dish towel to keep warm while cooking the remaining rotis. Serve warm.

BREADS OF INDIA AND THE MIDDLE EAST

Chapatis, rotis and pooris are typical unleavened Indian flat breads. Chiles, herbs and spices are popular additions. The tradition of baking flat breads continues into the Middle East, although their specialities—crisp lavash, onion breads and barbari—include yeast. All these breads are perfect for serving with soups or dips. In southern India flour is replaced with rice and lentils or beans, which are fermented to make a pancake-style flat bread.

BHATURAS

*These light, fluffy leavened breads, made with semolina and flour and
flavored with butter and yogurt, taste delicious served warm.*

*1/2 ounce fresh yeast
1 teaspoon sugar
1/2 cup lukewarm water
1 3/4 cups all-purpose flour
1/2 cup semolina
1/2 teaspoon salt
1 tablespoon butter or ghee
2 tablespoons plain yogurt
oil, for frying*

MAKES 10 BHATURAS

COOK'S TIP

Ghee can be found in Asian and
Indian supermarkets, however, it is
easy to make at home. Melt unsalted
butter in a heavy-bottomed pan over
low heat. Simmer very gently until the
residue changes to a light golden
color, then leave to cool. Strain
through cheesecloth before using.

1 Mix the yeast with the sugar and
water in a bowl. Sift the flour into a
large bowl and stir in the semolina and
salt. Rub in the butter or ghee.

2 Add the yeast mixture and yogurt and
mix to a dough. Turn out on to a lightly
floured surface and knead for
10 minutes until smooth and elastic.

3 Place in a lightly oiled bowl, cover
with lightly oiled plastic wrap and let
rise, in a warm place, for about 1 hour,
or until doubled in bulk.

4 Turn out on to a lightly floured surface
and punch down. Divide into 10 equal
pieces and shape each one into a ball.
Flatten into disks with the palm of your
hand. Roll out on a lightly floured
surface into 5-inch rounds.

5 Heat oil to a depth of 1/2-inch in a
deep frying pan and slide one bhatura
into the oil. Fry for about 1 minute,
turning over after 30 seconds, then
drain on paper towels. Keep warm in a
low oven while frying the remaining
bhaturas. Serve warm.

TANDOORI ROTIS

There are numerous varieties of breads in India, most of them unleavened. This one, as its name suggests, would normally be baked in a tandoor—a clay oven which is heated with charcoal or wood. The oven becomes extremely hot, cooking the bread in minutes.

3 cups atta or fine whole-wheat flour
1 teaspoon salt
1 cup water
2–3 tablespoons melted ghee or butter, for brushing

MAKES 6 ROTIS

COOK'S TIP
The rotis are ready when light brown bubbles appear on the surface.

1 Sift the flour and salt into a large bowl. Add the water and mix to a soft dough. Knead on a lightly floured surface for 3–4 minutes until smooth. Place in a lightly oiled bowl, cover with lightly oiled plastic wrap; let rest for 1 hour.

2 Turn out on to a lightly floured surface. Divide the dough into 6 pieces and shape each piece into a ball. Press out into a larger round with the palm of your hand, cover with lightly oiled plastic wrap and let rest for 10 minutes.

3 Meanwhile, preheat the oven to 450°F. Place 3 baking sheets in the oven to heat. Roll the rotis into 6-inch rounds, place 2 on each baking sheet and bake for 8–10 minutes. Brush with ghee or butter and serve warm.

NAAN

From the Caucasus through the Punjab region of northwest India and beyond, all serve these leavened breads. Traditionally cooked in a very hot clay oven known as a tandoor, naan are usually eaten with dry meat or vegetable dishes, such as tandoori.

2 cups unbleached white bread flour
1/2 teaspoon salt
1/2 ounce fresh yeast
4 tablespoons lukewarm milk
1 tablespoon vegetable oil
2 tablespoons plain yogurt
1 egg
2–3 tablespoons melted ghee or butter, for brushing

MAKES 3 NAAN

1 Sift the flour and salt together into a large bowl. In a smaller bowl, cream the yeast with the milk. Set aside for 15 minutes.

2 Add the yeast mixture, oil, yogurt and egg to the flour and mix to a soft dough.

3 Turn out the dough on to a lightly floured surface and knead for about 10 minutes until smooth and elastic. Place in a lightly oiled bowl, cover with lightly oiled plastic wrap and let rise, in a warm place, for 45 minutes, or until doubled in bulk.

4 Preheat the oven to its highest setting, at least 450°F. Place 3 heavy baking sheets in the oven to heat.

5 Turn the dough out on to a lightly floured surface and punch down. Divide into 3 equal pieces and shape into balls.

6 Cover two of the balls of dough with oiled plastic wrap and roll out the third into a teardrop shape about 10 inches long, 5 inches wide and with a thickness of about 1/4–1/3 inch.

7 Preheat the broiler on its highest setting. Meanwhile, place the naan on the hot baking sheets and bake for 3–4 minutes, or until puffed up.

8 Remove the naan from the oven and place under the hot broiler for a few seconds, or until the top of the naan browns slightly. Wrap the cooked naan in a dish towel to keep warm while rolling out and cooking the remaining naan. Brush with melted ghee or butter and serve warm.

VARIATIONS
You can flavor naan in numerous different ways:
• To make spicy naan, add 1 teaspoon each ground coriander and ground cumin to the flour in step 1. If you would like the naan to be extra fiery, add 1/2–1 teaspoon hot chile powder.
• To make cardamom-flavored naan, lightly crush the seeds from 4–5 green cardamom pods and add to the flour in step 1.
• To make poppy seed naan, brush the rolled-out naan with a little ghee and sprinkle with poppy seeds. Press lightly to make sure that they stick.
• To make peppered naan, brush the rolled-out naan with a little ghee and dust generously with coarsely ground black pepper.
• To make onion-flavored naan, add 1/2 cup finely chopped or coarsely grated onion to the dough in step 2. You may need to reduce the amount of egg if the onion is very moist to prevent making the dough too soft.
• To make whole-wheat naan, substitute whole-wheat bread flour for some or all of the white flour.

COOK'S TIP
To help the naan dough to puff up and brown, place the baking sheets in an oven preheated to the maximum temperature for at least 10 minutes before baking to ensure that they are hot. Preheat the broiler while the naan are baking.

RED LENTIL DOSAS

Dosas and idlis are the breads of southern India. They are very different from traditional north Indian breads as they are made from lentils or beans and rice rather than flour. Dosas are more like pancakes; they are eaten freshly cooked, often at breakfast time, with chutney.

3/4 cup long-grain rice
1/4 cup red lentils
1 cup warm water
1 teaspoon salt
1/2 teaspoon ground turmeric
1/2 teaspoon freshly ground
black pepper
2 tablespoons chopped
fresh cilantro
oil, for frying and drizzling

MAKES 6 DOSAS

VARIATION
Add 4 tablespoons grated coconut, 1 tablespoon grated fresh ginger and 1 finely chopped chile to the batter just before cooking.

1 Place the rice and lentils in a bowl, cover with the water and let soak for 8 hours.

2 Drain off the water and reserve. Place the rice and lentils in a food processor and blend until smooth. Blend in the reserved water.

3 Scrape into a bowl, cover with plastic wrap and leave in a warm place to ferment for about 24 hours.

4 Stir in the salt, turmeric, pepper and cilantro. Heat a heavy-based frying pan over a medium heat for a few minutes until hot. Smear with oil and add about 2–3 tablespoons batter.

5 Using the rounded bottom of a soup spoon, gently spread the batter out, using a circular motion, to make a 6-inch diameter dosa.

6 Cook for 1 1/2–2 minutes, or until set. Drizzle a little oil over the dosa and around the edges. Turn over and cook for about 1 minute, or until golden. Keep warm in a low oven over simmering water while cooking the remaining dosas. Serve warm.

PARATHAS

These triangular-shaped breads, made from a similar dough to that used for chapatis, are enriched with layers of ghee or butter to create a wonderfully rich, flaky bread.

*1 1/4 cups unbleached
all-purpose flour
1 cup whole-wheat flour
1/2 teaspoon salt
1 tablespoon vegetable oil
1/2–2/3 cup water
scant 1/2 cup melted ghee or
clarified butter*

MAKES 9 PARATHAS

1 Sift the flours and salt together into a large bowl. Add the oil with sufficient water to mix to a soft dough. Turn out the dough on to a lightly floured surface and knead vigorously for 8–10 minutes until smooth.

2 Place in a lightly oiled bowl and cover with a damp dish towel. Let rest for 30 minutes.

3 Turn out on to a lightly floured surface. Divide the dough into 9 equal pieces. Cover 8 pieces of dough with oiled plastic wrap. Shape the remaining piece into a ball and then flatten it. Roll into a 6-inch round.

4 Brush with a little of the melted ghee or clarified butter and fold in half. Brush and fold again to form a triangular shape. Repeat with the remaining dough. Stack, layered between plastic wrap, to keep moist. Heat a griddle or heavy-bottomed frying pan.

5 Keeping the shape, roll each piece of dough to a larger triangle, with each side measuring 6–7 inches. Brush with ghee or butter and place on the griddle or in the pan, brushed side down. Cook for about 1 minute, brush with ghee or butter and turn over. Cook for about 1 minute, or until crisp and dotted with brown speckles. Keep warm in a low oven while cooking the remaining parathas. Serve the parathas warm.

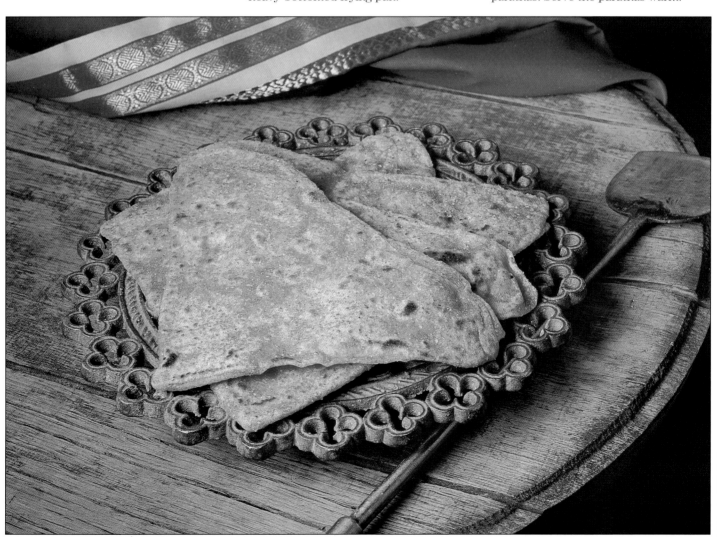

POORIS

Pooris are small disks of dough that when fried, puff up into light airy breads. They will melt in your mouth!

*1 cup unbleached
all-purpose flour
1 cup whole-wheat flour
1/2 teaspoon salt
1/2 teaspoon chile powder (optional)
2 tablespoons vegetable oil
scant 1/2 cup water
oil, for frying*

MAKES 12 POORIS

1 Sift the flours, salt and chile powder, if using, into a large bowl. Add the vegetable oil then add sufficient water to mix to a dough. Turn out on to a lightly floured surface and knead for 8–10 minutes until smooth.

2 Place in a lightly oiled bowl and cover with lightly oiled plastic wrap. Let rest for 30 minutes.

3 Turn out on to a lightly floured surface. Divide the dough into 12 equal pieces. Keeping the rest of the dough covered, roll one piece into a 5-inch round. Repeat with the remaining dough. Stack the pooris, layered between plastic wrap, to keep moist.

4 Heat oil to a depth of 1 inch in a deep frying pan to 350°F. Using a spatula, lift one poori and gently slide it into the oil; it will sink but return to the surface and begin to sizzle. Gently press the poori into the oil. It will puff up. Turn over after a few seconds and cook for 20–30 seconds.

5 Remove the poori from the pan and drain on paper towels. Keep warm in a low oven while cooking the remaining pooris. Serve warm.

VARIATION
To make spinach-flavored pooris, thaw 2 ounces frozen chopped spinach, drain it well and add it to the dough with a little grated fresh ginger root and 1/2 teaspoon ground cumin.

CHAPATIS

These chewy, unleavened breads are eaten throughout Northern India. They are usually served as an accompaniment to spicy dishes.

*1 1/2 cups atta or whole-wheat flour
1/2 teaspoon salt
scant scant 1/2 cup water
1 teaspoon vegetable oil
melted ghee or butter, for brushing
(optional)*

MAKES 6 CHAPATIS

2 Knead for 5–6 minutes until smooth. Place in a lightly oiled bowl, cover with a damp dish towel and let rest for 30 minutes. Turn out on to a floured surface. Divide the dough into 6 equal pieces. Shape each piece into a ball.

3 Press the dough into a larger round with the palm of your hand, then roll into a 5-inch round. Stack, layered between plastic wrap, to keep moist.

4 Heat a griddle or heavy-based frying pan over a medium heat for a few minutes until hot. Take one chapati, brush off any excess flour, and place on the griddle. Cook for 30–60 seconds, or until the top begins to bubble and white specks appear on the underside.

5 Turn the chapati over using a spatula and cook for a further 30 seconds. Remove from the pan and keep warm, layered between a folded dish towel, while cooking the remaining chapatis. If you like, the chapatis can be brushed lightly with melted ghee or butter immediately after cooking. Serve warm.

COOK'S TIP
Atta or *ata* is a very fine whole-wheat flour, which is only found in Indian stores and supermarkets. It is sometimes simply labeled chapati flour. *Atta* can also be used for making rotis and other Indian flat breads.

1 Sift the flour and salt into a bowl. Add the water and mix to a soft dough. Knead in the oil, then turn out on to a lightly floured surface.

MISSI ROTIS

These flavor-packed unleavened breads are eaten in northern India. They are made with gram flour—grams or chana dhal are a variety of chickpea, which are milled to make this gluten-free flour.

1 cup gram flour
1 cup whole-wheat flour
1 green chile, seeded and chopped
1/2 onion, finely chopped
1 tablespoon chopped fresh cilantro
1/2 teaspoon ground turmeric
1/2 teaspoon salt
1 tablespoon oil or melted butter
1/2–2/3 cup lukewarm water
2–3 tablespoons melted butter or ghee

MAKES 4 ROTIS

VARIATION
Use 1/4–1/2 teaspoon chile powder in place of the fresh chile.

1 Mix the flours, chile, onion, cilantro, turmeric and salt together in a large bowl. Stir in the 1 tablespoon oil or melted butter.

2 Mix in sufficient water to make a pliable soft dough. Turn out the dough on to a lightly floured surface and knead until smooth.

3 Place in a lightly oiled bowl, cover with lightly oiled plastic wrap and let rest for 1 hour.

4 Turn the dough out on to a lightly floured surface. Divide into 4 equal pieces and shape into balls. Roll out each ball into a thick round 6–7 inches in diameter.

5 Heat a griddle or heavy-based frying pan over a medium heat for a few minutes until hot.

6 Brush both sides of one roti with the melted butter or ghee. Add it to the griddle or frying pan and cook for about 2 minutes, turning after 1 minute. Brush the cooked roti lightly with melted butter or ghee again, slide it on to a plate and keep warm in a low oven while cooking the remaining rotis in the same way. Serve the rotis warm.

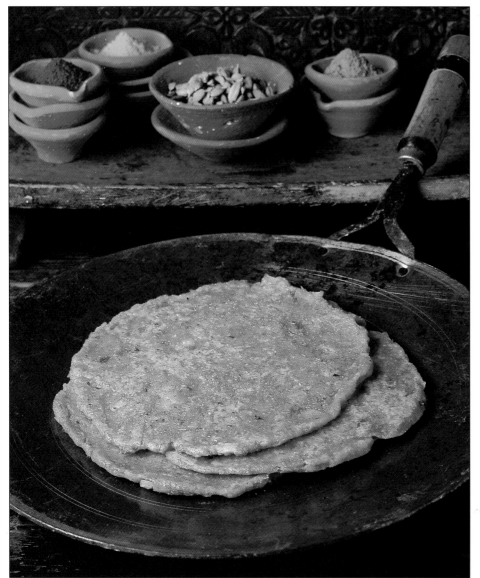

LAVASH

Thin and crispy, this flat bread is universally eaten throughout the Middle East. It's ideal for serving with soups and starters, and can be made in any size and broken into pieces as desired.

*2¹/2 cups unbleached white
bread flour
1¹/2 cups whole-wheat flour
1 teaspoon salt
¹/2 ounce fresh yeast
1 cup lukewarm water
4 tablespoons plain yogurt or milk*

MAKES 10 LAVASH

1 Sift the white and whole-wheat flours and salt together into a large bowl and make a well in the center. Mix the yeast with half the lukewarm water until creamy, then stir in the remaining water.

2 Add the yeast mixture and yogurt or milk to the center of the flour and mix to a soft dough. Turn out on to a lightly floured surface and knead for 8–10 minutes until smooth and elastic. Place in a lightly oiled bowl, cover with lightly oiled plastic wrap and let rise, in a warm place, for about 1 hour, or until doubled in bulk. Punch down the dough, re-cover with lightly oiled plastic wrap and let rise for 30 minutes.

3 Turn the dough back out on to a lightly floured surface. Punch down gently and divide into 10 equal pieces. Shape into balls, then flatten into disks with the palm of your hand. Cover and let rest for 5 minutes. Meanwhile, preheat the oven to the maximum temperature – at least 450°F. Place 3 or 4 baking sheets in the oven to heat.

4 Roll the dough as thinly as possible, then lift it over the backs of your hands and gently stretch and turn the dough. Let rest in between rolling for a few minutes if necessary to avoid tearing.

5 As soon as they are ready, place 4 lavash on the baking sheets and bake for 6–8 minutes, or until starting to brown. Stack the remaining uncooked lavash, layered between plastic wrap or waxed paper, and cover, to keep moist. Transfer to a wire rack to cool and cook the remaining lavash.

4 cups unbleached white bread flour
1 teaspoon salt
³/₄ ounce fresh yeast
scant 1¼ cups lukewarm water

FOR THE TOPPING
4 tablespoons finely chopped onion
1 teaspoon ground cumin
2 teaspoons ground coriander
2 teaspoons chopped fresh mint
2 tablespoons olive oil

MAKES 8 BREADS

COOK'S TIP
If you haven't any fresh mint to hand, then add 1 tablespoon dried mint. Use the freeze-dried variety if you can as it has much more flavor.

SYRIAN ONION BREAD

The basic Arab breads of the Levant and Gulf have traditionally been made with a finely ground whole-wheat flour similar to chapati flour, but now are being made with white flour as well. This Syrian version has a tasty, aromatic topping.

1 Lightly flour 2 baking sheets. Sift the flour and salt together into a large bowl and make a well in the center. Cream the yeast with a little of the water, then mix in the remainder.

2 Add the yeast mixture to the center of the flour and mix to a firm dough. Turn out on to a lightly floured surface and knead for 8–10 minutes until smooth and elastic.

3 Place in a lightly oiled bowl, cover with lightly oiled plastic wrap and leave to rise, in a warm place, for about 1 hour, or until doubled in size.

4 Punch down the dough and turn out on to a lightly floured surface. Divide into 8 equal pieces and roll into 5–6-inch rounds. Make them slightly concave. Prick all over and space well apart on the baking sheets. Cover with lightly oiled plastic wrap and let rise for 15–20 minutes.

5 Meanwhile, preheat the oven to 400°F. Mix the chopped onion, ground cumin, ground coriander and chopped mint in a bowl. Brush the breads with the olive oil for the topping, sprinkle them evenly with the spicy onion mixture and bake for 15–20 minutes. Serve the onion breads warm.

BARBARI

—

*These small Iranian flat breads can be made in a variety of sizes. For a
change, make two large breads and break off pieces to scoop up dips.*

*2 cups unbleached white bread flour
1 teaspoon salt
1/2 ounce fresh yeast
scant 2/3 cup lukewarm water
oil, for brushing*

MAKES 6 BARBARI

1 Lightly dust 2 baking sheets with flour.
Sift the flour and salt together into a
bowl and make a well in the center.

3 Place in a lightly oiled bowl, cover
with lightly oiled plastic wrap and let
rise for 45–60 minutes, or until doubled.

2 Mix the yeast with the water. Pour
into the center of the flour, sprinkle a
little flour over and leave in a warm
place for 15 minutes. Mix to a dough,
then turn out on to a lightly floured
surface and knead for 8–10 minutes
until smooth and elastic.

4 Punch down the dough and turn out
on to a lightly floured surface. Divide
into 6 equal pieces and shape into
rectangles. Roll each one out to about
4 × 2 inches and about 1/2-inch thick.
Space well apart on the baking sheets,
and make four slashes in the tops.

5 Cover the breads with lightly oiled
plastic wrap and let rise, in a warm
place, for 20 minutes. Meanwhile,
preheat the oven to 400°F. Brush
the breads with oil and bake for
12–15 minutes, or until pale golden.
Serve warm.

VARIATION
Sprinkle with sesame or caraway
seeds before baking.

Shopping for Bread and Flour

The following flour mills, bakeries and food stores are worth visiting. Most mills sell flour direct, but it is best to telephone before visiting.

UNITED STATES

King Arthur Flour
P.O. Box 876
Norwich, VT 05055-0876
Tel: (800) 827-6836

Bob's Red Mill
5209 S.E. International Way
Milwaukie, OR 97222
Tel: (503) 654-3215
Fax: (503) 653 1339

Walnut Acres Organic Farms
Penns Creek, PA 17862
Tel: (800) 433-3998

Arrowhead Mills
P.O. Box 866
Hereford, TX 79045
Tel: (806) 364-0730

Community Mill and Bean
267 Route 89 South
Savannah, NY 13146
Tel: (800) 755-0554

New Hope Mills, Inc.
RR2, Box 269A
Moravia, NY 13119
Tel: (315) 497-0783

Kenyon Cornmeal Company
Osquepough, RI 02836
Tel: (401) 783-4054

San Francisco French
Bread Co.
580 Julie Ann Way
Oakland, CA 94629
Tel: (888) 661-7687
or (510) 568-7697

Poulsbo Bakery
P.O. Box 2778
18924 Front Street NE
Poulsbo, WA 98370
Tel: (360) 779-2798
Fax: (360) 677-3581

N.Y. Cake & Bake
 Distributor
56 West 22nd Street
New York, NY 10010
Tel: (800)94-CAKE-9
Fax: (212) 675-7099

Williams-Sonoma
P.O. Box 7456
San Francisco
CA 94120-7456
Tel: (800) 541-2233

Commodities
117 Hudson Street
New York, NY 10013
Tel: (212) 334-8330

Dean & Deluca
110 Greene Street
Suite 304
New York, NY 10012
Tel: (800) 221-7714

Von Snedaker's Magic
 Baking Sheet
12021 Wilshire Boulevard
Suite 231
Los Angeles, CA 90025
Tel: (310) 395-6365

FBM (French Baking
 Machines)
2666 Route 130
Cranbury
NJ 08512
Tel: (609) 860-0577

The Chef's Catalogue
3215 Commercial Avenue
Northbrook
IL 60062-1900
Tel: (800) 338-3232

Bread Baker's Guild of America
P.O. Box 22254
Pittsburgh, PA 15222
Tel: (412) 322-8275

AUSTRALIA

Bowan Island Bakery
202 Lyons Road
Drummoyne
NSW 2047
Tel: (02) 9181 3524

Brown's Bakeries
PO Box 1298
Windsor, VIC 3181
Tel: (03) 9510 9520

Dallas Bread
28 Cross Street
Brookvale
NSW 2100
Tel: (02) 9905 6021

David Jones Food Hall
Cnr. Market and
 Castlereagh Streets
Sydney, NSW 2000
Tel: (02) 9266 6005

Haberfield Bakery
153 Ramsay Road
Haberfield, Sydney, NSW
Tel: (02) 9797 7715

Il Gianfornaio
414 Victoria Avenue
Chatswood, Sydney, NSW
Tel: (02) 413 4833

Infinity Sourdough Bakery
225 Victoria Street
Darlinghurst, NSW 2031
Tel: (02) 9380 4320

La Gerbe d'Or
257 Glenmore Road
Paddington, Sydney, NSW
Tel: (02) 9331 10710

New Norcia Bakeries
163A Scarborough
 Beach Road
Mt Hawthorn, WA 6016
Tel: (08) 9443 9437

Quinton's Sourdough and
 Danish Shop
179 The Mall
Leura, NSW 2780
Tel: (02) 9266 6065

Simon Johnson
181 Harris Street
Pyrmont, Sydney NSW 2009
NSW 2009
Tel: (02) 9552 2522

ENGLAND

& Clarke's
122 Kensington Church Street
London W8 4BH
Tel: 0171 229 2190

Baker & Spice
46 Walton Street
London SW3 1RB
Tel: 0171 589 4734

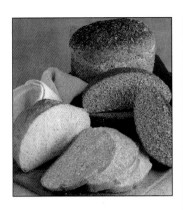

Crowdy Mill
Bow Road
Habertonford, Totnes
Devon TQ9 7HU
Tel: 01803 732 340

Euphorium Bakery
203 Upper Street
London N1 1RQ
Tel: 0171 359 7146

Funchal Patisserie
141 Stockwell Road
London SW9 9TN
Tel: 0171 733 3134

Hobb's House Bakery
39 High Street
Chipping Sodbury
Bristol BS37 6BA
Tel: 01454 321 629

Konditor & Cook
22 Cornwall Street
London SE1 8TW
Tel: 0171 261 0456

Letheringsett Watermill
Riverside Road
Letheringsett
Norfolk NR25 7YD
Tel: 01263 713 153

Maison Blanc
102 Holland Park Avenue
London W11 4UA
Tel: 0171 221 2494

Neal's Yard Bakery
6 Neal's Yard
London WC2H 9DP
Tel: 0171 836 5199

Pimhill Organic Centre
Lea Hall, Harmer Hill
Nr Shrewsbury SY4 3DY
Tel: 01939 290 075

Sally Lunn's
4 North Parade Passage
Bath BA1 1NX
Tel: 01225 461 634

Selfridges
Food Hall
400 Oxford Street
London W1A 1AB
Tel: 0171 629 1234

Shipton Mill Limited
Long Newton
nr Tetbury
Gloucestershire
GL8 8RP
Tel: 01666 505 050

The Old Farmhouse Bakery
Steventon
nr Abingdon
Oxon OX13 6RP
Tel: 01235 831 230

Villandry Foodstore
    Restaurant
170 Great Portland Street
London W1N 5TB
Tel: 0171 631 3131

SCOTLAND

Aberfeldy Water Mill
Mill Street
Aberfeldy
Tayside
PH15 2BG
Tel: 01887 820 803

Ian Mellis
205 Bruntsfield Place
Edinburgh EH10 4DH
Tel: 0131 447 8889

Star Continental Bakery
158 Fore Street
Scottoun
Glasgow
G14 0AE
Tel: 0141 959 7307

Taylor's of Waterside Bakery
Waterside Street
Strathaven
ML10 6AW
Tel: 01357 521 260

Valvona & Crolla
19 Elm Row
Edinburgh EH7 4AA
Tel: 0131 556 6066

Victor Hugo
26–7 Melville Terrace
Edinburgh EH9 2PR
Tel: 0131 667 1827

WALES

The Village Bakery
Melmerby Road
Melberby
Penrith
Cumbria
CA10 1HE
Tel: 01768 881 515

Derwen Bakehouse
Museum of Welsh Life
St Fagans
Cardiff
Glamorgan
CF5 6XB
Tel: 01222 573 500

ACKNOWLEDGMENTS

—

PUBLISHER'S ACKNOWLEDGMENTS

The Publishers would like to thank Jo Lethaby and Jenni Fleetwood for their skilful editing; Jill Jones, who tracked down almost all the breads for the Breads of the World section; Jenny Blair for sourcing the Scottish breads; Amy Willenski, who tracked down or specially baked all the US breads; Angus Henderson and Jacky Lannel at Villandry Foodstore Restaurant, who specially baked the fougasse, épi and pane au cioccolato loaves; Christine Gough, the baker at the Welsh Museum of Life, for baking and supplying traditional Welsh breads; and Giacomo and Nuala Farruggia at Il Forno for baking and supplying many of the Italian breads, as well as the harvest loaf and hot cross buns.

PHOTOGRAPHY ACKNOWLEDGMENTS

All recipe pictures and chapter openers are by Nicki Dowey. The pictures on pages 6–125 are by Amanda Heywood, except for the following that have been reproduced with the kind permission of those listed: p. 6t, p. 7t, p. 14b and p. 250 Maison Blanc Limited; p. 7b Jan Suttle/Life File; p. 9t and 13b Emma Lee/Life File; p. 12 t Lionel Moss/ Life File; p.12b Jeff Griffin/Life File; p. 8t and b e.t. archive; p. 9b English Heritage Photographic Library; p. 10t e.t. archive; p. 10b Biblioteca Estense, Modena/e.t. archive; p. 11t Andreas von Einsiedel/National Trust Photographic Library; p. 11b Eric Crichton/National Trust Photographic Library; p. 13 Food Features.

INDEX